FIRST PRINCIPLES • DE-RISKING • PREMATURE OPTIMIZATION •
FALLACY • OVERFITTING • FRAME OF REFERENCE • FRAMING •
MBERS • THE THIRD STORY • MOST RESPECTFUL INTERPRETATION
SERVING BIAS • VEIL OF IGNORANCE • BIRTH LOTTERY • JUST
ADIGM SHIFT • SEMMELWEIS REFLEX • CONFIRMATION BIAS •
THINKING GRAY • DEVIL'S ADVOCATE POSITION • INTUITION •
IC PROBABILITY BIAS • TRAGEDY OF THE COMMONS • TYRANNY
UNITY • EXTERNALITIES • SPILLOVER EFFECTS • COASE THEOREM
ASYMMETRIC INFORMATION • ADVERSE SELECTION • MARKET
ITIVES • COBRA EFFECT • STREISAND EFFECT • HYDRA EFFECT •
CK • BOILING FROG • SHORT-TERMISM • TECHNICAL DEBT • PATH
INFORMATION OVERLOAD • ANALYSIS PARALYSIS • PERFECT IS
ONS • HICK'S LAW • PARADOX OF CHOICE • DECISION FATIGUE •
S • MULTITASKING • THE TOP IDEA IN YOUR MIND • DEEP WORK
OPPORTUNITY COST • OPPORTUNITY COST OF CAPITAL • BEST
IGH-LEVERAGE ACTIVITIES • PARETO PRINCIPLE • POWER LAW
G UTILITY • NEGATIVE RETURNS • BURNOUT • PRESENT BIAS •
HYPERBOLIC DISCOUNTING • COMMITMENT • DEFAULT EFFECT •
FALLACY • DESIGN PATTERN • ANTI-PATTERN • BRUTE FORCE
S OF SCALE • PARALLEL PROCESSING • DIVIDE AND CONQUER •
N • SCIENTIFIC METHOD • INERTIA • STRATEGY TAX • SHIRKY
ASIS • POTENTIAL ENERGY • CENTER OF GRAVITY • ACTIVATION
CTION • TIPPING POINT • TECHNOLOGY ADOPTION LIFE CYCLE •
E • BUTTERFLY EFFECT • LUCK SURFACE AREA • ENTROPY • 2 X 2
TISM • OUT-GROUP BIAS • ZERO-SUM VS. WIN-WIN • ANECDOTAL
NG FACTOR • HYPOTHESIS • TEXAS SHARPSHOOTER FALLACY •
PECTANCY BIAS • PLACEBO EFFECT • PROXY • SELECTION BIAS •
BLER'S FALLACY • CLUSTERING ILLUSION • REGRESSION TO THE
ATION • NORMAL DISTRIBUTION • PROBABILITY DISTRIBUTION •

Super Thinking

Super Thinking

The Big Book of Mental Models

GABRIEL WEINBERG

[AND]

LAUREN McCANN

PORTFOLIO / PENGUIN

PORTFOLIO / PENGUIN
An imprint of Penguin Random House LLC
penguinrandomhouse.com

Image credits appear on pages 321–326

Most Portfolio books are available at a discount when purchased in quantity for
sales promotions or corporate use. Special editions, which include personalized
covers, excerpts, and corporate imprints, can be created when purchased in large
quantities. For more information, please call (212) 572-2232 or e-mail
specialmarkets@penguinrandomhouse.com. Your local bookstore can also
assist with discounted bulk purchases using the Penguin Random House
corporate Business-to-Business program. For assistance in locating a
participating retailer, e-mail B2B@penguinrandomhouse.com.

LIBRARY OF CONGRESS CATALOGING-IN-PUBLICATION DATA

Names: Weinberg, Gabriel, author. | McCann, Lauren, author.
Title: Super Thinking: The Big Book of Mental Models /
Gabriel Weinberg and Lauren McCann.
Description: New York: Portfolio/Penguin, [2019] | Includes index.
Identifiers: LCCN 2019002099 (print) | LCCN 2019004235 (ebook) |
ISBN 9780525533597 (ebook) | ISBN 9780525542810 (international edition) |
ISBN 9780525533580 (hardcover)
Subjects: LCSH: Thought and thinking. | Cognition. | Reasoning.
Classification: LCC BF441 (ebook) | LCC BF441 .W4446 2019 (print) |
DDC 153.4/2—dc23
LC record available at https://lccn.loc.gov/2019002099

Printed in the United States of America
3 5 7 9 10 8 6 4 2

BOOK DESIGN BY TANYA MAIBORODA

Contents

Introduction

The Super Thinking Journey

EACH MORNING, AFTER OUR KIDS head off to school or camp, we take a walk and talk about our lives, our careers, and current events. (We're married.) Though we discuss a wide array of topics, we often find common threads—recurring concepts that help us explain, predict, or approach these seemingly disparate subjects. Examples range from more familiar concepts, such as opportunity cost and inertia, to more obscure ones, such as Goodhart's law and regulatory capture. (We will explain these important ideas and many more in the pages that follow.)

These recurring concepts are called **mental models**. Once you are familiar with them, you can use them to quickly create a *mental* picture of a situation, which becomes a *model* that you can later apply in similar situations. (Throughout this book, major mental models appear in boldface when we introduce them to you. We use italics to emphasize words in a model's name, as well as to highlight common related concepts and phrases.)

In spite of their usefulness, most of these concepts are not universally taught in school, even at the university level. We picked up some of them in our formal education (both of us have undergraduate and graduate degrees from MIT), but the bulk of them we learned on our own through reading, conversations, and experience.

We wish we had learned about these ideas much earlier, because they not only help us better understand what is going on around us, but also make us more effective decision makers in all areas of our lives. While we can't go back in time and teach our younger selves these ideas, we can provide this guide for others, and for our children. That was our primary motivation for writing this book.

An example of a useful mental model from physics is the concept of **critical mass**, the *mass* of nuclear material needed to create a *critical* state whereby a nuclear chain reaction is possible. Critical mass was an essential mental model in the development of the atomic bomb.

Every discipline, like physics, has its own set of mental models that people in the field learn through coursework, mentorship, and firsthand experience. There is a smaller set of mental models, however, that are useful in general day-to-day decision making, problem solving, and truth seeking. These often originate in specific disciplines (physics, economics, etc.), but have metaphorical value well beyond their originating discipline.

Critical mass is one of these mental models with wider applicability: ideas can attain critical mass; a party can reach critical mass; a product can achieve critical mass. Unlike hundreds of other concepts from physics, critical mass is broadly useful outside the context of physics. (We explore critical mass in more detail in Chapter 4.)

We call these broadly useful mental models *super models* because applying them regularly gives you a *super* power: **super thinking**—the ability to *think* better about the world—which you can use to your advantage to make better decisions, both personally and professionally.

We were introduced to the concept of super models many years ago through Charlie Munger, the partner of renowned investor Warren Buffett. As Munger explained in a 1994 speech at University of Southern California Marshall Business School titled "A Lesson on Elementary, Worldly Wisdom as It Relates to Investment Management and Business":

What is elementary, worldly wisdom? Well, the first rule is that you can't really know anything if you just remember isolated facts and try and bang 'em back. If the facts don't hang together on a latticework of theory, you don't have them in a usable form.

You've got to have models in your head. And you've got to array your experience—both vicarious and direct—on this latticework of models.

As the saying goes, "History doesn't repeat itself, but it does rhyme." If you can identify a mental model that applies to the situation in front of you, then you immediately know a lot about it. For example, suppose you are thinking about a company that involves people renting out their expensive power tools, which usually sit dormant in their garages. If you realize that the concept of critical mass applies to this business, then you know that there is some threshold that needs to be reached before it could be viable. In this case, you need enough tools available for rent in a community to satisfy initial customer demand, much as you need enough Lyft drivers in a city for people to begin relying on the service.

That is super thinking, because once you have determined that this business model can be partially explained through the lens of critical mass, you can start to reason about it at a higher level, asking and answering questions like these: What density of tools is needed to reach the critical mass point in a given area? How far away can two tools be to count toward the same critical mass point in that area? Is the critical mass likely to be reached in an area? Why or why not? Can you tweak the business model so that this critical mass point is reachable or easier to reach? (For instance, the company could seed each area with its own tools.)

As you can see, super models are shortcuts to higher-level thinking. If you can understand the relevant models for a situation, then you can bypass lower-level thinking and immediately jump to higher-level thinking. In contrast, people who don't know these models will likely never reach this higher level, and certainly not quickly.

Think back to when you first learned multiplication. As you may recall, multiplication is just repeated addition. In fact, all mathematical operations based on arithmetic can be reduced to just addition: subtraction is just adding a negative number, division is just repeated subtraction, and so on. However, using addition for complex operations can be really slow, which is why you use multiplication in the first place.

For example, suppose you have a calculator or spreadsheet in front of you. When you have 158 groups of 7 and you want to know the total, you could use your tool to add 7 to itself 158 times (slow), or you could just multiply 7×158 (quick). Using addition is painfully time-consuming when you are aware of the higher-level concept of multiplication, which helps you work quickly and efficiently.

When you don't use mental models, strategic thinking is like using addition when multiplication is available to you. You start from scratch every time without using these essential building blocks that can help you reason about problems at higher levels. And that's exactly why knowing the right mental models unlocks super thinking, just as subtraction, multiplication, and division unlock your ability to do more complex math problems.

Once you have internalized a mental model like multiplication, it's hard to imagine a world without it. But very few mental models are innate. There was a time when even addition wasn't known to most people, and you can still find whole societies that live without it. The Pirahã of the Amazon rain forest in Brazil, for example, have no concept of specific numbers, only concepts for "a smaller amount" and "a larger amount." As a result, they cannot easily count beyond three, let alone do addition, as Brian Butterworth recounted in an October 20, 2004, article for *The Guardian*, "What Happens When You Can't Count Past Four?":

> Not having much of number vocabulary, and no numeral symbols, such as one, two, three, their arithmetical skills could not be tested in the way we would test even five-year-olds in Britain. Instead, [linguist Peter] Gordon used a matching task. He would lay out up to eight objects in front of him on a table, and the Pirahã participant's task was to place the same number of objects in order on the table. Even when the objects were placed in a line, accuracy dropped off dramatically after three objects.

Consider that there are probably many disciplines where you have only rudimentary knowledge. Perhaps physics is one of them? Most of the concepts from physics are esoteric, but some—those physics mental models that we present in this book—do have the potential to be repeatedly useful in your day-to-day life. And so, despite your rudimentary knowledge of the discipline, you can and should still learn enough about these particular concepts to be able to apply them in non-physics contexts.

For instance, unless you are a physicist, Coriolis force, Lenz's law, diffraction, and hundreds of other concepts are unlikely to be of everyday use to you, but we contend that critical mass will prove useful. That's the difference between regular mental models and super models. And this pattern repeats for each of the major disciplines. As Munger said:

> And the models have to come from multiple disciplines—because all the wisdom of the world is not to be found in one little academic department. . . . You've got to have models across a fair array of disciplines.
>
> You may say, "My God, this is already getting way too tough." But, fortunately, it isn't that tough—because 80 or 90 important models will carry about 90 percent of the freight in making you a worldly-wise person. And, of those, only a mere handful really carry very heavy freight.

Munger expanded further in an April 19, 1996, speech at Stanford Law School similarly titled "A Lesson on Elementary, Worldly Wisdom, Resulted":

> When I urge a multidisciplinary approach . . . I'm really asking you to ignore jurisdictional boundaries. If you want to be a good thinker, you must develop a mind that can jump these boundaries. You don't have to know it all. Just take in the best big ideas from all these disciplines. And it's not that hard to do.

You want to have a broad base of mental models at your fingertips, or else you risk using suboptimal models for a given situation. It's like the expression "If all you have is a hammer, everything looks like a nail." (This phrase is associated with another super model, *Maslow's hammer*, which we cover in Chapter 6.) You want to use the right tool for a given situation, and to do that, you need a whole toolbox full of super models.

This book is that toolbox: it systematically lists, classifies, and explains all the important mental models across the major disciplines. We have woven all these super models together for you in a narrative fashion through nine chapters that we hope are both fun to read and easy to understand. Each chapter has a unifying theme and is written in a way that should be convenient to refer back to.

We believe that when taken together, these super models will be useful to you across your entire life: to make sense of situations, help generate ideas, and aid in decision mak-

ing. For these mental models to be most useful, however, you must apply them at the right time and in the right context. And for that to happen, you must know them well enough to associate the right ones with your current circumstances. When you deeply understand a mental model, it should come to you naturally, like multiplication does. It should just pop into your head.

Learning to apply super mental models in this manner doesn't happen overnight. Like Spider-Man or the Hulk, you won't have instant mastery of your powers. The superpowers you gain from your initial knowledge of these mental models must be developed. Reading this book for the first time is like Spider-Man getting his spider bite or the Hulk his radiation dose. After the initial transformation, you must develop your powers through repeated practice.

When your powers are honed, you will be like the Hulk in the iconic scene from the movie *The Avengers* depicted on the previous page. When Captain America wants Bruce Banner (the Hulk's alter ego) to turn into the Hulk, he tells him, "Now might be a really good time for you to get angry." Banner replies, "That's my secret, Captain. . . . I'm always angry."

This is the book we wish someone had gifted us many years ago. No matter where you are in life, this book is designed to help jump start your super thinking journey. This reminds us of another adage, "The best time to plant a tree was twenty years ago. The second best time is now."

Being Wrong Less

YOU MAY NOT REALIZE IT, but you make dozens of decisions every day. And when you make those decisions, whether they are personal or professional, you want to be right much more often than you are wrong. However, consistently being right more often is hard to do because the world is a complex, ever-evolving place. You are steadily faced with unfamiliar situations, usually with a large array of choices. The right answer may be apparent only in hindsight, if it ever becomes clear at all.

Carl Jacobi was a nineteenth-century German mathematician who often used to say, "Invert, always invert" (actually he said, "*Man muss immer umkehren*," because English wasn't his first language). He meant that *thinking* about a problem from an *inverse* perspective can unlock new solutions and strategies. For example, most people approach investing their money from the perspective of making more money; the inverse approach would be investing money from the perspective of not losing money.

Or consider healthy eating. A direct approach would be to try to construct a healthy diet, perhaps by making more food at home with controlled ingredients. An inverse approach, by contrast, would be to try to avoid unhealthy options. You might still go to all the same eating establishment but simply choose the healthier options when there.

The concept of **inverse thinking** can help you with the challenge of making good decisions. The inverse of being *right more* is being *wrong less*. Mental models are a tool set that can help you be wrong less. They are a collection of concepts that help you more effectively navigate our complex world.

As noted in the Introduction, mental models come from a variety of specific disciplines, but many have more value beyond the field they come from. If you can use these mental models to help you make decisions as events unfold before you, they can help you be wrong less often.

Let us offer an example from the world of sports. In tennis, an **unforced error** occurs when a player makes a mistake not because the other player hit an awesome shot, but rather because of their own poor judgment or execution. For example, hitting an easy ball into the net is one kind of unforced error. To be wrong less in tennis, you need to make fewer unforced errors on the court. And to be consistently wrong less in decision making, you consistently need to make fewer unforced errors in your own life.

See how this works? Unforced error is a concept from tennis, but it can be applied as a metaphor in any situation where an avoidable mistake is made. There are unforced errors in baking (using a tablespoon instead of a teaspoon) or dating (making a bad first impression) or decision making (not considering all your options). Start looking for unforced errors around you and you will see them everywhere.

An unforced error isn't the only way to make a wrong decision, though. The best decision based on the information available at the time can easily turn out to be the wrong decision in the long run. That's just the nature of dealing with uncertainty. No matter how hard you try, because of uncertainty, you may still be wrong when you make decisions, more frequently than you'd like. What you can do, however, is strive to make fewer unforced errors over time by using sound judgment and techniques to make the best decision at any given time.

Another mental model to help improve your thinking is called **antifragile**, a concept explored in a book of the same name by financial analyst Nassim Nicholas Taleb. In his words:

> Some things benefit from shocks; they thrive and grow when exposed to volatility, randomness, disorder, and stressors and love adventure, risk, and uncertainty. Yet, in spite of the ubiquity of the phenomenon, there is no word for the exact opposite of fragile. Let us call it antifragile.

Antifragility is beyond resilience or robustness. The resilient resists shocks and stays the same; the antifragile gets better.

Just as it pays off to make your financial portfolio antifragile in the face of economic shocks, it similarly pays off to make your thinking antifragile in the face of new decisions. If your thinking is antifragile, then it gets better over time as you learn from your mistakes and interact with your surroundings. It's like working out at the gym—you are shocking your muscles and bones so they grow stronger over time. We'd like to improve your thought process by helping you incorporate mental models into your day-to-day thinking, increasingly matching the right models to a given situation.

By the time you've finished reading this book, you will have more than three hundred mental models floating around in your head from dozens of disciplines, eager to pop up at just the right time. You don't have to be an expert at tennis or financial analysis to benefit from these concepts. You just need to understand their broader meaning and apply them when appropriate. If you apply these mental models consistently and correctly, your decisions will become *wrong* much *less*, or inverted, *right* much *more*. That's super thinking.

In this chapter we're going to explore solving problems without bias. Unfortunately, evolution has hardwired us with several mind traps. If you are not aware of them, you will make poor decisions by default. But if you can recognize these traps from afar and avoid them by using some tried-and-true techniques, you will be well on the path to super thinking.

KEEP IT SIMPLE, STUPID!

Any science or math teacher worth their salt stresses the importance of knowing how to derive every formula that you use, because only then do you really know it. It's the difference between being able to attack a math problem with a blank sheet of paper and needing a formula handed to you to begin with. It's also the difference between being a chef—someone who can take ingredients and turn them into an amazing dish without looking at a cookbook—and being the kind of cook who just knows how to follow a recipe.

Lauren was the teaching assistant for several statistics courses during her years at MIT. One course had a textbook that came with a computer disk, containing a simple application that could be used as a calculator for the statistical formulas in the book. On one exam, a student wrote the following answer to one of the statistical problems posed: "I would use the disk and plug the numbers in to get the answer." The student was not a chef.

The central mental model to help you become a chef with your thinking is **arguing from first principles**. It's the practical starting point to being wrong less, and it means thinking from the bottom up, using basic building blocks of what you think is true to build sound (and sometimes new) conclusions. *First principles* are the group of self-evident assumptions that make up the foundation on which your conclusions rest—the ingredients in a recipe or the mathematical axioms that underpin a formula.

Given a set of ingredients, a chef can adapt and create new recipes, as on *Chopped*. If you can argue from first principles, then you can do the same thing when making decisions, coming up with novel solutions to hard problems. Think MacGyver, or the true story depicted in the movie *Apollo 13* (which you should watch if you haven't), where a malfunction on board the spacecraft necessitated an early return to Earth and the creation of improvised devices to make sure, among other things, that there was enough usable air for the astronauts to breathe on the trip home.

NASA engineers figured out a solution using only the "ingredients" on the ship. In the movie, an engineer dumps all the parts available on the spacecraft on a table and says, "We've got to find a way to make this [holding up square canister] fit into the hole for this [holding up round canister] using nothing but that [pointing to parts on the table]."

If you can argue from first principles, then you can more easily approach unfamiliar

Arguing from First Principles

situations, or approach familiar situations in innovative ways. Understanding how to derive formulas helps you to understand how to derive new formulas. Understanding how molecules fit together enables you to build new molecules. Tesla founder Elon Musk illustrates how this process works in practice in an interview on the *Foundation* podcast:

> First principles is kind of a physics way of looking at the world. . . . You kind of boil things down to the most fundamental truths and say, "What are we sure is true?" . . . and then reason up from there. . . .
>
> Somebody could say . . . "Battery packs are really expensive and that's just the way they will always be. . . . Historically, it has cost $600 per kilowatt-hour, and so it's not going to be much better than that in the future." . . .
>
> With first principles, you say, "What are the material constituents of the batteries? What is the stock market value of the material constituents?" . . . It's got cobalt, nickel, aluminum, carbon, and some polymers for separation, and a seal can. Break that down on a material basis and say, "If we bought that on the London Metal Exchange, what would each of those things cost?" . . .
>
> It's like $80 per kilowatt-hour. So clearly you just need to think of clever ways to take those materials and combine them into the shape of a battery cell and you can have batteries that are much, much cheaper than anyone realizes.

When arguing from first principles, you are deliberately starting from scratch. You are explicitly avoiding the potential trap of conventional wisdom, which could turn out to be wrong. Even if you end up in agreement with conventional wisdom, by taking the first-principles approach, you will gain a much deeper understanding of the subject at hand.

Any problem can be approached from first principles. Take your next career move. Most people looking for work will apply to too many jobs and take the first job that is offered to them, which is likely not the optimal choice. When using first principles, you'll instead begin by thinking about what you truly value in a career (e.g., autonomy, status, mission, etc.), your required job parameters (financial, location, title, etc.), and your previous experience. When you add those up, you will get a much better picture of what might work best for your next career move, and then you can actively seek that out.

Thinking alone, though, even from first principles, only gets you so far. Your first principles are merely assumptions that may be true, false, or somewhere in between. Do you really value autonomy in a job, or do you just think you do? Is it really true you need to go back to school to switch careers, or might it actually be unnecessary?

Ultimately, to be wrong less, you also need to be testing your assumptions in the real world, a process known as **de-risking**. There is *risk* that one or more of your assumptions are untrue, and so the conclusions you reach could also be false.

As another example, any startup business idea is built upon a series of principled assumptions:

- My team can build our product.
- People will want our product.
- Our product will generate profit.
- We will be able to fend off competitors.
- The market is large enough for a long-term business opportunity.

You can break these general assumptions down into more specific assumptions:

- *My team can build our product.* We have the right number and type of engineers; our engineers have the right expertise; our product can be built in a reasonable amount of time; etc.
- *People will want our product.* Our product solves the problem we think it does; our product is simple enough to use; our product has the critical features needed for success; etc.
- *Our product will generate profit.* We can charge more for our product than it costs to make and market it; we have good messaging to market our product; we can sell enough of our product to cover our fixed costs; etc.
- *We will be able to fend off competitors.* We can protect our intellectual property; we are doing something that is difficult to copy; we can build a trusted brand; etc.
- *The market is large enough for a long-term business opportunity.* There are enough people out there who will want to buy our product; the market for our product is growing rapidly; the bigger we get, the more profit we can make; etc.

Once you get specific enough with your assumptions, then you can devise a plan to test (de-risk) them. The most important assumptions to de-risk first are the ones that are necessary conditions for success and that you are most uncertain about. For example, in the startup context, take the assumption that your solution sufficiently solves the problem it was designed to solve. If this assumption is untrue, then you will need to change what you are doing immediately before you can proceed any further, because the whole endeavor won't work otherwise.

Once you identify the critical assumptions to de-risk, the next step is actually going out and testing these assumptions, proving or disproving them, and then adjusting your strategy appropriately.

Just as the concept of first principles is universally applicable, so is de-risking. You can de-risk anything: a policy idea, a vacation plan, a workout routine. When de-risking, you want to test assumptions quickly and easily. Take a vacation plan. Assumptions could be around cost ("I can afford this vacation"), satisfaction ("I will enjoy this vacation"), coordination ("my relatives can join me on this vacation"), etc. Here, de-risking is as easy as doing a few minutes of online research, reading reviews, and sending an email to your relatives.

Unfortunately, people often make the mistake of doing way too much work before testing assumptions in the real world. In computer science this trap is called **premature optimization**, where you tweak or perfect code or algorithms (*optimize*) too early (*prematurely*). If your assumptions turn out to be wrong, you're going to have to throw out all that work, rendering it ultimately a waste of time.

It's as if you booked an entire vacation assuming your family could join you, only to finally ask them and they say they can't come. Then you have to go back and change everything, but all this work could have been avoided by a simple communication up front.

Back in startup land, there is another mental model to help you test your assumptions, called **minimum viable product**, or **MVP**. The MVP is the *product* you are developing with just enough features, the *minimum* amount, to be feasibly, or *viably*, tested by real people.

The MVP keeps you from working by yourself for too long. LinkedIn cofounder Reid Hoffman put it like this: "If you're not embarrassed by the first version of your product, you've launched too late."

As with many useful mental models, you will frequently be reminded of the MVP now that you are familiar with it. An oft-quoted military adage says: "No battle plan survives contact with the enemy." And boxer Mike Tyson (prior to his 1996 bout against Evander Holyfield): "Everybody has a plan until they get punched in the mouth." No matter the context, what they're all saying is that your first plan is probably wrong. While it is the best starting point you have right now, you must revise it often based on the real-world feedback you receive. And we recommend doing as little work as possible before getting that real-world feedback.

As with de-risking, you can extend the MVP model to fit many other contexts: mini-

Minimum Viable Product

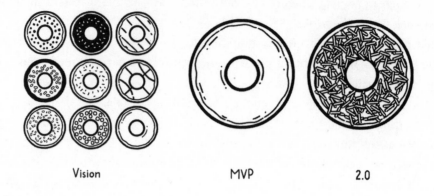

Vision   MVP   2.0

mum viable organization, minimum viable communication, minimum viable strategy, minimum viable experiment. Since we have so many mental models to get to, we're trying to do minimum viable explanations!

The MVP forces you to evaluate your assumptions quickly. One way you can be wrong with your assumptions is by coming up with too many or too complicated assumptions up front when there are clearly simpler sets you can start with. **Ockham's razor** helps here. It advises that the simplest explanation is most likely to be true. When you encounter competing explanations that plausibly explain a set of data equally well, you probably want to choose the simplest one to investigate first.

This model is a *razor* because it "shaves off" unnecessary assumptions. It's named after fourteenth-century English philosopher William of Ockham, though the underlying concept has much older roots. The Greco-Roman astronomer Ptolemy (*circa* A.D. 90–168) stated, "We consider it a good principle to explain the phenomena by the simplest hypotheses possible." More recently, the composer Roger Sessions, paraphrasing Albert Einstein, put it like this: "Everything should be made as simple as it can be, but not simpler!" In medicine, it's known by this saying: "When you hear hoofbeats, think of horses, not zebras."

A practical tactic is to look at your explanation of a situation, break it down into its constituent assumptions, and for each one, ask yourself: Does this assumption really need to be here? What evidence do I have that it should remain? Is it a false dependency?

For example, Ockham's razor would be helpful in the search for a long-term romantic partner. We've seen firsthand that many people have a long list of extremely specific criteria for their potential mates, enabled by online dating sites and apps. "I will only date a

Brazilian man with blue eyes who loves hot yoga and raspberry ice cream, and whose favorite *Avengers* character is Thor."

However, this approach leads to an unnecessarily small dating pool. If instead people reflected on whom they've dated in the past in terms of what underlying characteristics drove their past relationships to fail, a much simpler set of dating criteria would probably emerge. It is usually okay for partners to have more varied cultural backgrounds and looks, and even to prefer different *Avengers* characters, but they probably do need to make each other think and laugh and find each other attractive.

Therefore, a person shouldn't narrow their dating pool unnecessarily with overly specific criteria. If it turns out that dating someone who doesn't share their taste in superheroes really does doom the relationship, then they can always add that specific filter back in.

Ockham's razor is not a "law" in that it is always true; it just offers guidance. Sometimes the true explanation can indeed be quite complicated. However, there is no reason to jump immediately to the complex explanation when you have simpler alternatives to explore first.

If you don't simplify your assumptions, you can fall into a couple of traps, described in our next mental models. First, most people are, unfortunately, hardwired to latch onto unnecessary assumptions, a predilection called the **conjunction fallacy**, studied by Amos Tversky and Daniel Kahneman, who provided this example in the October 1983 *Psychological Review*:

Linda is 31 years old, single, outspoken, and very bright. She majored in philosophy. As a student, she was deeply concerned with issues of discrimination and social justice, and also participated in anti-nuclear demonstrations.
Which is more probable?
1. Linda is a bank teller.
2. Linda is a bank teller and is active in the feminist movement.

In their study, most people answered that number 2 is more probable, but that's impossible unless *all* bank tellers are also active in the feminist movement. The *fallacy* arises because the probability of two events in *conjunction* is always less than or equal to the probability of either one of the events occurring alone, a concept illustrated in the Venn diagram on the next page.

You not only have a natural tendency to think something specific is more probable than something general, but you also have a similarly fallacious tendency to explain data

Conjunction Fallacy

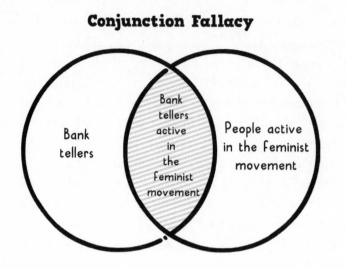

using too many assumptions. The mental model for this second fallacy is **overfitting**, a concept from statistics. Adding in all those overly specific dating requirements is over-fitting your dating history. Similarly, believing you have cancer when you have a cold is overfitting your symptoms.

Overfitting occurs when you use an overly complicated explanation when a simpler one will do. It's what happens when you don't heed Ockham's razor, when you get sucked into the conjunction fallacy or make a similar unforced error. It can occur in any situation where an explanation introduces unnecessary assumptions.

As a visual example, the data depicted on the next page can be easily explained by a straight line, but you could also *overfit* the data by creating a curved one that moves through every single point, as the wavy line does.

One approach to combatting both traps is to ask yourself: How much does my data really support my conclusion versus other conclusions? Do my symptoms really point only to cancer, or could they also point to a variety of other ailments, such as the common cold? Do I really need the curvy line to explain the data, or would a simple straight line explain just as much?

A pithy mnemonic of this advice and all the advice in this section is *KISS: Keep It Simple, Stupid!* When crafting a solution to a problem, whether making a decision or explaining data, you want to start with the simplest set of assumptions you can think of and de-risk them as simply as possible.

Overfitting

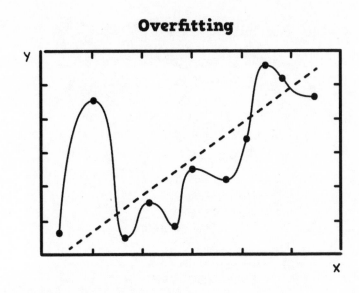

IN THE EYE OF THE BEHOLDER

You go through life seeing everything from your perspective, which varies widely depending on your particular life experiences and current situation.

In physics your perspective is called your **frame of reference**, a concept central to Einstein's theory of relativity. Here's an example from everyday life: If you are in a moving train, your *reference frame* is inside the train, which appears at rest to you, with objects inside the train not moving relative to one another, or to yourself. However, to someone outside the train looking in, you and all the objects in the train are moving at great speed, as seen from their different frame of reference, which is stationary to them. In fact, everything but the speed of light—even time—appears different in different frames of reference.

If you're trying to be as objective as possible when making a decision or solving a problem, you always want to account for your frame of reference. You will of course be influenced by your perspective, but you don't want to be unknowingly influenced. And if you think you may not have the full understanding of a situation, then you must actively try to get it by looking from a variety of different frames of reference.

A frame-of-reference mental trap (or useful trick, depending on your perspective) is **framing**. Framing refers to the way you present a situation or explanation. When you present an important issue to your coworker or family member, you try to *frame* it in a way that might help them best understand your perspective, setting the stage for a beneficial conversation. For example, if you want your organization to embark on an innovative

The BITTERSWEET MEETING of PERCEPTION and REALITY

www.cartoonstock.com

yet expensive project, you might frame it to your colleagues as a potential opportunity to outshine the competition rather than as an endeavor that would require excessive resources. The latter framing may have it rejected out of hand.

You also need to be aware that family members and coworkers are constantly framing issues for you as well, and your perception of their ideas can vary widely based on how they are framed. When someone presents a new idea or decision to you, take a step back and consider other ways in which it could be framed. If a colleague tells you they are leaving for another job to seek a better opportunity, that may indeed be true, but it also may be true that they want to leave the organization after feeling overlooked. Multiple framings can be valid yet convey vastly different perspectives.

If you visit news sites on the internet, then you probably know all about framing, or at least you should. For example, headlines have a framing effect, affecting the meaning people take away from stories. On August 31, 2015, three police officers responded to a 911 call about a burglary in progress. Unfortunately, the call did not specify an exact address, and the officers responded to the wrong house. Upon finding the back door unlocked, they entered, and encountered a dog. Gunfire ensued, and the dog, homeowner, and one of the officers were shot, all by officer gunfire. The homeowner and officer survived. Two headlines framed the incident in dramatically different ways.

Framing Effect

FOX NEWS

DANGEROUS CONFUSION
Ga. Officer Shot, Badly Hurt
Responding to Wrong House.

CNN

Cops at Wrong House Shoot
Owner

In a study by Ullrich Ecker and others, "The Effects of Subtle Misinformation in News Headlines," presented in the December 2014 issue of the *Journal of Experimental Psychology: Applied*, students read an article about a small increase in burglary rates over the last year (0.2 percent) that was anomalous in a much larger decline over the past decade (10 percent). The same article came with one of two different headlines: "Number of Burglaries Going Up" or "Downward Trend in Burglary Rate." The headline had a significant effect on which facts in the article were remembered:

> The pattern was clear-cut: A misleading headline impaired memory for the article. . . . A misleading headline can thus do damage despite genuine attempts to accurately comprehend an article. . . . The practical implications of this research are clear: News consumers must be [made] aware that editors can strategically use headlines to effectively sway public opinion and influence individuals' behavior.

A related trap/trick is **nudging**. Aldert Vrij presents a compelling example in his book *Detecting Lies and Deceit*:

> Participants saw a film of a traffic accident and then answered the question, "About how fast were the cars going when they *contacted* each other?" Other participants received the same question, except that the verb contacted was re-

placed by either hit, bumped, collided, or smashed. Even though the participants saw the same film, the wording of the question affected their answers. The speed estimates (in miles per hour) were 31, 34, 38, 39, and 41, respectively.

You can be *nudged* in a direction by a subtle word choice or other environmental cues. Restaurants will nudge you by highlighting certain dishes on menu inserts, by having servers verbally describe specials, or by just putting boxes around certain items. Retail stores and websites nudge you to purchase certain products by placing them where they are easier to see.

Nudging

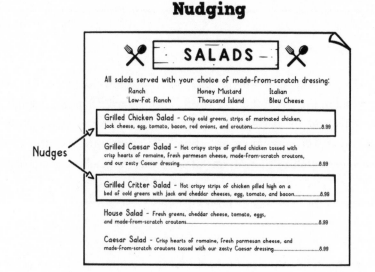

Another concept you will find useful when making purchasing decisions is **anchoring**, which describes your tendency to rely too heavily on first impressions when making decisions. You get *anchored* to the first piece of framing information you encounter. This tendency is commonly exploited by businesses when making offers.

Dan Ariely, behavioral economist and author of *Predictably Irrational*, brings us an illustrative example of anchoring using subscription offers for *The Economist*. Readers were offered three ways to subscribe: web only ($59), print only ($125), and print and web ($125).

Yes, you read that right: the "print only" version cost the same as the "print and web" version. Who would choose that? Predictably, no one. Here is the result when one hundred MIT students reported their preference:

Web only ($59): 16 percent
Print only ($125): 0 percent
Print and web ($125): 84 percent

So why include that option at all? Here's why: when it was removed from the question, this result was revealed:

Web only ($59): 68 percent
Print and web ($125): 32 percent

Just having the print-only option—even though no one chooses it—*anchors* readers to a much higher value for the print-and-web version. It feels like you are getting the web version for free, causing many more people to choose it and creating 43 percent more revenue for the magazine by just adding a version that no one chooses!

Shoppers at retailers Michaels or Kohl's know that these stores often advertise sales, where you can save 40 percent or more on selected items or departments. However, are those reduced prices a real bargain? Usually not. They're reduced from the so-called manufacturer's suggested retail price (MSRP), which is usually very high. Being aware of the MSRP anchors you so that you feel you are getting a good deal at 40 percent off. Often, that reduction just brings the price to a reasonable level.

Anchoring isn't just for numbers. Donald Trump uses this mental model, anchoring others to his extreme positions, so that what seem like compromises are actually agreements in his favor. He wrote about this in his 1987 book *Trump: The Art of the Deal*:

> My style of deal-making is quite simple and straightforward. I aim very high, and then I just keep pushing and pushing to get what I'm after. Sometimes I settle for less than I sought, but in most cases I still end up with what I want.

More broadly, these mental models are all instances of a more general model, **availability bias**, which occurs when a *bias*, or distortion, creeps into your objective view of reality thanks to information recently made *available* to you. In the U.S., illegal immigration has been a hot topic with conservative pundits and politicians in recent years, leading many people to believe it is at an all-time high. Yet the data suggests that illegal immigration via the southern border is actually at a five-decade low, indicating that the prevalence of the topic is creating an availability bias for many.

U.S. Southern Border Apprehensions at Five-Decade Low

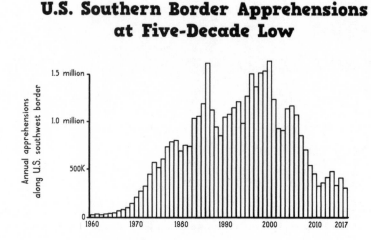

Availability bias can easily emerge from high media coverage of a topic. Rightly or wrongly, the media infamously has a mantra of "If it bleeds, it leads." The resulting heavy coverage of violent crime causes people to think it occurs more often than it does. The polling company Gallup annually asks Americans about their perception of changing violent crime rates and found in 2014 that "federal crime statistics have not been highly relevant to the public's crime perceptions in recent years."

U.S. Crime Rate: Actual vs. Perceived

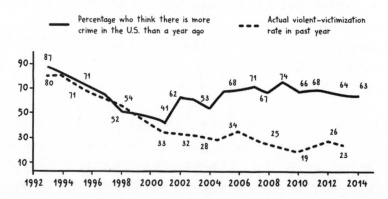

In a famous 1978 study, "Judged Frequency of Lethal Events," from the *Journal of Experimental Psychology*, Sarah Lichtenstein and others asked people about forty-one leading causes of death. They found that people often overstate the risk of sensationally over-reported causes of death, like tornados, by fifty times and understate the risk of common causes of death, like stroke, by one hundred times.

Mortality Rates by Cause: Actual vs. Perceived

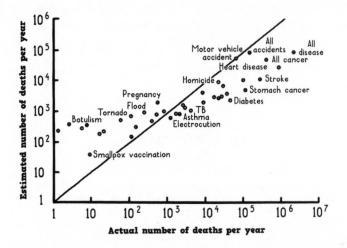

Availability bias stems from overreliance on your recent experiences within your frame of reference, at the expense of the big picture. Let's say you are a manager and you need to write an annual review for your direct report. You are supposed to think critically and objectively about her performance over the entire year. However, it's easy to be swayed by those really bad or really good contributions over just the past few weeks. Or you might just consider the interactions you have had with her personally, as opposed to getting a more holistic view based on interactions with other colleagues with different frames of reference.

With the rise of personalized recommendations and news feeds on the internet, availability bias has become a more and more pernicious problem. Online this model is called the **filter bubble**, a term coined by author Eli Pariser, who wrote a book on it with the same name.

Because of availability bias, you're likely to click on things you're already familiar with, and so Google, Facebook, and many other companies tend to show you more of what they *think* you already know and like. Since there are only so many items they can show you—only so many links on page one of the search results—they therefore *filter* out links they think you are unlikely to click on, such as opposing viewpoints, effectively placing you in a *bubble*.

In the run-up to the 2012 U.S. presidential election and again in 2018, the search engine DuckDuckGo (founded by Gabriel) conducted studies where individuals searched on Google for the same political topics, such as gun control and climate change. It discovered that people got significantly different results, personalized to them, when searching for the same topics at the same time. This happened even when they were signed out and in so-called incognito mode. Many people don't realize that they are getting tailored results based on what a mathematical algorithm thinks would increase their clicks, as opposed to a more objective set of ranked results.

The Filter Bubble

SAME SEARCH

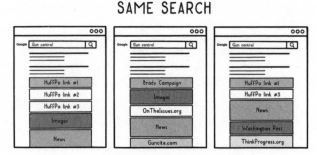

DIFFERENT RESULTS

When you put many similar filter bubbles together, you get **echo chambers**, where the same ideas seem to bounce around the same groups of people, *echoing* around the collective *chambers* of these connected filter bubbles. Echo chambers result in increased partisanship, as people have less and less exposure to alternative viewpoints. And because of availability bias, they consistently overestimate the percentage of people who hold the same opinions.

It's easy to focus solely on what is put in front of you. It's much harder to seek out an objective frame of reference, but that is what you need to do in order to be wrong less.

WALK A MILE IN THEIR SHOES

Most of the significant problems in the world involve people, so making headway on these problems often requires a deep understanding of the people involved. For instance, enough food is produced to feed everyone on the planet, yet starvation still exists because this food cannot be distributed effectively. Issues involving people, such as in corrupt governments, are primary reasons behind these distribution failures.

However, it is very easy to be wrong about other people's motivations. You may assume they share your perspective or context, think like you do, or have circumstances similar to yours. With such assumptions, you may conclude that they should also behave like you would or hold your beliefs. Unfortunately, often these assumptions are wrong.

Consequently, to be wrong less when thinking about people, you must find ways to increase your empathy, opening up a deeper understanding of what other people are really thinking. This section explores various mental models to help you do just that.

In any conflict between two people, there are two sides of the story. Then there is the **third story**, the *story* that a *third*, impartial observer would recount. Forcing yourself to think as an impartial observer can help you in any conflict situation, including difficult business negotiations and personal disagreements.

The third story helps you see the situation for what it really is. But how do you open yourself up to it? Imagine a complete recording of the situation, and then try to think about what an outside audience would say was happening if they watched or listened to the recording. What story would they tell? How much would they agree with your story? Authors Douglas Stone, Bruce Patton, and Sheila Heen explore this model in detail in their book *Difficult Conversations*: "The key is learning to describe the gap—or difference—between your story and the other person's story. Whatever else you may think and feel, you can at least agree that you and the other person see things differently."

If you can coherently articulate other points of view, even those directly in conflict with your own, then you will be less likely to make biased or incorrect judgments. You will dramatically increase your empathy—your understanding of other people's frames of reference—whether or not you agree. Additionally, if you acknowledge the perspective of the third story within difficult conversations, it can have a disarming effect, causing others involved to act less defensively. That's because you are signaling your willingness and ability to consider an objective point of view. Doing so encourages others involved to do the same.

Another tactical model that can help you empathize is the **most respectful interpre-**

tation, or **MRI**. In any situation, you can explain a person's behavior in many ways. MRI asks you to you *interpret* the other parties' actions in the *most respectful* way possible. It's giving people *the benefit of the doubt.*

For example, suppose you sent an email to your kid's school asking for information on the science curriculum for the upcoming year, but haven't heard back in a few days. Your first interpretation may be that they're ignoring your request. A more respectful interpretation would be that they are actively working to get back to you but haven't completed that work yet. Maybe they are just waiting on some crucial information before replying, like a personnel decision that hasn't been finalized yet, and that is holding up the response.

The point is you don't know the real answer yet, but if you approach the situation with the most respectful interpretation, then you will generally build trust with those involved rather than destroy it. With MRI, your follow-up email or call is more likely to have an inquisitive tone rather than an accusatory one. Building trust pays dividends over time, especially in difficult situations where that trust can serve as a bridge toward an amicable resolution. The next time you feel inclined to make an accusation, take a step back and think about whether that is really a fair assumption to make.

Using MRI may seem naïve, but like the third story, this model isn't asking you to give up your point of view. Instead, MRI asks you to approach a situation from a perspective of respect. You remain open to other interpretations and withhold judgment until necessary.

Another way of giving people the benefit of the doubt for their behavior is called **Hanlon's razor**: *never attribute to malice that which is adequately explained by carelessness.* Like Ockham's razor, Hanlon's razor seeks out the simplest explanation. And when people do something harmful, the simplest explanation is usually that they took the path of least resistance. That is, they *carelessly* created the negative outcome; they did not cause the outcome out of *malice.*

Hanlon's razor is especially useful for navigating connections in the virtual world. For example, we have all misread situations online. Since the signals of body language and voice intonation are missing, harmless lines of text can be read in a negative way. Hanlon's razor says the person probably just didn't take enough time and care in crafting their message. So the next time you send a message and all you get back is *OK*, consider that the writer is in a rush or otherwise occupied (the more likely interpretation) instead of coming from a place of dismissiveness.

The third story, most respectful interpretation, and Hanlon's razor are all attempts to overcome what psychologists call the **fundamental attribution error**, where you frequently make *errors* by *attributing* others' behaviors to their internal, or *fundamental*, motivations rather than external factors. You are guilty of the fundamental attribution error whenever you think someone was mean because she *is* mean rather than thinking she was just having a bad day.

You of course tend to view your own behavior in the opposite way, which is called **self-serving bias**. When you are the *actor*, you often have *self-serving* reasons for your behavior, but when you are the *observer*, you tend to blame the other's intrinsic nature. (That's why this model is also sometimes called *actor-observer bias*.)

For example, if someone runs a red light, you often assume that person is inherently reckless; you do not consider that she might be rushing to the hospital for an emergency. On the other hand, you will immediately rationalize your own actions when you drive like a maniac ("I'm in a hurry").

Another tactical model to help you have greater empathy is the **veil of ignorance**, put forth by philosopher John Rawls. It holds that when thinking about how society should be organized, we should do so by imagining ourselves *ignorant* of our particular place in the world, as if there were a *veil* preventing us from knowing who we are. Rawls refers to this as the "original position."

For example, you should not just consider your current position as a free person when contemplating a world where slavery is allowed. You must consider the possibility that you might have been born a slave, and how that would feel. Or, when considering policies regarding refugees, you must consider the possibility that you could have been one of those seeking refuge. The veil of ignorance encourages you to empathize with people across a variety of circumstances, so that you can make better moral judgments.

Suppose that, like many companies in recent years, you are considering ending a policy that has allowed your employees to work remotely because you believe that your teams perform better face-to-face. As a manager, it may be easy to imagine changing the policy from your perspective, especially if you personally do not highly value remote working. The veil of ignorance, though, pushes you to imagine the change from the original position, where you could be any employee. What if you were an employee caring for an elderly family member? What if you were a single parent? You may find that the new policy is warranted even after considering its repercussions holistically, but putting on the veil of ignorance helps you appreciate the challenges this might pose for your staff and might even help you come up with creative alternatives.

Speaking of privilege, we (the authors) often say we are lucky to have won the **birth lottery**. Not only were we not born into slavery, but we were also not born into almost any disadvantaged group. At *birth*, we were no more deserving of an easier run at life than a child who was born into poverty, or with a disability, or any other type of disadvantage. Yet we are the ones who won this *lottery* since we do not have these disadvantages.

It can be challenging to acknowledge that a good portion of your success stems from luck. Many people instead choose to believe that the world is completely fair, orderly, and predictable. This view is called the **just world hypothesis**, where people always get what they deserve, good or bad, because of their actions alone, with no accounting for luck or randomness. This view is summed up as *you reap what you sow.*

Ironically, belief in a just world can get in the way of actual *justice* by leading people to **victim-blame**: The sexual assault victim "should have worn different clothes" or the welfare recipient "is just lazy." *Victims* of circumstance are actually *blamed* for their circumstances, with no accounting for factors of randomness like the birth lottery.

The problem with the just world hypothesis and victim-blaming is that they make broad judgments about why things are happening to people that are often inaccurate at the individual level. You should also keep in mind that the model of **learned helplessness** can make it hard for some people to strive for improvement without some assistance. Learned helplessness describes the tendency to stop trying to escape difficult situations because we have gotten used to difficult conditions over time. Someone *learns* that they are *helpless* to control their circumstances, so they give up trying to change them.

In a series of experiments summarized in "Learned Helplessness" in the February 1972 *Annual Review of Medicine,* psychologist Martin Seligman placed dogs in a box where they were repeatedly shocked at random intervals. Then he placed them in a similar box where they could easily escape the shocks. However, they did not actually try to escape; they simply lay down and waited for the shocks to stop. On the other hand, dogs who were not shocked would quickly jump out of the box.

Learned helplessness can be overcome when animals or people see that their actions can make a difference, that they aren't actually helpless. A shining light in the reduction of chronic homelessness has been a strategy that directly combats learned helplessness, helping people take back control of their lives after years on the streets. The strategy, known as Housing First, involves giving apartments to the chronic homeless and, at the same time, assigning a social worker to help each person reintegrate into society, including finding work and living day-to-day in their apartment. Utah has been the leader in this strategy, reducing its chronic homeless population by as much as 72 percent. And the strategy actually saves on average eight thousand dollars per person in annual expenses, as the chronic homeless tend to use a lot of public resources, such as hospitals, jails, and shelters.

Learned helplessness is not found only in dire situations. People can also exhibit learned helplessness in everyday circumstances, believing they are incapable of doing or learning certain things, such as public speaking or using new technologies. In each of these cases, though, they are probably capable of improving their area of weakness if guided by the right mentor, a topic we cover in more detail later in Chapter 8. You don't want to make a fundamental attribution error by assuming that your colleague is incapable of doing something when they really just need the proper guidance.

All the mental models in this section—from the third story to learned helplessness— can help you increase your empathy. When applying them, you are effectively trying to understand people's actual circumstances and motivations better, trying as best you can to *walk a mile in their shoes*.

PROGRESS, ONE FUNERAL AT A TIME

Just as you can be anchored to a price, you can also be anchored to an entire way of thinking about something. In other words, it can be very difficult to convince you of a new idea when a contradictory idea is already entrenched in your thinking.

Like many kids in the U.S., our sons are learning "Singapore math," an approach to arithmetic that includes introducing pictorial steps in order to develop a deeper understanding of basic concepts. Even to mathematically inclined parents, this alternative

Singapore Math: Addition

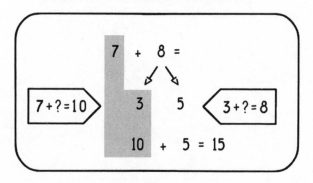

Singapore math teaches addition using "number bonds" that break apart numbers so that students can add in groups of ten.

way of doing arithmetic can feel foreign after so many years of thinking about it another way.

In science, this phenomenon is documented in Thomas Kuhn's book *The Structure of Scientific Revolutions*, which popularized the **paradigm shift** model, describing how accepted scientific theories change over time.

Instead of a gradual, evolving progression, Kuhn describes a bumpy, messy process in which initial problems with a scientific theory are either ignored or rationalized away. Eventually so many issues pile up that the scientific discipline in question is thrown into a crisis mode, and the *paradigm shifts* to a new explanation, entering a new stable era.

Essentially, the old guard holds on to the old theories way too long, even in the face of an obvious-in-hindsight alternative. Nobel Prize–winning physicist Max Planck explained it like this in his *Scientific Autobiography and Other Papers*: "A new scientific truth does not triumph by convincing its opponents and making them see the light, but rather because its opponents eventually die, and a new generation grows up that is familiar with it," or, more succinctly, "Science progresses one funeral at a time."

In 1912, Alfred Wegener put forth the theory of continental drift that we know to be true today, in which the continents *drift* across the oceans. Wegener noticed that the different continents fit together nicely like a jigsaw puzzle. Upon further study, he found that fossils seemed strikingly similar across continents, as if the continents indeed were put together this way sometime in the past.

Distribution of Fossils Across the Southern Continents of Pangea

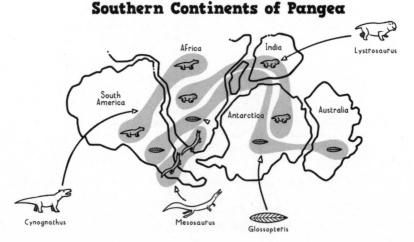

We now know this to be the case—all of our continents were previously grouped together into one supercontinent now called Pangea. However, his theory was met with harsh criticism because Wegener was an outsider—a meteorologist by training instead of a geologist—and because he couldn't offer an explanation of the mechanism causing continental drift, just the idea that it likely had taken place. It basically sat uninvestigated by mainstream geologists for forty years, until the new science of paleomagnetism started creating additional data in support of it, reviving the theory.

The major theory that held during this time was that there must have been narrow land bridges (called Gondwanian bridges) sometime in the past that allowed the animals to cross between continents, even though there was never any concrete evidence of their existence. Instead of helping to investigate Wegener's theory (which certainly wasn't perfect but had promise), geologists chose to hold on to this incorrect land bridge theory until the evidence for continental drift was so overwhelming that a paradigm shift occurred.

Gondwanian Bridges

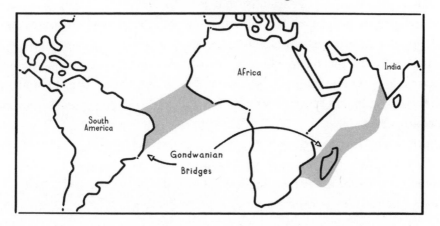

The work of Ignaz Semmelweis, a nineteenth-century Hungarian doctor, met a similar fate. He worked at a teaching hospital where doctors routinely handled cadavers and also delivered babies, without appropriately washing their hands in between. The death rate of mothers who gave birth in this part of the hospital was about 10 percent! In another part of the same hospital, where babies were mostly delivered by midwives who did not routinely handle cadavers, the comparable death rate was 4 percent.

Semmelweis obsessed about this difference, painstakingly eliminating all variables until he was left with just one: doctors versus midwives. After studying doctor behavior, he concluded that it must be due to their handling of the cadavers and instituted a practice of washing hands with a solution of chlorinated lime. The death rate immediately dropped to match that in the other part of the hospital.

Despite the clear drop in the death rate, his theories were completely rejected by the medical community at large. In part, doctors were offended by the idea that they were killing their patients. Others were so hung up on the perceived deficiencies of Semmelweis's theoretical explanation that they ignored the empirical evidence that the hand-washing was improving mortality. After struggling to get his ideas adopted, Semmelweis went crazy, was admitted to an asylum, and died at the age of forty-seven. It took another twenty years after his death for his ideas about antiseptics to start to take hold, following Louis Pasteur's unquestionable confirmation of germ theory.

Like Wegener, Semmelweis didn't fully understand the scientific mechanism that underpinned his theory and crafted an initial explanation that turned out to be somewhat incorrect. However, they both noticed obvious and important empirical truths that should have been investigated by other scientists but were *reflexively* rejected by these scientists because the suggested explanations were not in line with the conventional thinking of the time. Today, this is known as a **Semmelweis reflex**.

Individuals still hang on to old theories in the face of seemingly overwhelming evidence—it happens all the time in science and in life in general. The human tendency to gather and interpret new information in a *biased* way to *confirm* preexisting beliefs is called **confirmation bias**.

Unfortunately, it's extremely easy to succumb to confirmation bias. Correspondingly, it is hard to question your own core assumptions. There is a reason why many startup companies that disrupt industries are founded by industry outsiders. There is a reason why many scientific breakthroughs are discovered by outsiders to the field. There is a reason why "fresh eyes" and "outside the box" are clichés. The reason is because outsiders aren't rooted in existing paradigms. Their reputations aren't at stake if they question the status quo. They are by definition "free thinkers" because they are *free* to *think* without these constraints.

Confirmation bias is so hard to overcome that there is a related model called the **backfire effect** that describes the phenomenon of digging in further on a position when faced with clear evidence that disproves it. In other words, it often *backfires* when people try to change your mind with facts and figures, having the opposite *effect* on you than it should; you become more entrenched in the original, incorrect position, not less.

"I trust this site to tell the truth."

In one 2008 Yale study, pro-choice Democrats were asked to give their opinions of Supreme Court nominee John Roberts before and after hearing an ad claiming he supported "violent fringe groups and a convicted [abortion] clinic bomber." Unsurprisingly, disapproval went from 56 percent to 80 percent. However, disapproval stayed up at 72 percent when they were told the ad was refuted and withdrawn by the abortion rights advocacy group that created it.

You may also succumb to holding on to incorrect beliefs because of **disconfirmation bias**, where you impose a stronger burden of proof on the ideas you don't want to believe. Psychologist Daniel Gilbert put it like this in an April 16, 2006, article for *The New York Times*, "I'm O.K., You're Biased":

> When our bathroom scale delivers bad news, we hop off and then on again, just to make sure we didn't misread the display or put too much pressure on one foot. When our scale delivers good news, we smile and head for the shower. By uncritically accepting evidence when it pleases us, and insisting on more when it doesn't, we subtly tip the scales in our favor.

The pernicious effects of confirmation bias and related models can be explained by **cognitive dissonance**, the stress felt by holding two contradictory, *dissonant*, beliefs at once. Scientists have actually linked cognitive dissonance to a physical area in the brain that plays a role in helping you avoid aversive outcomes. Instead of dealing with the underlying cause of this stress—the fact that we might actually be wrong—we take the easy way out and rationalize the conflicting information away. It's a survival instinct!

Once you start looking for confirmation bias and cognitive dissonance, we guarantee you will spot them all over, including in your own thoughts. A real trick to being wrong less is to fight your instincts to dismiss new information and instead to embrace new ways of thinking and new paradigms. The meme on the next page perfectly illustrates how cognitive dissonance can make things we take for granted seem absurd.

There are a couple of tactical mental models that can help you on an everyday basis to overcome your ingrained confirmation bias and tribalism. First, consider **thinking gray**, a concept we learned from Steven Sample's book *The Contrarian's Guide to Leadership*. You may *think* about issues in terms of black and white, but the truth is somewhere in between, a shade of *gray*. As Sample puts it:

> Most people are binary and instant in their judgments; that is, they immediately categorize things as good or bad, true or false, black or white, friend or foe. A truly effective leader, however, needs to be able to see the shades of gray inherent in a situation in order to make wise decisions as to how to proceed.
>
> The essence of thinking gray is this: don't form an opinion about an important matter until you've heard all the relevant facts and arguments, or until circumstances force you to form an opinion without recourse to all the facts (which happens occasionally, but much less frequently than one might imagine). F. Scott Fitzgerald once described something similar to thinking gray when he observed that the test of a first-rate mind is the ability to hold two opposing thoughts at the same time while still retaining the ability to function.

This model is powerful because it forces you to be patient. By delaying decision making, you avoid confirmation bias since you haven't yet made a decision to confirm! It can be difficult to think gray because all the nuance and different points of view can cause cognitive dissonance. However, it is worth fighting through that dissonance to get closer to the objective truth.

A second mental model that can help you with confirmation bias is the **Devil's advocate position**. This was once an official position in the Catholic Church used during the process of canonizing people as saints. Once someone is canonized, the decision is eter-

nal, so it was critical to get it right. Hence this *position* was created for someone to *advocate* from the *Devil's* point of view against the deceased person's case for sainthood.

More broadly, playing the Devil's advocate means taking up an opposing side of an argument, even if it is one you don't agree with. One approach is to force yourself literally to write down different cases for a given decision or appoint different members in a group to do so. Another, more effective approach is to proactively include people in a decision-making process who are known to hold opposing viewpoints. Doing so will help everyone involved more easily see the strength in other perspectives and force you to craft a more compelling argument in favor of what you believe. As Charlie Munger says, "I never allow myself to have an opinion on anything that I don't know the other side's argument better than they do."

DON'T TRUST YOUR GUT

You make most of your everyday decisions using your **intuition**, with your subconscious automatically *intuiting* what to do from instinct or encoded knowledge. It's your common or sixth sense, your *gut feeling*, drawing on your past experiences and natural programming to react to circumstances.

In his book *Thinking, Fast and Slow*, economics Nobel laureate Daniel Kahneman makes a distinction between this intuitive fast thinking and the more deliberate, logical thinking you do when you slow down and question your intuitive assumptions.

He argues that when you do something frequently, it gradually gets encoded in your brain until at some point your intuition, via your fast thinking, takes over most of the time and you can do the task mindlessly: driving on the highway, doing simple arithmetic, saying your name. However, when you are in uncertain situations where you do not have encoded knowledge, you must use your slower thinking: driving on new roads, doing complex math, digging into your memory to recall someone you used to know. These are not mindless tasks.

You can run into trouble when you blindly trust your gut in situations where it is unclear whether you should be thinking fast or slow. Following your intuition alone at times like these can cause you to fall prey to anchoring, availability bias, framing, and other pitfalls. Getting physically lost often starts with you thinking you intuitively know where to go and ends with the realization that your intuition failed you.

Similarly, in most situations where the mental models in this book will be useful, you will want to slow down and deliberately look for how to best apply them. You may use intuition as a guide to where to investigate, but you won't rely on it alone to make decisions. You will need to really take out the map and study it before making the next turn.

You probably do not have the right experience intuitively to handle everything that life throws at you, and so you should be especially wary of your intuition in any new or unfamiliar situation. For example, if you're an experienced hiker in bear country, you know that you should never stare down a bear, as it will take this as a sign of aggression and may charge you in response. Suppose now you're hiking in mountain lion country and you come across a lion—what should you do? Your intuition would tell you not to stare it down, but in fact, you should do exactly that. To mountain lions, direct eye contact signals that you aren't easy prey, and so they will hesitate to attack.

At the same time, intuition can help guide you to the right answer much more quickly. For example, the more you work with mental models, the more your intuition about which one to use in a given situation will be right, and the faster you will get to better decisions working with these models.

In other words, as we explained at the beginning of this chapter, using mental models over time is a slow and steady way to become more antifragile, making you better able to deal with new situations over time. Of course, the better the information you put into your brain, the better your intuition will be.

One way to accelerate building up useful intuition like this is to try consistently to argue from first principles. Another is to take every opportunity you can to figure out what is actually causing things to happen. The remaining mental models in this chapter can help you do just that.

At 11:39 A.M. EST on January 28, 1986, the space shuttle *Challenger* disintegrated over the Atlantic Ocean, just seventy-three seconds into its flight, killing the seven crew members on board. It was a sad day we both remember vividly. A U.S. presidential commission was appointed to investigate the incident, ultimately producing the Rogers Commission Report, named after its chairman, William Rogers.

When something happens, the **proximate cause** is the thing that immediately *caused* it to happen. In the case of the *Challenger*, the Rogers Commission Report showed that the proximate cause was the external hydrogen tank igniting.

The **root cause**, by contrast, is what you might call the *real* reason something happened. People's explanations for their behavior are no different: anyone can give you a reason for their behavior, but that might not be the *real* reason they did something. For example, consistent underperformers at work usually have a plausible excuse for each incident, but the real reason is something more fundamental, such as lack of skills, motivation, or effort.

The Rogers Commission, in its June 6, 1986, report to the president, concluded that the root cause of the *Challenger* disaster was organizational failure:

> Failures in communication . . . resulted in a decision to launch 51-L based on incomplete and sometimes misleading information, a conflict between engineering data and management judgments, and a NASA management structure that permitted internal flight safety problems to bypass key Shuttle managers.

As part of its work, the commission conducted a **postmortem**. In medicine, a postmortem is an examination of a dead body to determine the root cause of death. As a metaphor, *postmortem* refers to any examination of a prior situation to understand what happened and how it could go better next time. At DuckDuckGo, it is mandatory to conduct a postmortem after every project so that the organization can collectively learn and become stronger (antifragile).

One technique commonly used in postmortems is called **5 Whys**, where you keep asking the question "Why did that happen?" until you reach the root causes.

1. *Why did the* Challenger's *hydrogen tank ignite?* Hot gases were leaking from the solid rocket motor.
2. *Why was hot gas leaking?* A seal in the motor broke.
3. *Why did the seal break?* The O-ring that was supposed to protect the seal failed.
4. *Why did the O-ring fail?* It was used at a temperature outside its intended range.
5. *Why was the O-ring used outside its temperature range?* Because on launch day, the temperature was below freezing, at 29 degrees Fahrenheit. (Previously, the coldest launch had been at 53 degrees.)
6. *Why did the launch go forward when it was so cold?* Safety concerns were ignored at the launch meeting.
7. *Why were safety concerns ignored?* There was a lack of proper checks and balances at NASA. That was the root cause, the real reason the *Challenger* disaster occurred.

As you can see, you can ask as many questions as you need in order to get to the root cause—five is just an arbitrary number. Nobel Prize–winning physicist Richard Feynman was on the Rogers Commission, agreeing to join upon specific request even though he was then dying of cancer. He uncovered the organizational failure within NASA and threatened to resign from the commission unless its report included an appendix consisting of his personal thoughts around root cause, which reads in part:

> It appears that there are enormous differences of opinion as to the probability of a failure with loss of vehicle and of human life. The estimates range from roughly 1 in 100 to 1 in 100,000. The higher figures come from the working engineers, and the very low figures from management. . . .
>
> It would appear that, for whatever purpose, be it for internal or external consumption, the management of NASA exaggerates the reliability of its product, to the point of fantasy. . . .
>
> For a successful technology, reality must take precedence over public relations, for nature cannot be fooled.

Sometimes you may want something to be true so badly that you fool yourself into thinking it is likely to be true. This feeling is known as **optimistic probability bias**, because you are too *optimistic* about the *probability* of success. NASA managers were way too optimistic about the probability of success, whereas the engineers who were closer to the analysis were much more on target.

Root cause analysis, whether you use 5 Whys or some other framework, helps you cut through optimistic probability bias, forcing you to slow down your thinking, push through your intuition, and deliberately uncover the truth.

The reason that root causes are so important is that, by addressing them, you can prevent the same mistakes from happening in the future. An apt analogy is that by investigating root causes, you are not just treating the symptoms but treating the underlying disease.

We started this chapter explaining that to be wrong less, you need to both work at getting better over time (antifragile) and make fewer avoidable mistakes in your thinking (unforced errors). Unfortunately, there are a lot of mental traps that you actively need to try to avoid, such as relying too much on recent information (availability bias), being too wed to your existing position (confirmation bias), and overstating the likelihood of your desired outcome (optimistic probability bias). As Feynman warned Caltech graduates in 1974: "You must not fool yourself—and you are the easiest person to fool."

- To avoid mental traps, you must think more objectively. Try **arguing from first principles**, getting to **root causes**, and seeking out the **third story**.

- Realize that your intuitive interpretations of the world can often be wrong due to **availability bias, fundamental attribution error, optimistic probability bias**, and other related mental models that explain common errors in thinking.

- Use **Ockham's razor** and **Hanlon's razor** to begin investigating the simplest objective explanations. Then test your theories by **de-risking** your assumptions, avoiding **premature optimization**.

- Attempt to **think gray** in an effort to consistently avoid **confirmation bias**.

- Actively seek out other perspectives by including the **Devil's advocate position** and bypassing the **filter bubble**. Consider the adage "You are what you eat." You need to take in a variety of foods to be a healthy person. Likewise, taking in a variety of perspectives will help you become a super thinker.

Anything That Can Go Wrong, Will

ALL YOUR ACTIONS HAVE CONSEQUENCES, but sometimes those consequences are unexpected. On the surface, these unintended consequences seem unpredictable. However, if you dig deeper, you will find that unintended consequences often follow predictable patterns and can therefore be avoided in many situations. You just need to know which patterns to look out for—the right mental models.

Here is an example. In 2016, the UK government asked the public to help name a new polar research ship. Individuals could submit names and then vote on them in an online poll. More than seven thousand names were submitted, but one name won easily, with 124,109 votes: RSS *Boaty McBoatface*. (The ship was eventually named RSS *Sir David Attenborough* instead.)

Could the government have predicted this result? Well, maybe not that the exact name RSS *Boaty McBoatface* would triumph. But could they have guessed that someone might turn the contest into a joke, that the joke would be well received by the public, and that the joke answer might become the winner? You bet.

People turn open contests like this into jokes all the time. In 2012, Mountain Dew held a similar campaign to name a new soda, but they quickly closed it down when "Diabeetus" and "Hitler Did Nothing Wrong" appeared near the top of the rankings. Also that year, Walmart teamed up with Sheets Energy Strips and offered to put on a concert by international recording artist Pitbull at the Walmart location that received the most new Facebook likes. After an internet prankster took hold of the contest, Walmart's most remote store, in Kodiak, Alaska, won. Walmart and Pitbull still held the concert there and they even had the prankster who rigged the contest join Pitbull on the trip!

Unintended consequences are not a laughing matter under more serious circumstances. For instance, medical professionals routinely prescribe opioids to help people with chronic pain. Unfortunately, these drugs are also highly addictive. As a result, pain patients may abuse their prescribed medication or even seek out similar, cheaper, and more dangerous drugs like street heroin. According to the National Institutes of Health, in the U.S., nearly half of young people who inject heroin started abusing prescription opioids first.

Patients' susceptibility to opioid addiction and abuse has substantially contributed to the deadliest drug crisis in American history. As reported by *The New York Times* on November 29, 2018, more people died from drug overdoses in 2017 than from HIV/AIDS, car crashes, or gun deaths in the years of their respective peaks. Of course, no doctor prescribing painkillers intends for their patients to die—these deaths are unintended consequences.

Through this chapter, we want to help you avoid unintended consequences like these. You will be much less likely to fall into their traps if you are equipped with the right mental models to help you better predict and deal with these situations.

HARM THY NEIGHBOR, UNINTENTIONALLY

There is a class of unintended consequences that arise when a lot of people choose what they think is best for them individually, but the sum total of the decisions creates a worse outcome for everyone. To illustrate how this works, consider Boston Common, the oldest public park in the United States.

Before it was a park, way back in the 1630s, this fifty-acre plot of land in downtown Boston, Massachusetts, was a grazing pasture for cows, with local families using it collectively as common land. In England, this type of land is referred to legally as *commons*.

Pasture commons present a problem, though: Each additional cow that a farmer gets benefits their family, but if all the farmers keep getting new cows, then the commons can be depleted. All farmers would experience the negative effects of overgrazing on the health of their herds and land.

In an 1833 essay, "Two Lectures on the Checks to Population," economist William Lloyd described a similar, but hypothetical, overgrazing scenario, now called the **tragedy of the commons**. However, unbeknownst to him, his hypothetical situation had really occurred in Boston Common two hundred years earlier (and many other times before and since). More affluent families did in fact keep buying more cows, leading to overgrazing, until, in 1646, a limit of seventy cows was imposed on Boston Common.

Any shared resource, or *commons*, is vulnerable to this *tragedy*. Overfishing, deforestation, and dumping waste have obvious parallels to overgrazing, though this model extends far beyond environmental issues. Each additional spam message benefits the spammer who sends it while simultaneously degrading the entire email system. Collective overuse of antibiotics in medicine and agriculture is leading to dangerous antibiotic resistance. People make self-serving edits to Wikipedia articles, diminishing the overall reliability of the encyclopedia.

In each of these cases, an individual makes what appears to be a rational decision (e.g., prescribing an antibiotic to a patient who might have a bacterial infection). They use the common resource for their own benefit at little or no cost (e.g., each course of treatment has only a small chance of increasing resistance). But as more and more people make the

same decision, the common resource is collectively depleted, reducing the ability for everyone to benefit from it in the future (e.g., the antibiotic becomes much less useful).

More broadly, the tragedy of the commons arises from what is called the **tyranny of small decisions**, where a series of *small*, individually rational *decisions* ultimately leads to a system-wide negative consequence, or *tyranny*. It's *death by a thousand cuts.*

You've probably gone out to dinner with friends expecting that you will equally split the check. At dinner, each person is faced with a decision to order an expensive meal or a cheaper one. When dining alone, people often order the cheaper meal. However, when they know that the cost of dinner is shared by the whole group, people tend to opt for the expensive meal. If everyone does this then everyone ends up paying more!

Ecologist William E. Odum made the connection between the tyranny of small decisions and environmental degradation in his 1982 *BioScience* article: "Much of the current confusion and distress surrounding environmental issues can be traced to decisions that were never consciously made, but simply resulted from a series of small decisions."

It's the individual decision to place a well here, cut down some trees there, build a factory over there—over time these isolated decisions aggregate to create widespread problems in our environment that are increasingly difficult to reverse.

You can also find the tyranny of small decisions in your own life. Think of those small credit card purchases or expenses that seem individually warranted at the time, but collectively add up to significant credit card bills or cash crunches. Professionally, it may be the occasional distractions and small procrastinations that, in aggregate, make your deadlines hard to reach.

The tyranny of small decisions can be avoided when someone who has a view over the whole system can veto or curb particular individual decisions when broad negative impacts can be foreseen. When the decisions are all your own, you could do this for yourself. For example, to stop your out-of-control spending, you could self-impose a budget, checking each potential purchase against the budget to see if it's compatible with your spending plan. You could do the same for your time management, by more strictly regulating your calendar.

When decisions are made by more than just you, then a third party is usually needed to fill this role, just as the city of Boston did when it restricted the number of cows on Boston Common. Company expense policies that help prevent overspending are an organizational example.

Another cause of issues like the tragedy of the commons is the **free rider problem**, where some people get a *free ride* by using a resource without paying for it. People or companies who cheat on their taxes are free riders to government services they use, such as infrastructure and the legal system. If you've ever worked on a team project where one person didn't do anything substantive, that person was free-riding on the rest of the group. Another familiar example: Has anyone ever leeched off your wi-fi or Netflix account? Or perhaps you've been the free rider?

Free-riding is commonplace with **public goods**, such as national militaries, broadcast television, even the air we breathe. As you can see from these examples, it is usually difficult to exclude people from using public goods, because they are broadly available (*public*). Since one person's use does not significantly reduce a public good's availability to others, it might seem as though there is no harm in free-riding. However, if enough people free-ride on a public good, then it can degrade to the point of creating a tragedy of the commons.

Vaccinations provide an illustrative example that combines all these models (tragedy of the commons, free rider problem, tyranny of small decisions, public goods), plus one more: **herd immunity**. Diseases can spread only when they have an eligible host to infect. However, when the vast majority of people are vaccinated against a disease, there are very few eligible new hosts, since most people (in the *herd*) are *immune* from infection due to getting vaccinated. As a result, the overall public is less susceptible to outbreaks of the disease.

In this example, the public good is a disease-free environment due to herd immunity, and the free riders are those who take advantage of this public good by not getting vaccinated. The tyranny of small decisions can arise when enough individuals choose not to get vaccinated, resulting in an outbreak of the disease, creating a tragedy of the commons.

In practice, the percentage of people who need to be vaccinated for a given disease to achieve herd immunity varies by how contagious the disease is. For measles, an extremely contagious disease, the threshold is about 95 percent. That means an outbreak is possible if the measles vaccination rate in a community falls below 95 percent!

Before the measles vaccine was introduced in 1963, more than 500,000 people a year contracted measles in the United States, resulting in more than 400 annual deaths. After the vaccine was in popular use, measles deaths dropped to literally zero.

In recent years, some parents have refused to vaccinate their kids for measles and other diseases due to the belief that vaccines are linked to autism, based on since-discredited and

Herd Immunity

Disease	Pre-vaccine Average annual deaths	Post-vaccine Annual deaths (2004)
Diphtheria	1,822 (1936–1945)	0
Measles	440 (1953–1962)	0
Mumps	39 (1963–1968)	0
Pertussis	4,034 (1934–1943)	27
Polio	3,272 (1941–1954)	0
Rubella	3,17 (1966–1968)	0
Smallpox	337 (1900–1949)	0
Tetanus	472 (1947–1949)	4

known-to-be-fraudulent research. These people who choose not to vaccinate are free-riding on the herd immunity from the people who do choose to vaccinate.

Historically, vaccination rates stayed above the respective herd immunity thresholds to prevent outbreaks, so free riders didn't realize the harm they could be inflicting on themselves and others. In recent years, however, vaccination rates have dipped dangerously low in some places. For example, in 2017, more than seventy-five people in Minnesota, most of whom were unvaccinated, contracted measles. We can expect outbreaks like this to continue as long as there exist communities with vaccination rates below the herd immunity threshold.

Unfortunately, some people cannot be medically immunized, such as infants, people with severe allergies, and those with suppressed immune systems. At no fault of their own, they face the potentially deadly consequences of the anti-vaccination movement, a literal tragedy of the commons.

Herd immunity as a concept is useful beyond the medical context. It applies directly in maintaining social, cultural, business, and industry norms. If enough infractions are left unchecked, their incidence can start increasing quickly, creating a new negative norm that can be difficult to unwind. For example, in Italy, a common phrase is used to describe the current cultural norm around paying taxes: "Only fools pay." Though Italy has been actively fighting tax evasion in the past decade, this pervasive cultural norm of tax avoidance took hold over a longer period and is proving hard to reverse.

In situations like these, dropping below a herd immunity threshold can create lasting harm. It can be difficult to *put the genie back in the bottle.* Imagine a once pristine place that is now littered with garbage and graffiti. Once it has become dirtied, that state can quickly become the new normal, and the longer it remains dirty, the more likely it will remain in the dirty state.

Hollowed-out urban centers like Detroit or disaster-ridden areas like parts of New Orleans have seen this scenario play out in the recent past. People who don't want to live with the effects of the degradation but also don't want to do the hard work to clean it up may simply move out of the area or visit less, further degrading the space due to lack of a tax base to fund proper maintenance. It then takes a much larger effort to revitalize the area than it would have taken to keep it nice in the first place. Not only do the funds need to be found for the revitalization effort, but the expectation that it should be a nice place has to be reset, and then people need to be drawn back to it.

All these unintended consequences we've been talking about have a name from economics: **externalities**, which are consequences, good or bad, that affect an entity without its consent, imposed from an *external* source. The infant who cannot be vaccinated, for example, receives a positive externality from those who choose to vaccinate (less chance of getting the disease) and a negative externality from those who do not (more chance of getting the disease). Similarly, air pollution by a factory creates a negative externality for the people living nearby—low air quality. If that same company, though, trained all its workers in first aid, residents would receive a positive externality if some of those workers used that training to save lives outside of work.

Externalities occur wherever there are **spillover effects**, which happen when an *effect* of an activity *spills over* outside the core interactions of the activity. The effects of smoking spill over to surrounding people through secondhand smoke and, more broadly, through increased public healthcare expenditures. Sometimes spillover effects can be more subtle. When you buy a car, you add congestion to the roads you drive on, a cost borne by everyone who drives on the same roads. Or when you keep your neighbors up with loud music, you deprive them of sleep, causing them to be less productive.

Over the next few days, look out for externalities. When you see or hear about someone or some organization taking an action, think about people not directly related to the action who might experience benefit or harm from it. When you see someone litter, be aware of the negative externality borne by everyone else who uses that space. Consider that if enough people litter, the herd immunity threshold could be breached, plunging the space into a much worse state.

Addressing negative externalities is often referred to as *internalizing* them. Internalizing is an attempt to require the entity that causes the negative externality to pay for it. Ideally the "price" attached to the unwanted activity is high enough that it totally covers the cost of dealing with that activity's consequences. A high price can also stop the harm from occurring in the first place. If you see a sign warning of a five-hundred-dollar fine for littering, you will be sure to find a trash can.

There are many ways to internalize negative externalities, including taxes, fines, regulation, and lawsuits. Smoking externalities are internalized via cigarette taxes and higher health insurance premiums for smokers. Traffic congestion externalities are internalized through tolls. On a personal level, your neighbor might file a noise complaint against you if you consistently play music too loud.

Another way to internalize externalities is through a marketplace. Ronald Coase won the Nobel Prize in economics in 1991 in part for what has become known as the **Coase theorem**, essentially a description of how a natural marketplace can internalize a negative externality. Coase showed that an externality can be internalized efficiently without further need for intervention (that is, without a government or other authority regulating the externality) if the following conditions are met:

1. Well-defined property rights
2. Rational actors
3. Low transaction costs

When these conditions are met, entities surrounding the externality will transact among themselves until the extra costs are internalized. If you recall the Boston Common example, the externality from overgrazing was internalized by setting a limit on the number of cows per farmer (regulation). There were no property rights though.

The Coase theorem holds that instead of limiting the cows, another solution would have been to simply divide the grazing rights to the commons property among the farmers. The farmers could then trade the grazing rights among themselves, creating an efficient marketplace for the use of the commons.

Governments have similarly tried to address the negative externalities from the burning of fossil fuels (e.g., climate change) through **cap-and-trade** systems, which are modern-day applications of the Coase theorem. The way these systems work is that the government requires emitters to hold permits for the amount of pollutants they emit. The government also sets a fixed number of total permits, which serves as the emission *cap* in the market, similar to the imposed limit on the number of cows that could graze on Boston Common. Then companies can *trade* permits on an open exchange. Such a system satisfies the conditions of the Coase theorem because property rights are well defined

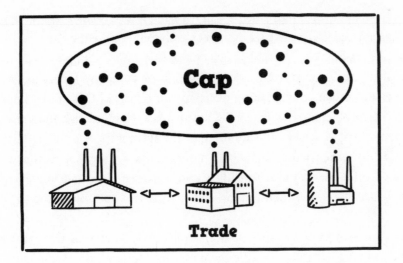

through the permitting process, companies act rationally to maximize their profits, and the open market provides low transaction costs.

If you're in charge of any system or policy, you want to think through the possible negative externalities ahead of time and devise ways to avoid them. What spillover effects could occur, and who would be affected by them? Is there a common resource that free riders could abuse or that could degrade into a tragedy of the commons? Is there another way to set up the policy or system that would reduce possible negative effects?

RISKY BUSINESS

Another set of unintended consequences can arise when people assess risk differently based on their individual positions and perspectives. These types of complications happen a lot with insurance, where risk assessments create financial consequences. For example, will you drive more recklessly in a rental car after you purchase extra rental insurance, simply because you're more protected financially from a crash? On average, people do.

This phenomenon, known as **moral hazard**, is where you take on more risk, or *hazard*, once you have information that encourages you to believe you are more protected. It has been a concern of the insurance industry since the seventeenth century! Sometimes moral hazard may involve only one person: wearing a bike helmet may give you a *false sense of security*, leading you to bike more recklessly, but you are the one who bears all the costs of a bike crash.

Moral hazards can also occur when a person or company serves as an *agent* for another person or company, making decisions on behalf of this entity, known as the *principal*. The problem arises when the agent takes on more risk than the principal would if the principal were acting alone, since the agent is more protected when things go wrong. For instance, when financial advisers manage your money, they try to stick to your risk profile, but they are more likely to take greater risks than you would on your own, simply because it isn't their money, and so losses do not impact their net worth as much.

Agency can lead to other issues as well, collectively known as the **principal-agent problem**, where the self-interest of the agent may lead to suboptimal results for the principal across a wide variety of circumstances. Politicians don't always act in the best interest of their constituents; real estate agents don't always act in the best interest of their sellers; financial brokers don't always act in the best interest of their clients; corporate management doesn't always act in the best interest of its shareholders—you get the idea. The agent's self-interest can trump the principal's interests.

Some fascinating studies of this concept have measured the behavior of agents when they are serving themselves compared with how they serve others. Real estate agents tend to sell their own houses at higher prices compared with their clients' houses, in large part because they are willing to leave them on the market longer. In *Freakonomics*, Steven Levitt and Stephen Dubner dig into the reason why:

> Only 1.5 percent of the purchase price goes directly into your agent's pocket.
> So on the sale of your $300,000 house, her personal take of the $18,000 commission is $4,500. . . . Not bad, you say. But what if the house was actually worth more than $300,000? What if, with a little more effort and patience and a few more newspaper ads, she could have sold it for $310,000? After the commission, that puts an additional $9,400 in your pocket. But the agent's additional share— her personal 1.5 percent of the extra $10,000—is a mere $150. . . .
> It turns out that a real-estate agent keeps her own home on the market an average of ten days longer and sells it for an extra 3-plus percent, or $10,000 on a $300,000 house. When she sells her own house, an agent holds out for the best

offer; when she sells yours, she encourages you to take the first decent offer that comes along. Like a stockbroker churning commissions, she wants to make deals and make them fast. Why not? Her share of a better offer—$150—is too puny an incentive to encourage her to do otherwise.

Moral hazard and principal-agent problems can occur because of **asymmetric information**, where one side of a transaction has different *information* than the other side; that is, the available information is not *symmetrically* distributed. Real estate agents have more information about the real estate market than sellers, so it is hard to question their recommendations. Similarly, a financial adviser generally has more information about the financial markets than their clients.

It is also not always completely transparent to principals how agents are compensated, which might cause principals to make different decisions than they would if they had the full picture. If you knew that your financial adviser was getting paid to recommend a financial product to you, you might be less likely to invest in it. Disclosure laws and the increase in open information via the internet can reduce the effects of asymmetric information.

"Under disclosure rules, I'm required to tell you I own stock in the company whose drug I'm prescribing."

Sometimes, though, the consumer has the upper hand when it comes to asymmetric information. This is often the case with insurance products, where the person or company applying for insurance usually knows more about their own risk profile than the insurance company does.

When parties *select* transactions that they think will benefit them, based at least partially on their own private information, that's called **adverse selection**. People who know they are going to need dental work are more likely to seek out dental insurance. This unfortunately drives up the price for everyone. Two ways to mitigate adverse selection in the insurance market are to mandate participation, as many localities do for car insurance, and to distinguish subpopulations based on their risk profiles, as life insurers do for smokers.

Like crossing a herd immunity threshold, rampant and persistent asymmetric information in a market can lead to its collapse. Consider a used car market where the sellers know the quality of their cars, but the buyers cannot distinguish between lemons (bad cars) and peaches (good cars).

In such a market, buyers will want to pay only an average-quality price for the cars on the market, since they can't tell the difference between peaches and lemons. Sellers who know their cars are peaches, however, will not want to sell them in this market because they know their cars are worth more than the average price. As they pull their peaches out of the market, the average quality drops and, in turn, the price of the used cars left in the market keeps dropping. The sellers of lemons free-ride on the market until it collapses into just a market of lemons.

Adverse selection was an early concern with the state health insurance exchanges as part of the Affordable Care Act (ACA) in the United States. Extending the metaphor, the lemons are sick people applying to the exchanges, and the peaches are healthy people applying. There was an individual mandate requiring health insurance, but the penalties for not complying were low, so the concern was that many healthy people would just opt to pay the fine rather than participate. Sick people, who need the insurance, would therefore make up more of the applicants, causing premiums to rise so that health insurers could cover their costs to care for them. This would, in turn, eject from the market more healthy participants not willing to pay these higher premiums, further raising prices. This situation is still unfolding, with those invested in the success of the ACA trying to ensure that it doesn't spiral out of control.

Sometimes there are ways to break the cycle. In the case of the used car market, services like Carfax try to restore symmetric information. This arrangement allows buyers to

The "Death Spiral" of Adverse Selection

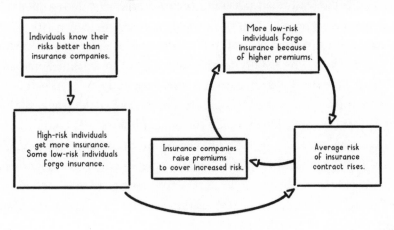

distinguish between lemons and peaches, and it eventually pushes lemons out of the market. In contrast, one of the goals of the ACA was to make sure that people with preexisting conditions were not pushed out of the market. The only way this system works, though, is if healthy, lower-risk people continue paying into the system, allowing insurers to spread out the cost of higher-risk individuals. This helps keep premiums from rising too high, making care more affordable for everyone. That's why the ACA mandate was so important to the viability of the overall system.

The mental models from the last section (tragedy of the commons, externalities, etc.) and those from this section (moral hazard, information asymmetry, etc.) are signs of **market failure**, where open *markets* without intervention can create suboptimal results, or *fail*. To correct a market failure, an outside party must intervene in some way. Unfortunately, these interventions themselves can also fail, a result called **government failure** or **political failure**.

Antibiotics present a good case study in market and political failure. As we described earlier, overuse of antibiotics can reduce their efficacy as a common resource because bacteria have a chance of evolving to develop resistance each time an antibiotic is used. Overprescription of antibiotics therefore contributes to the negative externality of widespread antibiotic resistance.

Before antibiotics, bacterial infections were a leading cause of death. Scarlet fever, a complication of untreated strep infections (usually strep throat) regularly killed children in the early 1900s, and at its peak tuberculosis caused 25 percent of all deaths in Europe. Anything that could lead to an infection, such as surgery or even a small cut, could be deadly.

If bacteria develop resistance to all antibiotics, large-scale bacterial outbreaks could be a reality again. That's why public health officials want to sideline some antibiotics for which bacteria have not yet developed any resistance, to be used in potential doomsday outbreak scenarios. We need a supply of new antibiotics to defend against these bacterial "superbugs" that cannot be killed by any current antibiotics.

For these new antibiotics to be useful in future doomsday scenarios, though, they must be used sparingly, only in cases where they are absolutely necessary. That's because each time they are used, the risk of bacteria developing resistance to them goes up. Let's suppose the government addresses the market failure of overuse of these antibiotics by permitting their use only in dire circumstances.

There is the clear need for these new antibiotics to be created, but at the same time they would not be able to be regularly used or sold. Assuming that their development and production continue to be left primarily to the private market, the government failure from this regulatory environment emerges: How can pharmaceutical companies get a return on their investment given current patent laws? Drug patents are likely to expire or come close to expiring before the drugs are needed, effectively erasing most potential profits for the pharmaceutical companies. Also, throughout this period, some amount of the drugs still need to be continually produced in case they are needed, with batches of them continually expiring before they can be sold. (Unfortunately, it is not possible to cost-effectively sideline large-scale manufacturing capacity while waiting for peak demand.)

These uncertainties lead to a second market failure of severe underinvestment in the development of new antibiotics, leaving us collectively vulnerable to future outbreaks. In fact, most large pharmaceutical companies have long since totally discontinued research-and-development investment in this area.

According to a 2014 report commissioned by the U.S. Department of Health and Human Services, there is a huge disconnect between the value of a new antibiotic for society and the value to the private market. In some cases, as for bacterial ear infections, the expected value to the private market is actually *negative*, while the value to society is estimated to be approximately $500 billion!

These future antibiotics are a public good (since they protect the public's health), and so there ought to be significant government-provided incentives to correct this market failure—for example, extended patent protection or shared development costs. Otherwise, we will remain in a tragedy-of-the-commons situation, because without such incentives we are all free-riding on the development of these drugs, directly leading to their underproduction.

No one knows when these drugs will be needed, and given their typical ten-year development timeline, there is no time to waste. A deadly bacterial outbreak could be around the corner. In any situation where risk and reward are separated across different entities, like this one, you want to look out for risk-related unintended consequences.

BE CAREFUL WHAT YOU WISH FOR

"The best laid schemes o' mice an' men [often go awry]," penned poet Robert Burns in 1785. In other words, things don't always go as planned. Consider Gosplan, the agency charged with central economic planning for the Soviet Union for most of the twentieth century. Their plans often involved setting economy-wide target amounts for commodities (wheat, tires, etc.), which broke down into production targets for specific facilities. In 1990, economist Robert Heilbroner described some of the complications with this system in "After Communism," published in *The New Yorker*:

> For many years, targets were given in physical terms—so many yards of cloth or tons of nails—but that led to obvious difficulties. If cloth was rewarded by the yard, it was woven loosely to make the yarn yield more yards. If the output of nails was determined by their number, factories produced huge numbers of pin-like nails; if by weight, smaller numbers of very heavy nails. The satiric magazine *Krokodil* once ran a cartoon of a factory manager proudly displaying his record output, a single gigantic nail suspended from a crane.

Goodhart's law summarizes the issue: *When a measure becomes a target, it ceases to be a good measure.* This more common phrasing is from Cambridge anthropologist Marilyn Strathern in her 1997 paper "'Improving Ratings': Audit in the British University System." However, the "law" is named after English economist Charles Goodhart, whose original formulation in a conference paper presented at the Reserve Bank of Australia in 1975 stated: "Any observed statistical regularity will tend to collapse once pressure is placed upon it for control purposes."

Social psychologist Donald T. Campbell formulated a similar "law" (known as *Camp-*

bell's law) in his 1979 study, "Assessing the Impact of Planned Social Change." He explains the concept a bit more precisely: "The more any quantitative social indicator is used for social decision-making, the more subject it will be to corruption pressures and the more apt it will be to distort and corrupt the social processes it is intended to monitor."

Both describe the same basic phenomenon: When you try to incentivize behavior by setting a measurable target, people focus primarily on achieving that measure, often in ways you didn't intend. Most importantly, their focus on the measure may not correlate to the behavior you hoped to promote.

High-stakes testing culture—be it for school examinations, job interviews, or professional licensing—creates **perverse incentives** to "teach to the test," or worse, cheat. In the city of Atlanta in 2011, 178 educators were implicated in a widespread scandal involving correcting student answers on standardized tests, ultimately resulting in eleven convictions and sentences of up to twenty years on racketeering charges. Similarly, hospitals and colleges have been increasingly criticized for trying to achieve rankings at the expense of providing quality care and education, the very things the rankings are supposed to be measuring.

In *A Short History of Nearly Everything*, Bill Bryson describes a situation in which paleontologist Gustav Heinrich Ralph von Koenigswald accidentally created perverse incentives on an expedition:

> Koenigswald's discoveries might have been more impressive still but for a tactical error that was realized too late. He had offered locals ten cents for every piece of hominid bone they could come up with, then discovered to his horror that they had been enthusiastically smashing large pieces into small ones to maximize their income.

It's like a wish-granting genie who finds loopholes in your wishes, meeting the letter of the wish but not its spirit, and rendering you worse off than when you started. In fact, there is a mental model for this more specific situation, called the **cobra effect**, describing when an attempted solution actually makes the problem worse.

This model gets its name from a situation involving actual cobras. When the British were governing India, they were concerned about the number of these deadly snakes, and so they started offering a monetary reward for every snake brought to them. Initially the policy worked well, and the cobra population decreased. But soon, local entrepreneurs started breeding cobras just to collect the bounties. After the government found out and ended the policy, all the cobras that were being used for breeding were released, increasing the cobra population even further.

A similar thing happened under French rule of Vietnam. In Hanoi, the local government created a bounty program for rats, paying the bounty based on a rat's tail. Enterprising ratcatchers, however, would catch and release the rats after just cutting off their tails; that way the rats could go back and reproduce. Whenever you create an incentive structure, you must heed Goodhart's law and watch out for perverse incentives, lest you be overrun by cobras and rats!

The **Streisand effect** applies to an even more specific situation: when you unintentionally draw more attention to something when you try to hide it. It's named for entertainer Barbra Streisand, who sued a photographer and website in 2003 for displaying an aerial photo of her mansion, which she wanted to remain private. Before the suit, the image had been downloaded a total of six times from the site; after people saw news stories about the lawsuit, the site was visited hundreds of thousands of times, and now the photo is free to license and is on display on Wikipedia and many other places. As was said of Watergate, *It's not the crime, it's the cover-up.*

Streisand Effect

A related model to watch out for is the **hydra effect**, named after the Lernaean Hydra, a beast from Greek mythology that grows two heads for each one that is cut off. When you arrest one drug dealer, they are quickly replaced by another who steps in to meet the demand. When you shut down an internet site where people share illegal movies or music, more pop up in its place. Regime change in a country can result in an even worse regime.

An apt adage is *Don't kick a hornet's nest,* meaning don't disturb something that is going to create a lot more trouble than it is worth. With all these traps—Goodhart's law, along with the cobra, hydra, and Streisand effects—if you are going to think about changing a system or situation, you must account for and quickly react to the clever ways people may respond. There will often be individuals who try to game the system or otherwise subvert what you're trying to do for their personal gain or amusement.

If you do engage, another trap to watch out for is the **observer effect**, where there is an *effect* on something depending on how you *observe* it, or even who observes it. An everyday example is using a tire pressure gauge. In order to measure the pressure, you must also let out some of the air, reducing the pressure of the tire in the process. Or, when the big boss comes to town, everyone acts on their best behavior and dresses in nicer clothes.

The observer effect is certainly something to be aware of when making actual measurements, but you should also consider how people might indirectly change their behavior as they become less anonymous. Think of how hard it is to be candid when you know the camera is rolling. Or how differently you might respond to giving a colleague performance feedback in an anonymous survey versus one with your name attached to it.

In "Chilling Effects: Online Surveillance and Wikipedia Use," Oxford researcher Jonathon Penny studied Wikipedia traffic patterns before and after the 2013 revelations by Edward Snowden about the U.S. National Security Agency's internet spying tactics, finding a 20 percent decline in terrorism-related article views involving terms like *al-Qaeda*, *Taliban*, and *car bomb*. The implication is that when people realized they were being

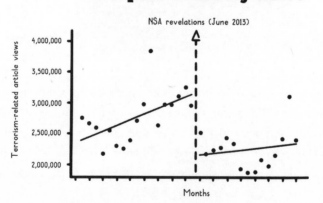

Wikipedia Chilling Effect

watched by their governments, some of them stopped reading articles that they thought could get them into trouble. The name for this concept is **chilling effect**.

In the legal context where the term *chilling effect* originated, it refers to when people feel discouraged, or *chilled*, from freely exercising their rights, for fear of lawsuits or prosecution. More generally, chilling effects are a type of observer effect where the threat of retaliation creates a change in behavior.

Sometimes chilling effects are intentional, such as when someone is made an example of to send a message to others about how offenders will be treated. For instance, a company will sue another aggressively over its patents to scare off other companies that might be thinking of competing with them.

Many times, though, chilling effects are unintentional. Mandated harassment reporting can give victims pause when contemplating reaching out for help, since they might not yet be ready for that level of scrutiny.

Fear of harassment also curbs usage of social media. In a June 6, 2017, Pew Research study, 13 percent of respondents said they stopped using an online service and 27 percent said they chose not to post something online after witnessing online harassment toward others.

In your personal relationships, you might find yourself walking on eggshells around a person you know has an anger management problem. Similarly, some romantic partners may not be totally honest about their relationship grievances if they perceive their partner as having one foot out the door.

Like the Wikipedia study discussed above, another unintentional chilling effect was found by an MIT study, "Government Surveillance and Internet Search Behavior," which showed that post-Snowden, people have also stopped searching for as many health-related terms on Google, even though the terms weren't directly related to illegal activity of any kind. As people understand more about corporate and government tracking, their searching of sensitive topics in general has been chilled. The authors noted: "Suppressing health information searches potentially harms the health of search engine users and, by reducing traffic on easy-to-monetize queries, also harms search engines' bottom line."

This negative unintended consequence could be considered **collateral damage**. In a military context, this term means injuries, *damage*, inflicted on unintended, *collateral*, targets. You can apply this model to any negative side effects that result from an action. The U.S. government maintains a No Fly List of people who are prohibited from commercial air travel within, into, or out of the U.S. There have been many cases of people with the same names as those on the list who experienced the collateral damage of being denied boarding and missing flights, including a U.S. Marine who was prevented from boarding a flight home from his military tour in Iraq. When people are deported or jailed, even for good reason, collateral damage can be inflicted on their family members. For instance, the loss of income could take a financial toll, or children could experience the trauma of growing up without one or both parents, possibly ending up in foster care.

Sometimes collateral damage can impact the entity that inflicted the damage in the first place, which is called **blowback**. Blowback sometimes can occur well after the initial action. The U.S. supported Afghan insurgents in the 1980s against the USSR. Years later these same groups joined al-Qaeda to fight against the U.S., using some of the very same weapons the U.S. had provided decades earlier.

Like Goodhart's law and related models, observer and chilling effects concern unintended consequences that can happen after you take a deliberate action—be it a policy, experiment, or campaign. Again, it is best to think ahead about what behaviors you are actually incentivizing by your action, how there might be perverse incentives at play, and what collateral damage or even blowback these perverse incentives might cause.

Take medical care as a modern example. Fee-for-service medicine, prevalent in the United States, pays healthcare providers based on how much treatment is provided. Quite simply, the more treatment that is provided, the more money that is made, effectively incentivizing quantity of treatment. If you have a surgery, any additional care required (follow-up surgeries, tests, physical therapy, medications, etc.) will be billed separately by the provider conducting the treatment, including any care resulting from surgical complications that might arise. Each piece of the treatment is generally individually profitable to the providers.

With value-based care, by contrast, there is usually just one reimbursement payment amount for everything related to the surgery, including much of the directly related additional care. This payment scheme therefore incentivizes quality over quantity, as the healthcare provider conducting the surgery is also on the hook for some of the additional care, sometimes even if it is administered by other providers. This payment scheme therefore focuses healthcare providers on determining the exact right amount of treatment because they face financial consequences for over- or under-providing care.

This straightforward change in how medicine is billed (one lump-sum payment to one provider versus many payments to multiple providers) significantly changes the incentives for healthcare providers. The Medicare system in the United States is shifting to this value-based reimbursement model both to reduce costs and to improve health out-comes, taking advantage of its better-aligned incentives between payment and quality care.

In other words, seemingly small changes in incentive structures can really matter. You should align the outcome you desire as closely as possible with the incentives you provide. You should expect people generally to act in their own perceived self-interest, and so you want to be sure this perceived self-interest directly supports your goals.

IT'S GETTING HOT IN HERE

In the first section of this chapter, we warned about the tyranny of small decisions, where a series of isolated and seemingly good decisions can nevertheless add up to a bad out-come. There is a broader class of unintended consequences to similarly watch out for, which also involve making seemingly good short-term decisions that can still add up to a bad outcome in the long term. The mental model often used to describe this class of un-intended consequences is called the **boiling frog**: Suppose a *frog* jumps into a pot of cold water. Slowly the heat is turned up and up and up, eventually boiling the frog to death.

It turns out real frogs generally jump out of the hot water in this situation, but the metaphorical boiling frog persists as a useful mental model describing how a gradual change can be hard to react to, or even perceive. The boiling frog has been used as a cau-tionary tale in a variety of contexts, from climate change to abusive relationships to the erosion of personal privacy. It is sometimes paired with another animal metaphor, also scientifically untrue—that of the ostrich with its *head in the sand*, ignoring the signs of danger. In each case the unintended consequence of not acting earlier is eventually an extremely unpleasant state that is hard to get out of—global warming, domestic violence, mass surveillance.

These unintended consequences are likely to arise when people don't plan for the long term. From finance, **short-termism** describes these types of situations, when you focus on *short-term* results, such as quarterly earnings, over long-term results, such as five-year profits. If you focus on just short-term financial results, you won't invest enough in the future. Eventually you will be left behind by competitors who are making those long-term investments, or you could be swiftly disrupted by new upstarts (which we cover in Chapter 9).

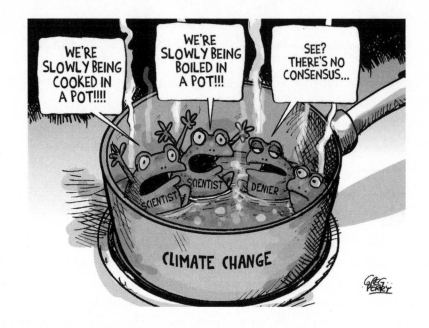

There are many examples of the deleterious effects of short-termism in everyday life. If you put off learning new skills because of the tasks in front of you, you will never expand your horizons. If you decorate your house one piece at a time in isolation, you won't end up with a cohesive décor. If there are additions to the tax code without any thought to long-term simplification, it eventually becomes a bloated mess.

The software industry has a name for the consequences of short-termism: **technical debt**. The idea comes from writing code: if you prioritize short-term code fixes, or "hacks," over long-term, well-designed code and processes, then you accumulate *debt* that will eventually have to be paid down by future code rewrites and refactors. Accumulating technical debt isn't necessarily harmful—it can help projects move along faster in the short term—but it should be done as a conscientious observer, not as an unaware boiling frog.

If you have been involved in any small home repairs, you're probably familiar with this model. When something small is broken, many people opt for a short-term fix today, DIY-style (or even duct-tape-style), because it is cheaper and faster. However, these "fixes," which may not be up to building standards, may cost you in the long run. In particular, the item may need to be repaired again at greater cost, such as when you want to sell your home.

Startup culture has extended this concept to other forms of "debt": *Management debt* is the failure to put long-term management team members or processes in place. *Design*

Technical Debt

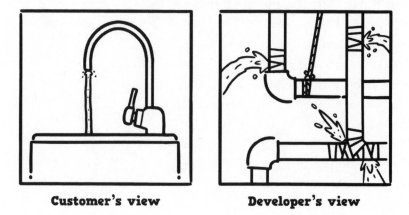

Customer's view   Developer's view

debt means not having a cohesive product design language or brand style guide. *Diversity debt* refers to neglecting to make necessary hires to ensure a diverse team. This model can likewise be extended to any area to describe the unintended consequences of short-term thinking: relationship debt, diet debt, cleaning debt.

In these scenarios, you need to keep up with your "payments" or else the debt can become overwhelming: the out-of-control messy house, the expanding waistline, or the deteriorating relationship. These outstanding debts impact your long-term flexibility. The general model for this impact comes from economics and is called **path dependence**, meaning that the set of decisions, or *paths*, available to you now is *dependent* on your past decisions.

Sometimes an initial decision or event may seem innocuous at first, but it turns out to strongly influence or limit your possible outcomes in the long run. As a small company, you may choose to use a piece of software for project management without giving it much thought. As you grow, though, you'll have a large group of people using this software, which may eventually turn out to be suboptimal; however, all your data is now stored there, and it would be a huge disruption to switch products.

On a personal level, many people are likely to stay near the town where they went to school once they graduate. This creates a massive long-term impact on their available career and family choices.

The same thing can happen on a larger scale. Similar types of businesses often congregate together—jewelry stores, furniture depots, car dealerships. In these cases, whichever store came first created a path dependence for all to follow.

The song "I Know an Old Lady," written by Rose Bonne and Alan Mills in 1952, captures the dangers of short-termism and path dependence if left unchecked.

There was an old lady who swallowed a fly;
I don't know why she swallowed a fly—perhaps she'll die!
There was an old lady who swallowed a spider;
That wriggled and jiggled and tickled inside her!
She swallowed the spider to catch the fly;
I don't know why she swallowed a fly—perhaps she'll die!
. . . There was an old lady who swallowed a cow;
I don't know how she swallowed a cow!
She swallowed the cow to catch the goat,
She swallowed the goat to catch the dog,
She swallowed the dog to catch the cat,
She swallowed the cat to catch the bird,
She swallowed the bird to catch the spider,
That wriggled and jiggled and tickled inside her!
She swallowed the spider to catch the fly;
I don't know why she swallowed a fly—perhaps she'll die!
There was an old lady who swallowed a horse;
. . . She died, of course!

To escape the fate of the old lady or the boiling frog, you need to think about the long-term consequences of short-term decisions. For any decision, ask yourself: What kind of debt am I incurring by doing this? What future paths am I taking away by my actions today?

Another model from economics offers some reprieve from the limitations of path dependence: **preserving optionality**. The idea is to make choices that *preserve* future *options*. Maybe as a business you put some excess profits into a rainy-day fund, or as an employee you dedicate some time to learning new skills that might give you options for future employment. Or, when faced with a decision, maybe you can delay deciding at all (see *thinking gray* in Chapter 1) and, instead, continue to wait for more information, keeping your options open until you are more certain of a better path to embark upon.

Many college freshmen have some idea of what they want to study, but most are not ready to immediately select their major. When selecting a college, it would be a good idea for a student to choose a school that is strong in several fields of interest, not just the one they think they might pick, which preserves their options until they are really ready to decide.

As with most things, though, preserving options must be done in moderation. Even if you choose a college with many possible majors, at some point you do need to pick one in order to be able to graduate on time. When selecting a graduate school, Lauren chose a program in operations research as a way of preserving optionality, rather than a more narrowly tailored program in biostatistics. However, not having a strong idea of what area she wanted to research for her dissertation ultimately resulted in an extra year of school.

The downside of keeping many options open is that it often requires more resources, increasing costs. Think of going to school while you also have a full-time job, maintaining multiple homes, or exploring several lines of business in one parent company. You need to find the right balance between preserving optionality and path dependence.

One model that can help you figure out how to strike this balance in certain situations is the **precautionary principle**: when an action could possibly create harm of an unknown magnitude, you should proceed with extreme *caution* before enacting the policy. It's like the medical principle of "First, do no harm."

For example, if there is reason to believe a substance might cause cancer, the precautionary principle advises that it is better to control it tightly now while the scientific community figures out the degree of harm, rather than risk people getting cancer unnecessarily because the substance has not been controlled. In 2012, the European Union adopted the precautionary principle formally with the Treaty on the Functioning of the European Union:

> Union policy on the environment shall aim at a high level of protection taking into account the diversity of situations in the various regions of the Union. It shall be based on the precautionary principle and on the principles that preventive action should be taken, that environmental damage should as a priority be rectified at source and that the polluter should pay.

On an individual level, the precautionary principle instructs you to take pause when an action could possibly cause you significant personal harm. That seems obvious, but people engage in risky behavior all the time (e.g., drunk or reckless driving). Beyond physical harm, the same concept applies to other kinds of harm: for example, financial harm (gambling or accepting a bad loan) and emotional harm (infidelity or going too far in an argument).

These mental models are the most useful when thinking about existential risks. After all, in the tale of the boiling frog, the frog dies. Therefore, you want first to assess what substantial harms could arise in the long term, then work backward to assess how your short-term decisions (or lack thereof) might be contributing to long-term negative scenarios (a process that we cover in more depth in Chapter 6). With this knowledge, you can then take the necessary level of precaution, paying down technical debt as needed, happily preventing yourself from becoming the boiling frog.

TOO MUCH OF A GOOD THING

On the side of an ancient Greek temple, home to the Oracle of Delphi, was inscribed the precept *Nothing in excess.* Our modern equivalent is *too much of a good thing.* It's natural to want more of something good, but too much of it can be bad. One slice of cookie dough cheesecake from The Cheesecake Factory is amazing; downing a whole cheesecake will probably cause you some problems, though.

The same goes for information. Complaints from people overwhelmed by too much information are not new. Roman writer Marcus Seneca said, "The abundance of books is a distraction"—in the first century A.D.! Today, researching almost anything online can make your head spin, from the mundane, such as wading through all the Amazon products and reviews for coffeemakers, to the life-changing, such as comparing colleges or choosing a new city to move to. There is just so much data and advice on almost any subject, it can easily be overwhelming.

Of course, you need some information to make good decisions, but too much information leads to **information overload**, which complicates a decision-making process. The excess *information* can *overload* the processing capacity of the system, be it a single person, group, or even computer, causing decision making to take too long.

There is a name for this unintended consequence: **analysis paralysis**, where your decision making suffers from *paralysis* because you are over-*analyzing* the large amount of information available. This is why you can spend too much time trying to make that coffeemaker decision or choosing where to go out to dinner when faced with an endless list of choices from Yelp. More seriously, people often stay in a job they don't like because they are unsure of what to do next given all the possibilities.

The model **perfect is the enemy of good** drives home this point—if you wait for the perfect decision, or perfect anything, really, you may be waiting a long time indeed. And by not making a choice, you are actually making a choice: you are choosing the status quo, which could be considerably worse than one of the other choices you could already have made.

© marketoonist.com

There is a natural conflict between the desire to make decisions quickly and the feeling that you need to accumulate more information to be sure you are making the right choice. You can deal with this conflict by categorizing decisions as either **reversible decisions** or **irreversible decisions**. Irreversible decisions are hard if not impossible to unwind. And they tend to be really important. Think of selling your business or having a kid. This model holds that these decisions require a different decision-making process than their reversible counterparts, which should be treated much more fluidly. In a letter to shareholders, Amazon CEO Jeff Bezos stressed the importance of this model:

Some decisions are consequential and irreversible or nearly irreversible—one-way doors—and these decisions must be made methodically, carefully, slowly, with great deliberation and consultation. If you walk through and don't like what you see on the other side, you can't get back to where you were before. . . . But most decisions aren't like that—they are changeable, reversible—they're two-way doors. If you've made a suboptimal [reversible] decision, you don't have to live with the consequences for that long. You can reopen the door and go back through. . . .

As organizations get larger, there seems to be a tendency to use the heavy-weight [irreversible] decision-making process on most decisions, including many [reversible] decisions. The end result of this is slowness, unthoughtful risk aversion, failure to experiment sufficiently, and consequently diminished invention.

Another way to help combat analysis paralysis is to limit choice, because the more choices you have, the harder it is to choose between them. In the early 1950s, psychologists William Hick and Ray Hyman separately conducted a number of experiments to try to quantify the mathematical relationship between the number of choices given and how long it takes to decide. They found that a greater number of choices increased the decision time logarithmically, in a formulation now known as **Hick's law**.

Hick's law is regularly cited as an important factor in user-experience designs, such as in the design of restaurant menus, website navigation, and forms (offline or online). For instance, on a menu, having a vegetarian section allows vegetarians to efficiently narrow the sections of the menu they should read through. Being able to determine quickly whether there are enough vegetarian options on a menu might be a big factor in whether a family with a vegetarian would choose to eat at your restaurant.

In your own life, you can use Hick's law to remember that decision time is going to increase with the number of choices, and so if you want people to make quick decisions, reduce the number of choices. One way to do this is to give yourself or others a multi-step decision with fewer choices at each step, such as asking what type of restaurant to go to (Italian, Mexican, etc.), and then offering another set of choices within the chosen category.

In addition to increased decision-making time, there is evidence that a wealth of options can create anxiety in certain contexts. This anxiety is known as the **paradox of choice**, named after a 2004 book of the same name by American psychologist Barry Schwartz.

Schwartz explains that an overabundance of choice, the fear of making a suboptimal decision, and the potential for lingering regret following missed opportunities can leave people unhappy. In the context of seeking romantic relationships, people are often reminded that there are "plenty of fish in the sea." With so many fish, this can leave you to question how you will know when you have found "the one." Similarly, you might be left questioning whether a past partner was "the one that got away." This anxiety also arises with smaller-scale decisions, such as when you have young kids and you find yourself finally with an opportunity to go out for the night: Do you go out with friends or with just your partner? Do you go to a nice restaurant or the movies? If the movies, which one? The more choices, the more chance you have for regret later.

While we, the authors, are reasonably happy people, we have experienced the anxiety surrounding the paradox of choice with our own life choices. We were lucky to have sold a startup company at a young age, leaving us with essentially unlimited career options. At the time of the sale, Lauren had just accepted a position at GlaxoSmithKline and was content with continuing down that path. However, over time she wondered whether this was the right path and found herself constantly reading job postings. She also spent a lot of time thinking about going back to school in a different field, fulfilling a different childhood dream, such as becoming an architect or designing prosthetics.

Gabriel was left with an entirely open-ended future and took some time off. But soon he started asking, What next? Should I start another for-profit company? Should Lauren and I start a nonprofit together? Write a book? The choices were and are endless. Don't get us wrong—we aren't complaining. We are just acknowledging that we personally sympathize with this model.

Hick's law and the paradox of choice explain downsides of having many choices. There is also a model that explains the downside of making many decisions in a limited period: **decision fatigue**. As you make more and more *decisions*, you get *fatigued*, leading to a worsening of decision quality. After taking a mental break, you effectively reset and start making higher-quality decisions again.

The 2011 study "Extraneous Factors in Judicial Decisions" describes the impact of decision fatigue on parole boards deciding whether to grant freedom to prisoners: "We find that the percentage of favorable rulings drops gradually from [about] 65% to nearly zero within each decision session and returns abruptly to [about] 65% after a break. Our findings suggest that judicial rulings can be swayed by extraneous variables that should have no bearing on legal decisions."

Some extremely productive people, including Steve Jobs and Barack Obama, have tried to combat decision fatigue by reducing the number of everyday decisions, such as what to eat or wear, so that they can reserve their decision-making faculties for more important decisions. Barack Obama chose to wear only blue or gray suits and said of this choice, "I'm trying to pare down decisions. I don't want to make decisions about what I'm eating or wearing. Because I have too many other decisions to make." Gabriel also tends to do this to some extent, usually wearing one of seven identical pairs of dark gray jeans and often eating the same lunch for weeks on end. He swears that it really does make things easier and saves time!

If you want more variety in your life, one suggestion is to front-load the decisions on your outfits and meals for the week to Sunday. Making these decisions on a usually lower-stress day can free up your decision-making capacity for the workweek. Meal planning and even some meal prep on the weekend can help keep you from making unhealthy choices when you are overwhelmed later in the week.

In this chapter we've covered an array of unintended consequences, from market failure to perverse incentives, from too much focus on the short term to too much of a good thing. Most generally, consider heeding **Murphy's law**: *Anything that can go wrong, will go wrong.* It's named after aerospace engineer Edward Murphy, from his remarks after his

measurement devices failed to perform as expected. It was intended as a defensive suggestion, to remind you to be prepared and to have a plan for when things go wrong.

It is unfortunately impossible to account for all possible unintended consequences. However, the mental models in this chapter can help you identify and avoid negative unintended consequences in a large array of situations. Look around—when you see unintended consequences in a situation, be it personal, professional, or in the wider world, one of these models is usually lurking behind. Next time, see if you can identify the underlying mental model behind the situation, and also try to think ahead about how it might apply to your own plans under consideration.

- In any situation where you can spot **spillover effects** (like a polluting factory), look for an **externality** (like bad health effects) lurking nearby. Fixing it will require intervention either by fiat (like government regulation) or by setting up a marketplace system according to the **Coase theorem** (like cap and trade).

- **Public goods** (like education) are particularly susceptible to the **tragedy of the commons** (like poor schools) via the **free rider problem** (like not paying taxes).

- Beware of situations with **asymmetric information**, as they can lead to **principal-agent problems**.

- Be careful when basing rewards on measurable incentives, because you are likely to cause unintended and undesirable behavior (**Goodhart's law**).

- **Short-termism** can easily lead to the accumulation of **technical debt** and create disadvantageous **path dependence**; to counteract it, think about **preserving optionality** and keep in mind the **precautionary principle**.

- Internalize the distinction between **irreversible** and **reversible decisions**, and don't let yourself succumb to **analysis paralysis** for the latter.

- Heed **Murphy's law**!

Spend Your Time Wisely

POLARIS IS THE BRIGHTEST STAR in the Little Dipper, a constellation also known as Ursa Minor, or Little Bear. You can easily find Polaris in the night sky because it is the last star in the handle of the Little Dipper, and the two outermost stars on the ladle of the Big Dipper point directly to it.

Since at least as far back as the Middle Ages, Polaris has played a critical role in naviga-

Finding Polaris

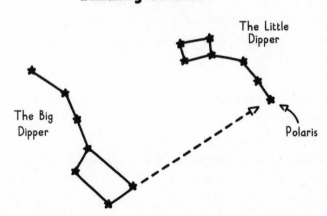

The Little Dipper

The Big Dipper

Polaris

tion. Given its unique location, almost directly above the North Pole, Polaris appears nearly fixed in the night sky, despite the Earth's rotation. You can know roughly what direction you're headed in just by looking up at it. If you want to head north, simply orient yourself toward Polaris.

A typical northern hemisphere star trail with Polaris in the center.

In the business world, there is a mental model that draws on Polaris for inspiration, called **north star**, which refers to the guiding vision of a company. For example, DuckDuckGo's north star is "to raise the standard of trust online." If you know your north star, you can point your actions toward your desired long-term future. Without a north star, you can be easily "lost at sea," susceptible to the unintended consequences of *short-termism* (see Chapter 2).

For an individual, it is important to have a personal north star, or mission statement. Do you have one? If not, you should think about drafting one for yourself. If you can orient yourself toward your north star and prioritize the right activities, you can accomplish amazing things over time. There are infinite possibilities, though here are a few examples to get you thinking:

- Being the best parent I can be
- Helping refugees as best I can
- Saving enough to retire by age forty
- Maximizing my positive impact on homelessness
- Living simply and being happy
- Advancing the science of human longevity

It's okay if your north star evolves as you progress toward it. You may discover greater clarity about what you want to accomplish, or a life event (e.g., marriage, kids, career/location change) may propel you in another direction. You may also need a new north star if you reach your destination! For instance, a teenager's north star might be getting into a certain university program, but once that has been reached, a new north star will be needed.

A north star is a long-term vision, so it is also okay if you don't reach it anytime soon. However, if you don't know where you want to go, how do you expect to ever get there? Your north star will help guide you through various life choices, slowly but steadily navigating you closer to your goals. In his 1996 book *The Road Ahead*, entrepreneur and philanthropist Bill Gates commented on this power of incremental progress: "People often overestimate what will happen in the next two years and underestimate what will happen in the next ten."

Gates wrote this statement in a business context, as a warning to not ignore far-off threats that can grow into major disrupters. That is, don't underestimate how far emerging competitors can advance or how much technology can change in ten years. Think of how Netflix progressed in a decade from a tiny niche to disrupting the entire cable-television industry.

This idea can also be powerful to you as an individual. Your incremental progress toward a goal may not be noticeable day to day. But over a long period of time, many small steps can get you really far if you stay pointed in the right direction.

If you put $1,000 in a savings account that pays 2 percent interest annually, the first year you will get $20 back. But the second year you will get a little more back ($20.40) because you also receive 2 percent interest on the $20 you received in interest the previous year. This is called **compound interest**, referring to the fact that your *interest* payments are growing over time, or *compounding*. Previous interest earned is added to the total amount each cycle, making a bigger base from which the next interest cycle is calculated.

Investor Warren Buffett, at one point the richest person in the world, said, "My wealth has come from a combination of living in America, some lucky genes, and compound interest" (see *birth lottery* in Chapter 1). Compound interest explains why it's easy for the rich to get richer. They can make more money from investing their already abundant capital, as opposed to having to earn more money just from their labor.

In a personal context, as long as you are pointed toward your north star, you have the opportunity to take advantage of the same concept by compounding your ability to move in your chosen direction. That's because what you can accomplish draws on your cumulative knowledge, skills, and network. As these grow, so does your impact potential. For example, as you progress in an industry, your industry contacts naturally expand, and it becomes increasingly likely that someone you've built a relationship with will help you progress higher in your career, such as recruiting you for your next job, serving as a reference, or acting as a mentor.

This chapter covers the mental models that you need (or need to avoid) to spend your precious time wisely, from the guiding light of the north star to the nitty-gritty of figuring out what to work on day to day, and how to complete those tasks most efficiently. Heed these mental models to get the most out of your future.

YOU CAN DO ANYTHING, BUT NOT EVERYTHING

Two-front wars played a major role in World Wars I and II, when Germany twice fought both Russia on its eastern front and Western allies on its western front. Each time, dividing its attention contributed significantly to Germany's eventual defeat. An anonymous saying captures this concept well: "If you chase two rabbits, both will escape."

If you've ever had to supervise two or more children who don't want to do the same activity, you understand how challenging it is to fight a two-front war. In business, a two-front war can happen if you have competitors attacking you on both sides, for example, on both the lower end and the higher end in terms of price, squeezing your customer base down. In the recent past in the U.S., mid-tier grocers like A&P have been driven to bankruptcy, squeezed by Walmart, Costco, Aldi, Amazon, and others entering the grocery business on the lower end, and Whole Foods, Wegmans, and others on the higher end.

Politicians often face a two-front war in which they are fighting on both sides of the political spectrum, with attacks from both the political right and left. A recent example is Hillary Clinton's 2016 U.S. presidential candidacy, where she faced a tough primary fight on the left from Bernie Sanders, and then in the general election she was still fighting for those voters while at the same time courting more-centrist voters.

You should be wary of fighting a two-front war, yet you probably do so every single day in the form of **multitasking**. When discussing *intuition* in Chapter 1, we explained that there are two types of thinking: low-concentration, autopilot thinking (for saying your name, walking, simple addition, etc.) and high-concentration, deliberate thinking (for everything else).

You can fully perform only one high-concentration activity at a time. Your brain just isn't capable of simultaneously focusing on two high-concentration activities at once. If you attempt this, you will be forced to context-switch between the two activities.

It's like when you are reading an article and pause to address an email that just came in. In that case, the context-switching is obvious, but the same thing happens if you're reading the article and someone starts talking to you at the same time. Your brain tries to handle both activities (reading and listening) by rapidly switching between them, and something has to give. This context-switching isn't instant, and so you end up either having to slow down one of the activities or doing one or both much more poorly.

The negative effects of multitasking (slow or poor performance) are sometimes acceptable if the activities are of low consequence, such as when you fold the laundry while watching TV, or listen to music while working out at the gym. In contrast, multitasking on activities of any significant consequence will be immediately problematic, or even deadly, as in the case of texting while driving.

Additionally, all the context-switching that occurs when multitasking is wasted time and effort. Extra mental overhead is also required to keep track of multiple activities at once. Therefore, you should try to avoid multitasking on any consequential activity.

Focusing on one high-concentration activity at a time can also help you produce dramatically better results. That's because the best results rely on creative solutions, which often come from concentrating intently on one thing. Startup investor Paul Graham calls it **the top idea in your mind** in his 2010 essay of the same name:

> Everyone who's worked on difficult problems is probably familiar with the phenomenon of working hard to figure something out, failing, and then suddenly seeing the answer a bit later while doing something else. There's a kind of thinking you do without trying to. I'm increasingly convinced this type of thinking is not merely helpful in solving hard problems, but necessary. The tricky part is, you can only control it indirectly.
>
> I think most people have one top idea in their mind at any given time. That's the idea their thoughts will drift toward when they're allowed to drift freely. And this idea will thus tend to get all the benefit of that type of thinking, while others are starved of it. Which means it's a disaster to let the wrong idea become the top one in your mind.

If you are constantly switching between activities, you don't end up doing much creative thinking at all. Author Cal Newport refers to the type of thinking that leads to breakthrough solutions as **deep work**. He advocates for dedicating long, uninterrupted periods of time to making progress on your most important problem. In a November 6, 2014, lecture titled "How to Operate," entrepreneur and investor Keith Rabois tells a story about how Peter Thiel used this concept when he was CEO of PayPal:

> [Peter] used to insist at PayPal that every single person could only do exactly one thing. And we all rebelled, every single person in the company rebelled to this idea. Because it's so unnatural, it's so different than other companies where people wanted to do multiple things, especially as you get more senior, you definitely want to do more things and you feel insulted to be asked to do just one thing.
>
> Peter would enforce this pretty strictly. He would say, I will not talk to you about anything else besides this one thing I assigned you. I don't want to hear about how great you are doing over here, just shut up, and Peter would run away. . . .
>
> The insight behind this is that most people will solve problems that they understand how to solve. Roughly speaking, they will solve B+ problems instead of A+ problems. A+ problems are high-impact problems for your company, but they are difficult. You don't wake up in the morning with a solution, so you tend to procrastinate them.
>
> So imagine you wake up in the morning and create a list of things to do today, there's usually the A+ one on the top of the list, but you never get around to it. And so you solve the second and third. Then you have a company of over a hundred people, so it cascades. You have a company that is always solving B+ things, which does mean you grow, which does mean you add value, but you never really create that breakthrough idea. No one is spending 100% of their time banging their head against the wall every day until they solve it.

Thiel's solution encourages deep work by strictly limiting multitasking. Of course, if you limit yourself to one activity at a time, it is critical that this top idea in your mind is an important one. Fortunately, there is also a mental model that can help you identify truly important activities.

U.S. President Dwight Eisenhower famously quipped, "What is important is seldom urgent and what is urgent is seldom important." This quote inspired Stephen Covey in *7 Habits of Highly Effective People* to create the **Eisenhower Decision Matrix**, a two-by-two grid (*matrix*) that helps you prioritize important activities across both your personal and your professional life by categorizing them according to their urgency and importance.

Eisenhower Decision Matrix

	Urgent	Not Urgent
Important	I-MANAGE • Crisis/emergency • Family obligations • Real deadlines	II-FOCUS • Strategic planning • Relationship-building • Deep work
Not Important	III-TRIAGE • Interruptions • Many "pressing" matters • Most events	IV-AVOID • Busywork • Picking out clothes • Most email and messages

Activities in quadrant I (Urgent/Important, such as handling a medical emergency) need to be done immediately. Activities in quadrant II (Not Urgent/Important, such as deep work) are also crucial, and should be prioritized just after the activities from quadrant I. You should focus your creative energies on these quadrant II activities as much as possible, because working on them will drive you fastest toward your long-term goals.

The activities in quadrant III (Urgent/Not Important, such as most events and many "pressing" matters) might be better delegated, outsourced, or just ignored. Finally, quadrant IV (Not Urgent/Not Important, such as busywork and most email) contains activities you should try to reduce or eliminate spending time on altogether.

The essential insight to be gained from this matrix is that the important activities in quadrant II are often overshadowed by the urgent distractions in quadrant III. You can be tricked into addressing the tasks in quadrant III immediately because they have urgency, vying for your attention. However, if you let those distractions in quadrant III take up a lot of your time, you may never get to the important tasks in quadrant II.

Similarly, the Not Urgent/Not Important things in quadrant IV can be attractive distractions because they provide immediate gratification (like completing a busywork task quickly) or are fun (like mindless phone games). It would be unhealthy to get rid of leisure completely in your life, but it is essential to evaluate how much of your time is being spent on leisure and unimportant activities so that they don't get in the way of achieving your long-term goals.

Quadrant IV activities also have the capacity to present with *false urgency* (like most email and texts). If you let them consistently interrupt you, you will suffer the negative effects of multitasking, context-switching between quadrant II and IV activities, significantly decreasing your performance on important matters. One approach to counteract this effect is to turn off notifications so that you do not succumb to this false urgency.

Using the Eisenhower Decision Matrix assumes that you can correctly categorize activities into each quadrant. Yet deciding what is important can be challenging, especially in an organizational context. Two mental models can offer insight on this difficulty.

Sayre's law, named after political scientist Wallace Sayre, offers that *in any dispute the intensity of feeling is inversely proportional to the value of the issues at stake.*

A related concept is *Parkinson's law of triviality*, named after naval historian Cyril Parkinson, which states that *organizations tend to give disproportionate weight to trivial issues.* Both of these concepts explain how group dynamics can lead the group to focus on the wrong things.

www.cartoonstock.com

**" We like to tackle the hard part first . . .
what we're ordering for lunch. "**

In his 1957 book *Parkinson's Law,* Parkinson presents an example of a budget committee considering an atomic reactor and a bike shed, offering that "the time spent on any item of the agenda will be in inverse proportion to the sum involved." The committee members are reluctant to deeply discuss all of the complicated aspects of the atomic reactor decision because it is challenging and esoteric. By contrast, everyone wants to weigh in with their opinion on the bike shed decision because it is easy and familiar relative to the reactor, even though it is also relatively unimportant. This phenomenon has become known as **bike-shedding**.

You must try not to let yourself get sucked into these types of debates, because they rob you of time that can be spent on important issues. In the budget meeting, the agenda could instead be structured so that time is pre-allocated proportionally to the relative importance of each item, and items can also be ordered by importance. That way much greater time will be apportioned to the reactor relative to the bike shed, and the reactor discussion will take place first. You can further set strict time limits for each agenda item (called *timeboxing*) to ensure that any bike-shedding that does arise doesn't take over the entire meeting.

For a real-life example, consider the recurring prominent debates about small items in the national budget each year in the United States. In the name of balancing the budget, politicians perennially suggest cutting national arts funding, science funding, and foreign aid.

No matter what you personally think of these programs, cutting them substantially will not significantly reduce the budget, as they respectively amount only to approximately 0.01 percent, 0.2 percent, and 1.3 percent of the total budget. In other words, if your goal is to significantly cut the budget, you would need to focus on much more major items in the budget. The sound and fury you hear over these relatively small items is therefore either a distraction from making any substantive progress on the stated goal or

U.S. Federal Spending in 2015

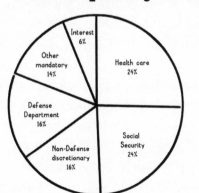

a misleading use of the idea of overall budget cuts to attack these programs for an unstated goal (like getting the federal government out of the business of funding these types of programs altogether).

That is, what is important versus what is not important is dependent on the particular goal being pursued. By putting potential activities in the context of this overall goal, using quantitative measures as much as possible, you can more clearly determine their relative importance.

Once you can correctly categorize activities as important and not important, you have another problem: for most people there is never enough time to work on the many important activities they've categorized. How do you choose what to do?

This section's theme is succinctly summarized by a quote from a *Fast Company* interview with productivity consultant David Allen, author of *Getting Things Done*: "You can do anything, but not everything." You must pick between the important activities in front of you, or else you will find yourself multitasking and lacking time for deep work. Allen also notes that "there is always more to do than there is time to do it, especially in an environment of so much possibility. We all want to be acknowledged; we all want our work to be meaningful. And in an attempt to achieve that goal, we all keep letting stuff enter our lives."

Luckily, there is an extremely powerful mental model from economics to guide you: **opportunity cost**. Every choice you make has a *cost*: the value of the best alternative *opportunity* you didn't choose. As a rule, you want to choose the option with the lowest opportunity cost.

Let's suppose you are thinking about quitting your job and starting your own business. The explicit costs of the new business are self-evident: any startup capital required for equipment, employees, legal costs, etc. If you need a loan, you have to add the explicit cost of interest payments (called the *cost of capital*). But there are also implicit costs, such as the wages and other benefits you would be giving up from your current job and the fact that the startup capital you provide could also be used for alternative investments (such as the stock market). Additionally, there are nonfinancial implicit costs (or benefits) to weigh, such as the impact on your family and personal fulfillment.

Your opportunity cost for starting this business is defined as the sum of all the explicit *and* implicit costs, based on an alternative future where you stayed at your job, continued earning your salary, and allocated what would have been your startup capital to other investments. What would your return be on path A versus on path B?

Opportunity cost extends to everyday decision making, such as when you drive farther to go to the "cheap" gas station. Suppose you can save 10 cents per gallon on a 20-gallon tank for a maximum savings of only $2.00. Even if this trip is an extra six minutes, you are essentially valuing your time at about $20 per hour, and this doesn't even account for the gas used in making the longer trip, the fact that you are saving less if your tank is not completely empty, or the mental overhead cost to fit a longer trip into your schedule. Of course, it may feel good to pay low prices or get a discount, but not when you need to spend a considerable amount of your limited time to do so. *Time is money!*

In business, opportunity cost is sometimes formalized as the **opportunity cost of capital**, the return you'd get on the best alternative use of that *capital*, your second-best *opportunity*. For example, suppose you're now running your business and you are returning 5 percent to the bottom line for every dollar you spend on an ongoing advertising campaign. You're now deciding the best way to reinvest some of these profits back into the business.

Whatever you select, you ought to be sure that you are making back at least 5 percent on your investment, because you could easily make that amount by investing more into the ad campaign. Thinking in terms of opportunity cost of capital pits your investment options against each other. Thus, you can make an informed choice among the array of projects and opportunities available to you.

Similarly, in negotiations there is another application of opportunity cost called **BATNA**, which stands for **best alternative to a negotiated agreement**. If you have a job offer, your BATNA is the best alternative job offer you have in hand, including your current job. You shouldn't accept an offer worse than your BATNA, because you can always take this better alternative offer (which could be the status quo).

In less clear-cut situations, it can be more challenging to understand your BATNA, and so it helps to brainstorm and literally list out all of your alternatives. This process can help you uncover additional alternatives that aren't immediately apparent. In any case, going into a negotiation knowing your BATNA is critical to making a decision that you won't regret.

Life and business can be thought of as just a series of such choices. These opportunity-cost models will help you consistently make better choices about what to work on, where to live, and whom to partner with. Generally, you want to choose things that have higher value than their opportunity costs, the best of all the alternatives in front of you. When put like that, it sounds simple, right?

Complications arise when you realize that you can't have it all. There are always trade-offs when you choose among the pursuits important to you.

We've tried to explain this concept to our kids in a simple way. Unfortunately, we have little to show for it so far. For our boys, there are only four to five hours from the time they get off the school bus until lights out at bedtime. During this time there are a few essential activities that need to happen, including homework, dinner, and nighttime routines.

They are often disappointed that there is little time left for stories, cuddles, or iPad after they take forever putting on pajamas and brushing their teeth because they are fooling around. We explain to them that the *cost* of fooling around is that they miss out on these other *opportunities*. It's a choice they are making. Similarly, if we go for a special trip out to dinner or ice cream, they lament the lack of time for free play before bed, not fully recognizing the trade-off. One day . . .

GETTING MORE BANG FOR YOUR BUCK

The *lever* is a simple machine consisting of a bar that sits atop a fulcrum. Through the placement of the fulcrum, the lever amplifies a small force over a large distance to create a much larger force over a small distance. Think of how you might use a crowbar to open a locked door. Back in the third century B.C., Archimedes famously boasted of the powers of the lever, "Give me a place to stand and I shall move the Earth."

The mechanical advantage gained by a lever, also known as **leverage**, serves as the basis of a mental model applicable across a wide variety of situations. The concept can be useful in any situation where applying force or effort in a particular area can produce outsized results, relative to similar applications of force or effort elsewhere.

In finance, leverage refers to borrowing money to purchase assets, which allows gains and losses to be multiplied. In this context, *leveraging up* means increasing debt, while

Leverage

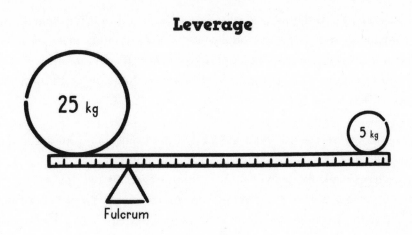

deleveraging is the opposite. A *leveraged buyout* takes place when one company buys out another, partially using other people's money.

In all these financial situations, the small force is the amount of money you initially put up, allowing you to wield a much larger force through the greater sum of money you have available via the debt you take on. For example, individuals usually purchase homes with down payments much smaller than the total price. In the United States this is typically 20 percent, but in the run-up to the 2007/2008 financial crisis, people bought houses with as little as zero percent down! But by taking on debt, people get to live in the homes they want.

In negotiation, leverage refers to the power one side has over another. If you have the ability to give or take more things than the other party, you have more leverage. No matter what the circumstances, small amounts of leverage can have large effects.

As applied to individuals, certain activities or actions have much greater leverage than others, and spending time or money on these **high-leverage activities** will produce the greatest effects. Therefore, you should take time to continually identify high-leverage activities. It's *getting more bang for your buck.*

You can apply this model in all areas of your life. The highest-leverage choice might not be the best fit every time, but the option that provides the most impact at the lowest cost always warrants consideration.

- Which job will give you the best opportunity to advance your career?
- Which home renovations might most increase the value of your home in an upcoming sale or most increase its livability?

- Which activities will most help your kids in the future, or bring them the most joy?
- To which causes or charities would your cash contributions make the most difference (a mental model itself called *effective altruism*)?
- How much and what type of exercise do you need to do to get the most benefits in the least amount of time?

Thinking about leverage helps you factor opportunity cost into your decision making. As a rule, the highest leverage activities have the lowest opportunity cost.

The **Pareto principle** can help you find high-leverage activities. It states that in many situations, 80 percent of the results come from approximately 20 percent of the effort. Addressing this 20 percent is therefore a high-leverage activity. This principle originated from observations in the late 1800s by economist Vilfredo Pareto detailed in his book *Manuel d'economie politique*: that 80 percent of the peas harvested in his garden came from only 20 percent of the pods, 80 percent of the land in Italy at the time was owned by 20 percent of the people, and so on.

Modern-day examples of this principle are easy to find. In the United States, about 80 percent of healthcare spending comes from 20 percent of the patients (see the figure below). Similarly, in 2007, 85 percent of U.S. wealth was owned by 20 percent of the people. While every relationship is not always 80/20, there is a common pattern for outcomes to be far from evenly distributed.

This particular 80/20 arrangement of outcomes is known as a **power law distribution**, where relatively few occurrences account for a significantly outsized proportion of

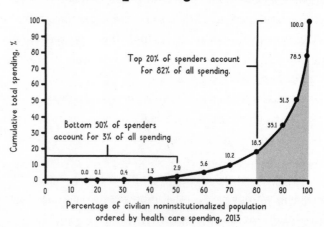

U.S. Health Spending Concentration

Top 20% of spenders account for 82% of all spending.

Bottom 50% of spenders account for 3% of all spending

Cumulative total spending, %

Percentage of civilian noninstitutionalized population ordered by health care spending, 2013

the total. (It is named after mathematical exponentiation, aka *power*, because the math that creates the distribution involves this operation.)

In the figure on the previous page, we see a power law distribution at work in the people who spend the most on healthcare. Other examples with similar patterns include the returns from venture capital, the strength of volcanic eruptions, and the size of power outages. When you're working to influence such a distribution, you're often looking toward those top outcomes, as they will have the most impact on the total.

Management consultant Joseph Juran popularized the Pareto principle in the 1940s, advising that the high-leverage plan is to find and focus on the smallest amount of the work that will bring about the best results. He called these high-leverage activities "the vital few." For example, if you want to improve the effectiveness of a web page, focus on the headline and leading image, often referred to as the "hero section." This is the first thing visitors will see, and the only thing many of them will read. The hero section is also what will be shared on social media. Small changes to this section—use of a catchier turn of phrase or a more engaging image—are simple, but have potential for a large effect.

The same principle applies to whole organizations. If you are trying to reduce costs and 80 percent of the budget is from 20 percent of the items, it makes sense to spend time seeing what you can do to make reductions in that 20 percent (as in our previous discussion of the U.S. budget). Similarly, if 80 percent of your company's sales come from 20 percent of its customers, you need to make sure these customers are satisfied, and find more like them. And if 80 percent of the usage of your website comes from 20 percent of the features, focus on those features. Incidentally, these are also the class of features that should go into an *MVP* (see Chapter 1).

After you determine *the 80/20* and address the *low-hanging fruit*, each additional hour of work will unfortunately produce less and less impactful results. In economics, this model is called the **law of diminishing returns**. It is the tendency for continued effort to *diminish* in effectiveness after a certain level of result has been achieved.

When Lauren was at GlaxoSmithKline, an external group was hired to evaluate the quality of clinical study reports and how efficiently they were written. The group evaluated report drafts to see how they evolved over time. For one report that had six drafts, the consultants found that the report's quality did not substantially improve from draft two to draft six—quite clearly a case of diminishing returns! The team obviously wasted time when making drafts three through six. Also, they placed undue pressure on colleagues who were waiting for the final report.

There is a similar concept called the **law of diminishing utility**, which says that the value, or *utility*, of consuming an additional item is usually, after a certain point, less than the value of the previous one consumed. Consider the difference between the enjoyment you receive from eating one donut versus eating a second or third donut. By the time you get to a sixth donut, you may no longer get any enjoyment out of it, and you might even start getting sick.

When continuing beyond a point like this can actually make things worse, you move from diminishing returns to **negative returns**. This can happen when you are striving for perfection and it becomes counterproductive. There are lots of phrases related to this concept—*overdoing it*, *trying too hard*, etc. (see the *Too Much of a Good Thing* section in Chapter 2).

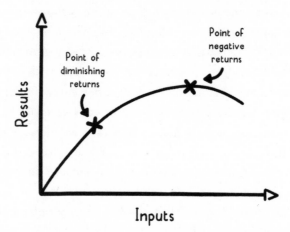

Law of Diminishing Returns

Overdoing it is also a quick path toward **burnout**, where high stress can take its toll and eventually extinguish your motivation, or worse. In the late 1970s in Japan the term *karoshi* was coined to describe the increasing number of people, some as young as their twenties and thirties, dying from strokes and heart attacks attributed to overwork.

Similar negative returns and burnout are prevalent in the high-stress environment of modern life throughout the world. In the quest for athletic success, for example, children all over the United States are suffering extreme injuries from overtraining—a clear sign of negative returns. Parents have started to sign their kids up for specialized coaching programs and commit them to playing one sport year-round at very young ages, which can easily result in overtaxing their young, growing bodies.

In baseball alone, hundreds of young pitchers each year are now having surgery on their elbows, colloquially named Tommy John surgery after the major league pitcher. This is a type of surgery that just a few decades ago was performed only on professional pitchers. Throwing more pitches in a year greatly increases your risk of injury, and so a heavy year-round schedule puts many teenagers in a dangerous situation. A lot of these kids are not even playing baseball two years later, whether it's because they never fully recovered or they just got completely burned out.

Another familiar example of negative returns is pulling an all-nighter. It is proven that cramming is not an effective method to retain material long term. All-night cram sessions can additionally be counterproductive because no one is at their best in a sleep-deprived state. If the all-nighter is to complete a paper, can the writer accurately evaluate the quality of the writing in the middle of the night? Probably not. Thus, the paper deteriorates as the night progresses.

So, once you've pushed through the highest-leverage pieces of a given project, when should you move on? Clearly, you ought to quit before you hit negative returns, but just because you've hit diminishing returns doesn't always mean you must stop what you're doing. It really comes down to opportunity cost. If you can identify another activity that can produce greater results for the same amount of effort, then you should jump to it.

Otherwise, you should keep at your current activity, since you're still making progress (even if it is slower progress) and you don't have anything better to do. However—and this is key—you should not assume there isn't anything better to do. You must periodically brainstorm and seek alternatives, making sure there aren't other high-leverage projects, with their own 80/20s, just out of view.

GET OUT OF YOUR OWN WAY

Applying leverage and related mental models will help you spend time on the right activities. The next step is getting those activities done in a timely manner. The path to doing this is fraught with traps. The first trap: procrastination.

Our kids are expert procrastinators, and if this is a genetically transferred trait, Lauren must take responsibility. Around the time we first met in 1999, Gabriel wrote an article in

– A FIELD GUIDE TO –
PROCRASTINATORS

The Cleaner

The Panicker

The List Maker

The Napper

The Sidetracker

The Social Sharer

The Internet Researcher

The Snacker

The Gamer

The Watcher

The Delegator

The Perpetuator

20PX.COM

The Tech, MIT's student newspaper, recommending that everyone stop procrastinating. While Lauren was not an expert procrastinator, she typically finished Friday's problem sets sometime late Thursday night. Gabriel was the only person Lauren knew at MIT who finished his weekly work by Tuesday; in fact, he procrastinated so little that he finished MIT in three years.

One reason why people procrastinate so much is **present bias**, which is the tendency to overvalue near-term rewards in the *present* over making incremental progress on long-term goals (see *short-termism* in Chapter 2). It's really easy to find reasons on any given day to skip going to the gym (too much work, bad sleep, feeling sick/sore, etc.), but if you do this too often, you'll never reach your long-term fitness goals.

Everyone discounts the future as compared with the present to some degree. For instance, given a choice between getting $100 today and $100 in a year, most everyone would choose to get it today. Suppose, though, you're offered $100 in a year, but you can pay a fee to get the $100 today (minus the fee). How much would you be willing to pay? Would you pay $20 to get the $100 right now (netting $80) versus getting $100 in a year?

When you cast this fee as a percentage, it effectively becomes an "interest rate," called the **discount rate** (in the example above, it would be 25 percent, since $80 × 125% = $100). Like any interest rate, it can compound, but instead of compounding positively as we discussed earlier, the discount rate compounds negatively. This negative compounding *discounts* payments out into the future more and more, since you won't be able to access them until much later.

The discount rate is the cornerstone of the **discounted cash flow** method of valuing assets, investments, and offers. This model can help you properly determine the worth of arrangements that involve future payments, such as investment properties, stocks, and bonds. For example, let's say you win the lottery and are offered a choice between getting one million dollars each year, forever, or a lump-sum payment today. How high does that lump-sum payment need to be before you will accept it? You might think initially it should be exceptionally high because the payments go out forever; but because of the compounding discount rate, the expected earnings far in the future aren't actually worth that much to you today.

At the discount rate of 5 percent per year, for example, the million dollars in *cash flow* from next year would be *discounted* to only $952,381 of value today ($1M/1.05). Two years out, because of compounding, the million that year becomes just $907,029 of value today ($1M/1.05^2). This continues with earnings further out being discounted more and more until they get discounted closer and closer to zero in today's dollars. Fifty years out, at the

5 percent discount rate, the million dollars that year is worth only $87,204 to you today ($1M/1.05^{50}).

When you add the discounted earnings together from all future years, you get the **net present value**, or **NPV**, of the lottery payments. In this case, the total comes to twenty million dollars. That is, if a 5 percent discount rate is appropriate, you would value this stream of cash flows of one million dollars a year forever at only twenty million dollars today, assuming you could get that twenty million dollars right now in the lump-sum payment. And in fact, around 5 percent is what is typically offered by lotteries.

Of course, this method is very sensitive to the discount rate (e.g., 5 percent versus 20 percent). At a 20 percent discount rate applied yearly, the NPV of this cash flow stream becomes valued at $5 million in today's dollars instead of $20 million at the 5 percent discount rate.

Net Present Value (NPV)

	Total NPV	NPVs of Payments in Year X					
		Year 1	Year 2	Year 3	Year 4	...	Year 50
0% Discount Rate	Infinite	$1,000,000	$1,000,000	$1,000,000	$1,000,000	...	$1,000,000
5% Discount Rate	$20,000,000	$952,381	$907,029	$863,838	$822,702	...	$87,204
10% Discount Rate	$10,000,000	$909,091	$826,446	$751,315	$683,013	...	$8,519
20% Discount Rate	$5,000,000	$833,333	$694,444	$578,704	$482,253	...	$110

The right discount rate to apply in a business and investing context is something we will explore a bit more in Chapter 6. Here, though, one thing to consider is what you could do with that money if you had it now. From a purely financial point of view, if you could guarantee investing at a rate greater than the discount rate, then you would be better off getting the lump-sum payment and investing it. For example, if you think you can invest at a 6 percent rate, then you'd be okay with a 5 percent discount rate. Lotteries usually offer rates around this 5 percent level for similar reasons (because they could invest at that rate).

Of course, you wouldn't consider just the financial point of view. If you had the lump-sum payment today, you might better enjoy your winnings because having more money now gives you more options in terms of spending. On the other hand, many actual lottery winners regret taking the lump-sum payment because they end up spending too much initially.

In personal situations, most people discount the future implicitly at relatively high discount rates. And they do so in a manner that is not actually fixed over time, which is called **hyperbolic discounting**. In other words, people really, really value instant gratification over delayed gratification, and this preference plays a central role in procrastination, along with other areas of life where people struggle with self-control, such as dieting, addiction, etc.

When you're on a diet, it's hard to avoid the pull of that donut in the office. That's because you get the short-term donut payoff right now, whereas the long-term dieting payoff, being so far in the future, is discounted in your mind close to zero (like company earnings fifty years in the future).

In studies, this preference is often revealed through asking people variations of the $100 question, finding points at which people are willing to get a lesser amount of money sooner rather than a greater amount later. One such study, "Some Empirical Evidence on Dynamic Inconsistency" by economist Richard Thaler, found that people on average were equally willing to receive $15 immediately, $30 after three months, $60 after one year, or $100 after three years. These values imply decreasing annual discount rates, declining from 277 percent to 139 percent to 63 percent as the delays get longer.

Once you are old enough (like us) to have plenty of regrets about procrastination, you can more easily appreciate that your future self is going to have even greater struggles if you continue to put things off. You must strive to keep these feelings of regret in mind as motivation to stay focused on the long-term benefits of your actions, viewing your present efforts as incremental progress toward your goals. In that way you can attempt to counteract your inherent present bias and resulting procrastination tendencies.

A mental model that can help you further combat your present bias is **commitment**, where you actively *commit* in some way to your desired future. Commitments can be formal or informal, but they are usually most effective when they have some sort of penalty attached to breaking the commitment.

For example, if you are trying to lose weight, you could sign up for a gym membership or make a bet with a friend. In these cases you are making a financial commitment and suffering a loss if you don't stick with it. Or you and a friend could agree to exercise and diet together or make some sort of public pronouncement about how much weight you both want to lose. In these cases, you are holding yourself accountable through social pressure.

Choosing to put money into a 401(k) program is another example, where you are committing to save for your retirement. The penalties for withdrawing from these accounts early are notoriously harsh, making it more likely that you will stick with your commitment.

Since many people take *the path of least resistance*, 401(k) programs also showcase the **default effect**, the *effect* stemming from the fact that many people just accept *default* options. Participation in a 401(k) or in programs such as organ donation or voter registration varies dramatically depending on whether the programs are default opt-in versus default opt-out.

Default Effect

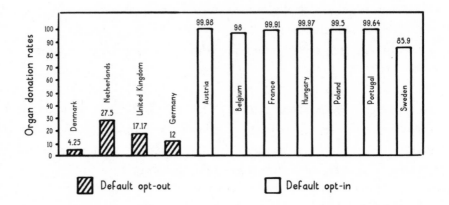

You can use the default effect to your personal advantage by making default commitments toward your long-term goals. A simple example is scheduling recurring time right into your calendar, such as an hour a week to look for a new job, deep-clean your living space, or work on a side project. Thereafter, by default your time is allocated to whichever long-term goal you choose. This same technique also works well for scheduling deep work. By putting deep-work blocks of time into your calendar, you can prevent yourself by default from booking this time with meetings since it is already committed.

Commitments have shortcomings, however. First, it is easy to put off making the commitment itself. Second, if the penalty isn't large, as in many social contracts or calendar commitments, you may decide it is worth it just to break it, defeating its purpose. Third, there are many ways to formulate an ineffective commitment, including making it unrealistic ("I will work out at the gym every day"), not specifying a clear timeline ("I will go to the gym more often"), and being too vague ("I will try to exercise more"). By contrast, a realistic, time-bound, and specific gym commitment might be: "I will go to the gym Wednesday and Sunday mornings with my friend for the next three months, doing twenty minutes of running and twenty minutes of weight training, and I will give my friend twenty dollars each time I miss a date."

Once you overcome procrastination and are actually making consistent progress toward a goal, the next trap you can fall into is failing to plan your time effectively. **Parkinson's law** (yes, another law by the same Parkinson of *Parkinson's law of triviality*) states that "work expands so as to fill the time available for its completion." Does that ring true for you? It certainly does for us.

When your top priority has a deadline far in the future, it doesn't mean that you need to spend all your time on it until the deadline. The sooner you finish, the sooner you can move on to the next item on your list. You also never know when finishing early might help you—for instance, when something important and urgent pops up in your Eisenhower Decision Matrix.

A couple of whimsical models capture the feelings surrounding end-of-project work. In his book *Gödel, Escher, Bach*, cognitive scientist Douglas Hofstadter coined **Hofstadter's law**: *It always takes longer than you expect, even when you take into account Hofstadter's Law.*

In other words, things take longer than you expect, even when you consider that they take longer than you expect! Tom Cargill was credited (in the September 1985 *Communications of the ACM*) for the similar *ninety-ninety rule* from his time programming at Bell Labs in the 1980s: *The first 90 percent of the code accounts for the first 90 percent of the development time. The remaining 10 percent of the code accounts for the other 90 percent of the development time.*

Both concepts highlight the fact that you're generally bad at estimating when things will get done, because, unless you put a lot of effort into continuous project planning, you don't realize all the little things that need to be completed to really button up a project. This has certainly proved true in writing this book!

The deeper point, however, is that you often have a choice of when to call the project "done." This choice can dramatically affect the project's time requirements, and periodically questioning what constitutes "done" can save you from wasted effort. In the case of the clinical study reports mentioned in the previous section, there could have been a step after each draft, comparing it with a predefined set of objectives for the project, and evaluating whether the group should move on.

Recall from Chapter 2 that *perfect is the enemy of good.* If you deliver that faultless and definitive report to your organization, you've probably waited too long. A less-than-perfect solution is often *good enough* to keep optimally moving forward. This model applies in other contexts as well: waiting until you are sure you are making the perfect decision, until you have crafted the flawless product, and so on. The best time to call something *done* is much earlier than it usually happens.

Of course, there are times when the circumstances call for getting things closer to perfect. However, those times are rarer than you think, and so it is worth considering ahead of time and again during a project what final quality level is acceptable, that is, what *done* means in this context (see *reversible decisions* versus *irreversible decisions* in Chapter 2).

Another often-overlooked option is to abandon the project altogether before it is done. Sometimes you need to acknowledge that you are just not on the path to success. Other times you may find that what it would take to get where you originally wanted to go is just not worth the effort anymore. Unfortunately, psychologically, your mind is working hard against you here, and **loss aversion** is the model that explains why. You are more inclined to avoid *losses*, to be *averse* to them, than you are to want to make similar gains.

Quite simply, you get more displeasure from losing fifty dollars than pleasure from gaining fifty dollars. Since you hate losing, loss aversion can cause you harm under many circumstances. You may hold losing stocks way too long, hoping they will recover back to the value they had when you bought them. You may stay in a house despite wanting to move, because you are waiting until its selling price exceeds your purchase price. These purchase prices are arbitrary numbers, independent of the current value of the assets, but they are meaningful to you because they represent losses or gains. Similarly, you may avoid killing a project because that would mean admitting the loss of your efforts up to that point.

Daniel Kahneman and Amos Tversky's work on this topic, detailed in the October 1992 issue of the *Journal of Risk and Uncertainty,* demonstrated that across many risky situations, such as winning or losing money based on a coin toss, people tend to want the potential payoff to be around double the potential loss before they are willing to take the gamble. That is, people want to have a fifty-fifty chance of winning one hundred dollars if they have to put fifty dollars on the line.

Loss aversion can be better understood using the *frame of reference* model (see Chapter 1). When you already have a win on your hands, you tend to want to *lock in your gains.* From this frame of reference, you tend to act more conservatively and are more likely to pass up a chance at a bigger gain if it means risking your current winnings.

Conversely, when you have a loss on your hands, you'd rather take a chance at breaking even than accept the sure loss. From this frame of reference, you tend to act more aggressively, not wanting to end with the loss.

From an objective frame of reference, however, you should approach both situations from the same standpoint of opportunity cost. By holding on to a loss too long, you are misallocating time or money that could be better used on another opportunity. Similarly, by walking away after a sure but small gain, you may be missing out on a potentially better opportunity.

When it comes to losses in particular, you need to acknowledge that they've already happened: you've already spent the resources on the project to date. When you allow these irrecoverable costs to cloud your decision making, you are falling victim to the **sunk-cost fallacy**. The *costs* of the project so far, including your time spent, have already been *sunk*. You can't get them back.

This can be a problem (*fallacy*) when these previous losses influence you to make a bad decision. An instance where sunk costs lead to an *escalation of commitment* is sometimes called the *Concorde fallacy*, named after the supersonic jet whose development program was plagued with prohibitive cost overruns and never came close to making a profit. Ask yourself: Is my project like the Concorde? Am I *throwing good money after bad* when it is better to just walk away?

Everyday sunk cost fallacy examples can run from less consequential decisions, such as finishing a movie or book that you don't like, to larger ones, such as investing more money into a failing business or staying in a career or relationship that is turning sour. You need to avoid thinking, *We've come too far to stop now*. Instead, take a realistic look at your chances of success and evaluate from an opportunity cost perspective whether your limited resources are best used continuing what you are doing or persuing another opportunity. You may have made a commitment, but given all you know now, this may be one of those situations where you should break it.

Evaluating your chances honestly can be difficult because you want so badly to believe that you can succeed. In a 1968 paper in the *Journal of Personality and Social Psychology*, Robert E. Knox and James A. Inkster described two experiments they conducted at two different horse tracks. They asked as many people as possible to rate the chances of their horses' winning. Some of the people were interviewed right before their bets were placed, and others right after. The group questioned after they made their bets rated their horses' chances significantly higher. This supported the scientists' prediction that, post-bet, bettors were more confident in their choices. Evidently, simply the act of committing to the bet convinced bettors that their odds of winning had increased (see *cognitive dissonance* in Chapter 1). Remaining data-driven can help you avoid this mistake. The "power of positive thinking" can only get you so far.

Some economists argue that considering sunk costs is okay when taking a loss may damage your reputation. However, you should also consider that holding on to something for too long because of pride can also damage how you're seen by those who are let down by your failure or stuck bailing you out. It is important to remember that flexibility is just as important to your success as tenacity, if not more so.

Sometimes, though, you can indeed right the ship. In these situations, admitting you are not on the right track is the best way to save a project. This admission can push you to change strategies and tactics and possibly call in reinforcements.

In Chapter 1, we discussed *postmortems*, where you analyze project failures so that you can do better next time. But you don't have to wait until the end of a project—you can also conduct *mid-mortems*, and occasionally even *pre-mortems*, where you predict ahead of time where things could go off track.

In Chapter 1, we also discussed the *third story*, where you look at conflicts from an objective point of view. You need to use the same point of view when evaluating your own projects. If you recognize that you cannot do that, then bring someone else in to help you get out of your own way.

SHORTCUT YOUR WAY TO SUCCESS

A good plan of attack ensures that you are using the right tools and processes to get the job done. For instance, in writing this book, our first step was to develop an outline. Rather than write without direction or move back and forth between disparate concepts, we wanted to make sure the book flowed properly. An outline helped us link related concepts and group them into coherent sections and chapters.

When starting something new, a good thing to remind yourself is that there is *no need to reinvent the wheel.* It is unlikely that you are the first person in the world who has faced this task, and, with the ubiquity of self-published experts, you are likely to be able to find a website, blog article, or how-to video on almost any topic. As Benjamin Franklin wrote in *The Way to Wealth,* "An investment in knowledge pays the best interest."

In many fields, leaders have agreed on *best practices* based on what has worked or what has not worked in the past. Architect Christopher Alexander introduced the concept of a **design pattern**, which is a reusable solution to a design problem. This idea has been adapted to other fields and is especially popular in computer science.

You are probably very familiar with common design patterns for everyday items.

Think of doorknobs being set at a certain height so they are easy for most people to use, or staircases being wide enough for most people to walk on. They are the same because they adhere to the same basic design patterns that have proven to be useful. In some cases, the patterns have been made official *standards*, as in building codes.

There are likely design patterns applicable to whatever you are doing as well. For writing books like this, there are many design patterns, from the way the book is laid out and printed to the length and writing style expected. The same is true in our careers: design patterns for startups (how they are commonly financed, managed, etc.), coding (how code is structured, common algorithms, etc.), and biostatistics (common drug trial designs, statistical methods, etc.).

The opposite of the well-tested design pattern is the **anti-pattern**, a seemingly intuitive but actually ineffective "solution" to a common problem that often already has a known, better solution. Most of the mental models in this book are either design patterns or anti-patterns, and learning them can help you avoid common mistakes. Anti-patterns in this chapter include bike-shedding, present bias, and negative returns. You can avoid anti-patterns by explicitly looking for them and then seeking out established design patterns instead.

While some amount of planning is always useful, sometimes the most efficient way to finish a task is to dive in quickly and start, rather than getting bogged down in *analysis paralysis* (see Chapter 2).

As a child, Lauren had a four-digit combination lock and she forgot the code to open it. Although one solution for an adult would be to just get a new lock, as a child she didn't have the funds, and after a quick calculation, she decided it would be easy enough to open the lock by doing an exhaustive search for the combination. And, lo and behold, it worked!

Exhaustive searches like this are a type of **brute force** solution. The term *brute force* is obviously applicable when referring to an activity that requires literal *force*, such as chopping down a tree with an ax. However, it is also used to refer to any solution that doesn't require an intellectually sophisticated method. For example, if you have to address ten envelopes, it can be faster to handwrite them than to print them.

Brute force solutions can be effective for many small-scale problems. However, they can quickly become untenable as the problem gets bigger, such as if you have a hundred envelopes to address. When this happens, using more sophisticated tools is an expedient though more expensive approach.

Consider again chopping down a tree. For a small tree, an ax or handsaw is okay. For a larger tree, you would want a chainsaw. For clearing a stand of trees, a "feller-buncher" is the preferred tool. In these cases, if you can afford it, it is effective to *throw more money at the problem* by spending on better tools.

However, some problems, such as large computational ones, can become intractable even with the help of sophisticated tools. For a password that is exactly eight characters long (letters or numbers, case sensitive), there are 218 trillion possible combinations— impossible to try by hand, and even extremely time-consuming for a computer. At 1,000 passwords a second, it would still take you 6,923 *years* to work through all those combinations.

A better method than trying every combination at random might be first to try combinations of words from the dictionary, recognizing that people often choose words for passwords. An even better method would consider common passwords, and words or numbers significant to this particular person, such as related birth dates, sports teams, or initials. This is a type of **heuristic** solution, a trial-and-error solution that is not guaranteed to yield optimal or perfect results, but in many cases is nevertheless very effective.

You should consider heuristics because they can be a shortcut to a solution for the problem in front of you, even if they may not work as well in other situations. If the problem persists, however, and you keep adding more heuristic rules, this type of solution can become unwieldy. That's what has happened to Facebook with content moderation. The company started out with a simple set of heuristic rules (e.g., no nudity), and gradually added more and more rules (e.g., nudity in certain circumstances, such as breastfeeding, is okay), until as of April 2018 it had amassed twenty-seven pages of heuristics.

Algorithms, step-by-step processes, are another approach. Algorithms are pervasive in modern life, solving many otherwise intractable problems, but we often don't even realize it. Consider travel: algorithms govern how traffic patterns are managed, how directions get calculated, how "best available" seats are selected, which hotels are recommended when you search for them . . . and that's just a start.

Algorithms can range from the simple (like a traffic light that changes every two minutes) to the complex (like a traffic a light that changes dynamically based on live sensors) to the highly complex (like an artificial intelligence that manages traffic lights across a whole city at once). Many algorithms operate as **black boxes**, which means they require very little understanding by the user of how they work. You don't care how you got the best seats, you just want the best seats! You can think of each algorithm as a *box* where inputs go in and outputs come out, but outside it is painted *black* so you can't tell what is going on inside. Common examples of black box algorithms include recommendation systems on Netflix or Amazon, matching on online dating sites, and content moderation on social media.

Physical tools can also be black boxes. Two sayings, "The skill is built into the tool" and "The craftsmanship is the workbench itself," suggest that the more sophisticated tools get, the fewer skills are required to operate them. Repairing or programming them is another story, though!

When you think about using tools to get your work done faster, you should start by discovering all the *off-the-shelf* options available to you. These are effectively design patterns you can purchase. For example, when printing address labels, you can use mail-merge programs, preprinted sheets of labels, and full-service copy centers.

You will want to invest some time in figuring out the pros and cons of your various options, because you can easily get yourself into trouble (in wasted money or time, or worse) if you select the wrong tool. Experts can help you identify your options, like when you go to a home improvement store and ask for tool advice on a DIY repair. Once a tool is selected, you will also want to invest additional time in understanding how to use it effectively, or hire an expert to operate it for you.

As you face the same problem again and again, not only do you want better tools and algorithms, but you also want better processes for interacting with those tools and algorithms. For example, if you want to produce a personal budget, you might start with pen, paper, and a calculator. After you figure out your expenses in the first month, you might quickly graduate to using a spreadsheet because it can do calculations faster and with fewer mistakes.

Further still, you could find another program to move the data into the spreadsheet automatically, which will save you even more time each month. **Automation** like this makes sense when the eventual time and money saved through more efficient processing and possibly better results outweigh the costs of setting it up.

Automation is also a great way to take advantage of **economies of scale**, when an operation becomes more efficient as its size increases. Economies of scale explain some of the advantages larger companies have relative to smaller ones. They can afford to pay the large up-front costs to have the biggest factories and warehouses with the most cutting-edge robots and machinery. Once set up, this technology means each new product moves through the factory and warehouse faster and cheaper.

The companies can then spread the initial fixed costs across a large volume of production, being able to produce or ship goods at much cheaper rates overall, even accounting for the up-front costs. This overall efficiency means they can charge less than competitors. Think Amazon.

Another way to speed things up is **parallel processing**, in which you solve a group of problems in *parallel*. In a computing context, you'd literally assign different calculations to different *processors*, such that multiple calculations are done simultaneously, as opposed to in *serial*, where calculations are done one after another. Amazon doesn't have just one big warehouse it ships from; it has more than a hundred! In this way it can break up the daily shipping logistics into many sub-problems at different facilities.

Parallel processing is an example of a **divide and conquer** strategy. If you can break a problem into independent pieces and hand these pieces out to different parties to solve, you can accomplish more, faster. Think of when you delegate parts of a project to different people or departments to work on.

"WE ALREADY HAVE QUITE A FEW PEOPLE WHO KNOW HOW TO DIVIDE. SO ESSENTIALLY, WE'RE NOW LOOKING FOR PEOPLE WHO KNOW HOW TO CONQUER."

Another strategy to get to a solution quicker when faced with a hard situation is to **reframe the problem**. Consider a central problem faced by Disney World: long lines. Most rides have limited seating, so the only way to move more people through the ride in the same amount of time is to build more apparatuses for the same ride. That's expensive, involves closing the ride for a substantial period, and may not even be realistically possible given space constraints. But what if the problem was reframed not as "How do we move people through the line faster?" but "How do we make people happier while they wait in line?"

When a problem is reframed, the *solution space* really opens up, and you can see that Disney has employed a variety of solutions to this reframed problem. Disney's FastPass system allows each guest a limited number of times to skip most of the wait of the line. The posted wait times outside the line take away the mystery behind the wait time, one of the most frustrating characteristics of other queuing systems. The lines also have features like games, artwork, animatronics, etc., to entertain guests so that the wait does not seem as long. Some of these features seem like they should be incorporated in any queuing system as design patterns. Once frequent Disney vacationers (like us!) experience them, it can be frustrating to visit amusement parks without them.

In math and science, problems are often reframed or manipulated into forms that are easier to solve. This is done by taking advantage of already known algorithms and design patterns, transforming the problem into one with a readily usable solution.

As passwords have become harder to crack, hackers have reframed their problem of "How can we best *guess* your password?" to "How can we best *get* your password?" From this angle, a better solution, unfortunately, is **social engineering**, where you are manipulated to give up your password willingly. Hackers literally *engineer* a *social* situation designed to get you to give up your password. Think of phishing emails pretending to be from your accounts but which actually originate from hackers. These social-engineering techniques have been behind most high-profile targeted hacks, including celebrities' iCloud photo accounts (2014), the release of emails from the Democratic National Committee and Hillary Clinton's campaign chair John Podesta (2016), and a breach at the U.S. Department of Justice exposing the names, phone numbers, and email addresses of thousands of FBI and Department of Homeland Security employees (2016).

From brute force to reframing the problem, the mental models in this section can all be used as tactical solutions to help you achieve project success faster. When you have a hard problem in front of you, take a moment to consider whether one or more of these models are applicable. A remark attributed to an anonymous woodsman is, "Give me six hours to chop down a tree and I will spend the first four sharpening the axe." More broadly, how to spend your time wisely really comes down to working smarter.

©2010 Scott Hilburn/Distributed by Universal Uclick

KEY TAKEAWAYS

- Choose activities to work on based on their relevance to your **north star**.

- Focus your time on just *one* of these truly important activities at a time (no **multi-tasking!**), making it the **top idea on your mind**.

- Select between options based on **opportunity cost** models.

- Use the **Pareto principle** to find the 80/20 in any activity and increase your **leverage** at every turn.

- Recognize when you've hit **diminishing returns** and avoid **negative returns**.

- Use **commitment** and the **default effect** to avoid **present bias,** and periodic evaluations to avoid **loss aversion** and the **sunk-cost fallacy**.

- Look for shortcuts via existing **design patterns**, tools, or clever **algorithms**. Consider whether you can **reframe the problem**.

Becoming One with Nature

BEFORE THE INDUSTRIAL REVOLUTION, most peppered moths in Manchester, England, were light-colored, using trees covered with pale bark and lichens as camouflage to avoid becoming prey for birds. The first reporting of a live dark moth was in 1811, but definitive proof of this variation didn't appear until the first was captured in 1848. A dark moth was extremely rare, estimated to represent only 0.01 percent of the peppered moth population around that time. But by 1895, the frequency of dark-colored peppered moths in Manchester had risen from 0.01 percent to 98 percent!

What happened? During this period, pollution from the new coal factories left the trees covered with soot and killed the pale lichens, resulting in darker trees. The light-colored moths' color became a liability rather than an asset. The dark-color genes, however, immediately became incredibly useful, as any moths that expressed them were now camouflaged against the dark trees. Birds picked off the light-colored moths in droves, leaving dark-colored moths to propagate and take over the gene pool. England's Clean Air Act of 1956 cleaned up the pollution, making the trees light again, reversing the trend, and ultimately making the dark-colored moths rare once more.

This rise and fall of the dark-colored peppered moth is a showcase of **natural selection**, the process that drives biological evolution. It was independently formulated by

Natural Selection

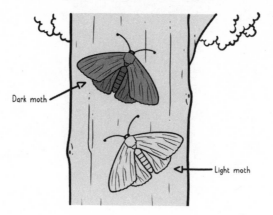

both Alfred Wallace and Charles Darwin, and later made famous by Darwin's 1859 book *On the Origin of Species by Means of Natural Selection.* Traits that provide reproductive advantages are *naturally selected* over generations, making them more prevalent as species evolve to fit their environment.

Beyond biological evolution, natural selection also drives societal evolution, the process by which society changes over time. In any part of society, you can trace the path of how ideas, practices, and products have adapted to ever-changing tastes, norms, and technology. If you magically transported successful companies, movies, and books from fifty years ago to the present day, and released them now for the first time, most would not be successful because society has evolved so much since their heyday.

Fifty years is a long time relative to the current rate of societal change. Think of the massive changes that can take place over the course of one generation. When Lauren was the same age as our youngest (seven), she had access to just seven TV channels (cable wasn't widespread at that time), but now our kids can watch essentially whatever they want whenever they want with Hulu, Netflix, Amazon, etc. No wonder they refer to the 1980s as the "olden days."

You will live through many more societal shifts: economic cycles, waves of innovation, evolving norms and standards. With more people than ever and everyone more connected through the internet and globalization, these shifts are happening faster than in the past. You must adapt to these changing environmental pressures to be successful.

Just as species develop biological adaptations over generations, you need to be open to

"In the old days this was considered a play station."

new ideas and paradigms, adjusting your thinking and behavior as necessary. Similarly, when organizations face disruption, they must find new ways to operate if they want to thrive. Professor Leon Megginson, paraphrasing Darwin, put it like this in a 1963 speech to the Southwestern Social Science Association: "It is not the most intellectual of the species that survives; it is not the strongest that survives; but the species that survives is the one that is able best to adapt and adjust to the changing environment in which it finds itself." That is, you need to change color like the peppered moth did.

As the CEO of a fast-growing company, Gabriel finds that his job and the jobs of his team look very different from how they looked just eighteen months ago. That's because as the company grows, what is required of its executives changes, moving initially from building a product (design, creation, etc.) to building a company (managing people, defining structure, etc.), to building a sustainable business (financial models, managing managers, etc.). In such a rapidly changing environment, you need a method for adapting quickly.

Luckily, science gives us such a mental model for making sure we stay among the "fittest": the **scientific method**. Formally, the scientific method is a rigorous cycle of making observations, formulating hypotheses, testing them, analyzing data, and developing new theories. But you can also apply it simply by embracing an experimental mindset. The most successful (and adaptive) people and organizations are constantly refining how they work and what they work on to be more effective.

As an example, think about your own productivity tools and methods. You can't expect to discover the setup that helps you do your best work right away. But if you keep experimenting (with different schedules, software, organization, processes, etc.), you will get closer and closer to the optimal setup, enabling you to go much further, faster.

The same mindset can be applied to other areas of your life, such as the all-important one of diet and exercise. What type of exercise program can you really stick to? What can you change in your diet or daily routines to make you eat healthier? When a scientific mindset is applied continuously via experimentation, you will improve your chances of being the fittest (some pun intended).

Natural selection and the scientific method are just the start. There are a host of natural laws that can help you understand the changes unfolding around you as well as how to adapt to them and even shape them. This chapter highlights many of these natural super models that can help you be more adaptive and manage change.

DON'T FIGHT NATURE

At some point you have likely heard someone paraphrase Isaac Newton's first law of motion, often referred to as the law of inertia: "An object at rest stays at rest and an object in motion stays in motion with the same speed and in the same direction unless acted upon by an unbalanced force."

Trucks have brakes.
But their cargo doesn't.

Inertia is a physical object's resistance to changing its current state of motion. The meme on the previous page illustrates this concept in practice.

As a metaphor, inertia can describe any resistance to a change in direction. In Chapter 1, we explained how you tend to have significant inertia in your beliefs because of *confirmation bias* and related models. This adherence to your beliefs can hamper your adaptability. By questioning your assumptions, you can adapt to new ways of thinking and overcome this personal inertia.

Inertia can increase the longer you hold on to your beliefs. If you're like most people, many of your core political, religious, and social beliefs can be traced to the family and geographic culture in which you were raised as a child. Have you reevaluated these views recently? If not, you are likely clinging to many beliefs that are in conflict with other beliefs you came to hold later, or that you never properly questioned. The more inertia you have, the more resistant you will be to changing these beliefs, and the less likely you will be to adapt your thinking when you need to.

Think about how scientific theories change over time, but how old "facts" still persist. When our parents were in school, they weren't taught about how an asteroid led to the extinction of the dinosaurs, because that theory wasn't put forth until 1980. And now, forty years later, this widely accepted asteroid theory has come under increased scrutiny in terms of how large a role it actually played in causing the mass extinction. Something different may very likely be in textbooks decades from now.

Have you heard that the latest research indicates that *Tyrannosaurus rex* had a form of feathers over parts of its body? Or that the war on saturated fat and dietary cholesterol that loomed large when we were kids in the 1980s has been completely revised, and now whole milk and eggs are thought to be part of a healthy diet? It can be hard to change old habits and beliefs once they are so ingrained, even if you now know them to be flawed. We are of course aware of both of these revisions, but still the image that comes to mind when we hear about *T. rex* is not that of a feathered dinosaur, and we still take pause at the idea of eating eggs every day.

Organizations face a similar danger because of inertia. A long-term commitment to an organizational strategy creates a lot of inertia toward that strategy. This inertia can lead to suboptimal decisions, referred to as a **strategy tax**. For example, most people would like to reduce their online footprint and be tracked less by advertisers. As a result, web browsers have incorporated more privacy features. For example, in 2017, Apple's Safari browser introduced a feature called Intelligent Tracking Prevention, which attempts to prevent ads from following you around the internet. However, we expect that Google will not add a feature like this to its Chrome browser, because Google itself is the company tracking you on most sites, since its long-term strategy is to dominate online advertising. Since Google tracks you, it can sell advertisers the ability to follow you around the internet with its ads.

Google's *strategy* of being the world's biggest advertising company requires it to pay the *tax* of not adding significant anti-tracking features to its browser, since doing so would counteract that strategy. Apple does not have to pay this tax since it does not have such a strategy.

Politicians and political parties create strategy tax when locking themselves into a long-term position. For example, the U.S. Republican Party has staked out a position that opposes climate change mitigation, with many politicians denying that man-made climate change is even taking place. As the negative effects of man-made climate change are becoming clearer through increased catastrophic weather incidents, this strategy tax may start to cost politically.

Reversing course once a strategy tax is established can be even more costly. In 1988, George H. W. Bush delivered this famous line at the Republican Party's national convention: "Read my lips: no new taxes." Later, this commitment caused significant problems for him when he faced a recession as president. Ultimately, Bush decided he had to break his pledge and raise taxes, and it cost him reelection.

The lesson here is that you should, as much as possible, avoid locking yourself into rigid long-term strategies, as circumstances can rapidly change. What strategy taxes are you currently paying?

A model related to the strategy tax is the **Shirky principle**, named after economics writer Clay Shirky. The Shirky principle states, *Institutions will try to preserve the problem to which they are the solution.* An illustrative example is TurboTax, a U.S. company that makes filing taxes easier, but also lobbies against ideas that would make it easier to file taxes directly with the government. For example, "return-free filing," a system in which the government would send you a pre-filled form based on information it already has available, would work well for most people. It is already a reality in some countries, saving time and money for millions. Yet TurboTax fights against the adoption of such a program because it wants tax filing to continue to be complex, since it is the solution to that problem.

Sometimes a person or department will try to preserve an inefficient process, even when a new idea or technology comes around that can make things easier. Think of the stodgy person at your office or school who is always talking about the "way it's always been done," constantly anxious about change and new technology. That person embodies the Shirky principle. You do not want to be that person.

Inertia in beliefs and behaviors allows entrenched ideas and organizations to persist for long periods of time. The **Lindy effect** is the name of this phenomenon. It was popularized by Nassim Taleb in his book *Antifragile*, which we mentioned in Chapter 1. Taleb explains:

> If a book has been in print for forty years, I can expect it to be in print for another forty years. But, and that is the main difference, if it survives another decade, then it will be expected to be in print another fifty years. This, simply, as a rule, tells you why things that have been around for a long time are not "aging" like persons, but "aging" in reverse. Every year that passes without extinction doubles the additional life expectancy. This is an indicator of some robustness. The robustness of an item is proportional to its life!

The Lindy effect applies to technologies, ideas, organizations, and other nonperishable things. Assuming that the thing in question is not falling out of favor, the longer it endures, the longer you can expect it to further endure.

The Lindy effect explains the continued relevance of Shakespeare and the Beatles. Since they show no signs of falling out of favor, the Lindy effect tells us we can expect Shakespeare plays to be performed for at least another four hundred years, and Beatles songs to be heard for at least another fifty.

Of course, things can and do eventually become unpopular, and there is another mental model to describe the point at which something's relevance begins to decline. This model is **peak**, as in *peak sexism*, *peak Facebook*. This concept was actually popularized with oil, as *peak oil* is usually defined as the point in time when the maximum amount of oil is being extracted from Earth. After peak oil, the decline may be a slow one, but it will have begun, with oil production falling each year instead of rising.

People have predicted peak oil many times. As far back as 1919, David White, the chief geologist of the U.S. Geological Survey, predicted in "The Unmined Supply of Petroleum in the United States" that the U.S. "peak of production will soon be passed, possibly within three years." Many similar predictions have come and gone, and peak oil has still not occurred. What has happened instead is that increased demand has driven innovation in how to get more oil out of the ground, continually increasing yearly production.

Now, though, a better argument for peak oil is starting to form as the oil market's underlying structure is proving to be unhealthy. The effects of climate change are looming. Solar energy is quickly becoming cost-competitive with oil on a global scale. Increasing cost-competitiveness of electric cars and the advent of autonomous vehicles and ride-sharing services are threatening to collapse the car and truck markets as we know them. All of these have the potential to create lasting effects on the oil market.

Whether you are a market observer or a market participant, these structural changes are worth considering when you're thinking about a possible new reality for the oil market. Should your next car be electric? Should you buy another car at all?

More generally, the Lindy effect and peak concepts can help you assess any idea or market opportunity and better predict how it might unfold. Is the market healthy? Has it already reached its peak? How long has it been around? Remember, markets that have been around a long time have more inertia. And the healthier the market is, the more difficult it will be to change.

In fact, something with a lot of inertia, even after its peak, can take an extremely long time to decline. Over the past decade, consumers have read fewer physical newspapers and have been "cutting the cord" with cable, yet plenty of newspapers and cable subscriptions are still sold and will continue to be sold for decades to come. Similarly, fax machines, video rental stores, and dial-up internet feel like relics of the nineties, but people still send plenty of faxes, and, as of the time of this writing, in late 2018, there still exists a Blockbuster video store in Bend, Oregon, and more than a million people still use AOL dial-up! As Samuel Clemens (aka Mark Twain) said, "The report of my death was an exaggeration."

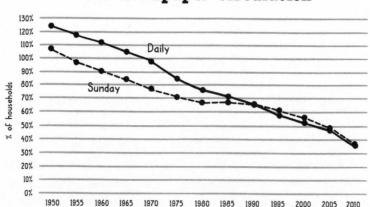

U.S. Newspaper Circulation

Momentum is a model that can help you understand how things change. Momentum and inertia are related concepts. In physics, momentum is the product (multiplication) of mass and velocity, whereas inertia is just a function of mass. That means a heavy object at rest has a lot of inertia since it is hard to move, but it has no momentum since its velocity is zero. However, a heavy object gets momentum quickly once it starts moving. The faster an object goes, the more momentum it has. However, its inertia remains the same (since its mass remains the same), and it is still similarly difficult to change its velocity.

To relate the concept to a real-world example, sending faxes is continually losing momentum. However, the act still has a lot of inertia since the technology is entrenched in many business processes. As a result, the momentum behind sending faxes decreases very slowly.

In your life, you can take advantage of this concept by seeking out things that are rapidly gaining momentum. For example, you could join an organization that is just starting to take off or start a new organization that leverages an innovative technology or idea that is beginning to go mainstream. In Chapter 3, we discussed the benefits of focusing on *high-leverage activities* to make the most out of your time. Activities associated with organizations or ideas with high and increasing momentum are very often high-leverage, because your efforts get amplified by the momentum.

Similarly, creating inertia by entrenching beliefs and processes in others is also a high-leverage activity. Once they are established, those beliefs or processes will be difficult to unwind, persisting for a long time. Think about those beliefs from childhood that we spoke about earlier and how hard they are to let go.

In an organizational context, establishing such beliefs and norms is the act of creating *culture,* which we will explore more fully in Chapter 8. Here, though, consider the relation of culture to inertia embodied in this saying: *Culture eats strategy for breakfast.* It is a warning that if you embark on a strategy that is in opposition to your organization's culture, which has much more inertia than even its strategy, it is very unlikely to succeed.

For example, in 2013 the U.S. government embarked on a strategy to create a website where citizens could directly apply for healthcare coverage. The website, HealthCare.gov, was to be made available on October 1, 2013, though unlike major technology firms, the U.S. government does not have a culture attuned to creating mainstream websites on a deadline. This culture/strategy mismatch was obvious when the government botched the launch of HealthCare.gov. In the first week of operations, only a small percentage of those interested were able to enroll. A strike team was assembled to fix the website, filled with top talent from major tech firms, a group steeped in a culture better matched to this strategy.

Quite simply, to be successful you need your organization's culture to align with its strategy. As an organizational leader, you must recognize if there is a mismatch and act accordingly. As the U.S. government eventually did, you could create a new team with a different culture more fit for the strategy. You could abandon the strategy or pursue a modified strategy more aligned with the existing culture. Or you could try to change the culture over time, steering it toward the desired long-term strategy, recognizing that it may be a slow and challenging process.

In new organizations, you have the opportunity to mold the culture toward long-term strategic directions. However, consider that the world can rapidly change around you. It follows, then, that you eventually may have to rapidly change your organization's strategy as well. Consequently, the best organizational culture in many situations is one that is highly adaptable, just as it is recommended for people themselves to be highly adaptable. That is, you likely want to craft an organizational culture that can readily accept new strategies or processes. A culture like this is agile, willing to experiment with new ideas, not tied down to existing processes.

The good news is that if you can establish inertia and momentum in an adaptable culture, or in any context really, it can have staying power. A mental model that captures this process well is the **flywheel**, a rotating physical disk that is used to store energy. Flywheels are still used in many industrial applications, though a more relatable example to get the concept is a children's merry-go-round. It takes a lot of effort to get a merry-go-round to start spinning, but once it is spinning, it takes little effort to keep it spinning.

Nonprofit marketing expert Tom Peterson credits the flywheel model for the growth

Flywheel

Flywheel

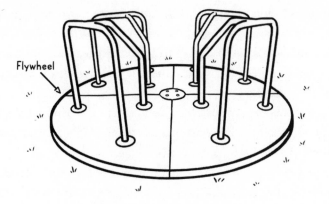

Flywheel

of the global anti-poverty nonprofit Heifer International from $3 million in revenue in 1992 to $90 million in 2008. In the 1970s, Heifer International created its gift catalog fundraising concept, encouraging people to give a gift like a goat or water buffalo to a family in need in order to make them more self-reliant. With Peterson's help, Heifer improved the catalog each year, running dozens of experiments through changes to its look, contents, production, distribution, and publicity. This constant testing and experimentation helped the company's revenue grow a little bit each year, never slowing down. It has continued to sustain higher and higher levels through today.

In his book *Good to Great*, Jim Collins relates many similar examples, using the flywheel metaphor to summarize how companies systematically and incrementally go from good to great.

> The flywheel image captures the overall feel of what it was like inside the companies as they went from good to great. No matter how dramatic the end result, the good-to-great transformations never happened in one fell swoop. There was no single defining action, no grand program, no one killer innovation, no solitary lucky break, no wrenching revolution. Good to great comes about by a cumulative process—step by step, action by action, decision, turn by turn of the flywheel— that adds up to sustained and spectacular results.

An example of a flywheel in everyday life is how it takes a lot of time and practice to become an expert on a topic, but once you are an expert it takes only minimal effort to remain on top of new developments in the field. On a shorter time scale, any personal or professional project can be viewed from the perspective of a flywheel. It is slow when you get started on the project, but once you gain some momentum, it seems easier to make progress. And as we discussed in Chapter 3, when we *multitask,* we never get enough momentum on any one task for it to start to feel easier. Instead, we are constantly spending energy starting and restarting the wheel rather than taking advantage of its momentum once we get it to start spinning.

The flywheel model tells you your efforts will have long-term benefits and will compound on top of previous efforts by yourself and others. It's the tactical way to apply the concepts of momentum and inertia to your advantage.

On the other hand, trying to change something that has a lot of inertia is challenging because of the outsized effort required. That doesn't mean it isn't worth the effort, but you should go in with eyes wide open, knowing that it can be difficult and time-consuming. If you do decide to try enacting such a change, there are several useful models to aid you in your quest.

First, from biology, there is **homeostasis**, which describes a situation in which an organism constantly regulates itself around a specific target, such as body temperature. When you get too cold, you shiver to warm up; when it's too hot, you sweat to cool off. In both cases, your body is trying to revert to its normal temperature. That's helpful, but the same effect also prevents change from the status quo when you want it to occur.

In general, societies, organizations, families, and individuals usually exhibit homeostasis around a set of core cultural values or metrics that relate to the status of the group. Doing so ensures their self-preservation (or so they think). For example, in the U.S., attempts at campaign finance reform have continually failed as lobbying groups have found new and innovative ways to react to regulations, and they continue to infuse their money into politics.

On a more mundane scale, within organizations or communities, people often naturally resist change, regularly responding with the mantra "If it ain't broke, don't fix it," "Don't rock the boat," or "That's how we do things around here." This reaction can be rationalized and justified because change can be disruptive, even if the proposed end state has attractive benefits.

In our kids' school district right now, there is a debate about changing the school start times based on solid research showing that teenagers do better with later start times. However, moving school times causes a decent amount of disruption to various pockets of the community, and would require many families and teachers to adjust their schedules and arrangements, such as for childcare. If the goal is to achieve the best educational outcome for the students, the data shows that start times should be moved, though the reaction to protect the status quo is nevertheless understandable.

Unfortunately, as a result of these types of homeostatic reactions, we stay in suboptimal arrangements for too long, from toxic personal relationships to poor organizational processes, all the way up to ineffective government policies. When you fight homeostasis—in yourself or in others—look out for the underlying mechanisms that are working against your efforts to make changes.

A good example would be exercising more to lose weight only to have your increased exercise lead to an increased appetite. Anticipating this reaction, some people eat protein after working out to mitigate the homeostatic effect, because certain types of slow-digesting proteins help you feel full for longer.

What is the "eating protein" equivalent in whatever situation you're dealing with? Finding the answer can help you overcome the status quo. One common approach is to get data that support the desired change, and then use that data to counteract objections to it. In the school start-times example, some people claim that making the start time later will just cause teenagers to stay up later, negating the effect. But studies from actual school districts that have already made the change show that is not the case, and that teenagers do in fact sleep more on average with later school times.

This concept of trying hard not to deviate from the status quo reminds us of a toy that is generically called a roly-poly toy (in the U.S., Playskool had a branded version called a

Potential Energy

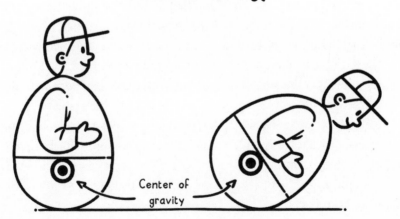

Center of gravity

Weeble—"Weebles wobble, but they don't fall down"), which rights itself when pushed over. These toys work using two useful concepts that are also metaphorical mental models that help you when enacting change: **potential energy** and **center of gravity**. Potential energy is the stored *energy* of an object, which has the *potential* to be released. Center of gravity is the *center* point in an object or system around which its mass is balanced.

Any time a roly-poly is tilted, its potential energy increases, as it takes in the energy used to tilt the toy. When released, this energy gets translated into a wobble around its center of gravity. Potential energy like this comes in many physical forms: gravitational, such as any object lifted up; elastic, such as a taut bowstring or spring; chemical, such as the energy locked up in food or fuel; etc.

Metaphorically, we talk about people and organizations having *pent-up energy*, energy waiting to be unlocked, released from its stored state, and unleashed on the world. Hidden potential energy is another thing you can look for when seeking change. Think of people in your organization who are motivated to make the change happen. They may be willing to help you. Talking to a diverse set of potential stakeholders can help you discover these hidden pockets of potential energy.

The term *center of gravity* is used notably in military strategy to describe the heart of an operation. Knowing an opponent's center of gravity tells you where to attack to inflict the most damage or what pieces of their infrastructure they will defend more than others. The closer to their center of gravity, the more damage you will cause, and the more they will risk defending it.

As applied tactically to enact change, if you can identify the center of gravity of an idea, market, or process—anything—then you might effect change faster by acting on that specific point. For example, you might convince a central influencer, someone other people or organizations look to for direction, that an idea is worthwhile.

Businesses often take advantage of this concept by seeking endorsements from celebrities, influencers, press, or marquee clients. One endorsement can have a cascading effect, as your idea is able to spread because you convinced the right person. In this context, it's a type of *pressure point*: press it, and you can move the whole system.

So far in this section we've discussed the power of inertia (strategy tax, Shirky principle), how to assess it (peak, Lindy effect), how to take advantage of it (flywheel), and how to think about reversing it through tactical models (homeostasis, potential energy, center of gravity). A couple other chemistry concepts will also be helpful to you tactically: **activation energy** and **catalyst**.

Activation energy is the minimum amount of *energy* needed to *activate* a chemical reaction between two or more reactants. Consider striking a match to ignite it: the friction from striking the match supplies the activation energy needed for it to ignite. A catalyst decreases the activation energy needed to start a chemical reaction. Think of how it is easier for a wildfire to start on a hot and dry day, with increased temperature and decreased moisture serving as catalysts.

More generally, activation energy can refer to the amount of effort it would take to start to change something, and catalyst to anything that would decrease this effort. When you are settled into the corner of the couch, it requires a lot of activation energy to get up. However, knowing there is ice cream in the freezer is a catalyst that lowers this activation energy. When attempting change, you want to understand the activation energy required and look for catalysts to make change easier.

In 2017, the U.S. saw both a rapid takedown of statues commemorating Confederate leaders and the accelerating takedown of sexual predators via the #MeToo movement. In both cases it seems that once there was enough activation energy, the movements pushed forward very quickly. It turns out there was a lot of potential energy waiting to be unleashed once those first steps were taken. Furthermore, social media posts and reporting by journalists were catalysts, serving as both a blueprint and an outlet for others to publicize these causes.

In Chapter 3 we described how *commitment* can help you overcome *present bias*; it can also serve as a great catalyst, or **forcing function**, to reach the activation energy required for a personal or organizational change. It usually takes the form of a prescheduled event, or *function*, that facilitates, or *forces*, you to take a desired action. A common example of a forcing function is the standing meeting, such as one-on-one meetings with a manager or coach, or a regular team meeting. These are set times, built into the calendar, when you can repeatedly bring up topics that can lead to change.

You can similarly build additional forcing functions directly into your personal or company culture. For instance, you can set the expectation of producing weekly project updates, which serve as catalysts to think critically about project status and communicate progress to stakeholders. A more personal forcing function would be a regular appointment with a trainer at a gym, or a weekly family meeting or budget review. These set blocks of time will grease the wheels for change.

The title of this section is *Don't Fight Nature*. You should be wary of fighting high-inertia systems blindly. Instead, you want to look at things more deeply, understand their underlying dynamics, and try to craft a high-leverage path to change that is more likely to succeed in a timely manner.

HARNESSING A CHAIN REACTION

Now we will discuss what often creates the underlying momentum behind new ideas as they permeate society: **critical mass**. As we noted in the Introduction, in physics critical mass is the *mass* of nuclear material needed to create a nuclear **chain reaction**, where the by-products of one *reaction* are used as the inputs for the next, *chaining* them together in a self-perpetuating fashion.

Nuclear Chain Reaction

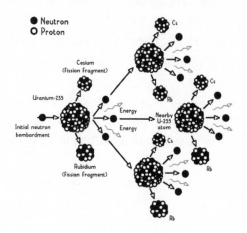

This piece of knowledge was essential for the creation of the atomic bomb. Below the critical mass, nuclear elements are relatively harmless; above, and you have enough material to drive an atomic explosion.

In 1944 in Los Alamos, New Mexico, Austrian-British physicist Otto Frisch was tasked with determining how much enriched uranium was required to create the critical mass for the first atomic bomb. Believe it or not, Frisch figured out the critical mass in part by physically stacking three-centimeter uranium bars, continually measuring their radioactive output as the stack grew larger. One day he almost caused a runaway reaction, the first known criticality accident, by simply leaning over the stack with his body. Some of the radiation reflected off his body and back into the stack, already near the critical mass, causing the radiation-detecting red lamps in the vicinity to shine continuously instead of flickering intermittently as usual. Noticing the lamps, Frisch scattered some of the bars quickly with his hand, and later wrote in his memoir, *What Little I Remember,* that if he "had hesitated for another two seconds before removing the material . . . the dose would have been fatal."

Critical mass as a super model applies to any system in which an accumulation can reach a threshold amount that causes a major change in the system. The point at which the system starts changing dramatically, rapidly gaining momentum, is often referred to as a **tipping point**. For example, a party needs to reach a critical mass of people before it feels like a party, and the arrival of the final person needed for the party to reach the critical number *tips* the party into high gear.

Sometimes this point is also referred to as an *inflection point*, where the growth curve bends, or *inflects*. However, note that mathematically the inflection point actually refers to a different point on the curve, when it changes from concave to convex, or vice versa.

Most popular technologies and ideas have had tipping points that propelled them further into the mainstream. If you graph their adoption curves, as in the chart below, you can plainly see these points.

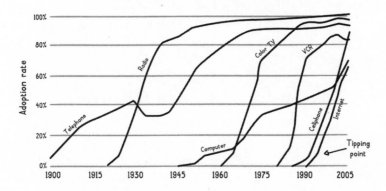

Technology Adoption Curves

When thinking about engaging with new ideas and technologies, you want to examine where they are along their adoption curves, paying special attention to tipping points. Did a tipping point just happen? Will one ever happen? What could be a catalyst? Being an expert in an area that is about to hit a tipping point is an advantageous position, since your expertise has increasing leverage as the idea or technology takes off. Conversely, specializing in an area that is a decade away from hitting a tipping point is a much lower-leverage situation.

The spreading, or diffusion, of an idea or technology is known as the **technology adoption life cycle**. In his 1962 book *Diffusion of Innovation*, sociologist Everett Rogers theorized that people belong to one of five groups based on how and when they adopt new things:

- *Innovators* (about 2.5 percent of the population) have the desire and financial wherewithal to take risks and are closely connected to the emerging field, usually because they are specifically interested in trying new things within it.
- *Early adopters* (13.5 percent) are willing to try out new things once they are a bit more fleshed out. Early adopters do not require social proof to use a product or idea. They are often the influencers that help push an idea past a tipping point, thus making it more broadly known.
- The *early majority* (34 percent) are willing to adopt new things once the value proposition has been clearly established by the early adopters. This group is not interested in wasting their time or money.
- The *late majority* (34 percent) are generally skeptical of new things. They will wait until something has permeated through the majority of people before adopting it. When they get on board, it is often at a lower cost.
- *Laggards* (16 percent) are the very last group to adopt something new, and they do so only because they feel it is necessity.

Technology Adoption Life Cycle

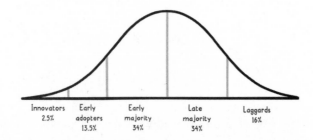

Consider the adoption of the cellphone, which, as you can see from the Technology Adoption figure, progressed in several stages. The initial users—the innovators and early adopters—were rich tinkerers or professionals (e.g., doctors) who were able and willing to pay the high expense because it helped them do their jobs better. Later, as the price came down and new use cases emerged (e.g., text messaging), the early and late majority adopted. And finally, when they felt left behind, the laggards bought cellphones. The smartphone has followed a similar pattern, albeit more quickly. Do you still know people who use flip phones? They are the laggards in the smartphone adoption lifecycle.

The curves that emerge from the technology adoption life cycle are known as **S curves** because they resemble an S shape. The bottom part of the S is the pace of initial slower adoption; then adoption kicks into high gear; and finally, adoption slows as the market saturates, creating the top part of the S.

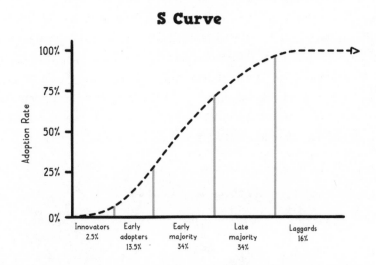

While developed as a theory about technological innovation, the concept of an adoption life cycle also applies to social innovations, including ideas of tolerance and social equality. In the past decades acceptance of same-sex marriage has swept through the early majority in the U.S., and even into the late majority among Independents and Democrats (see chart on next page).

Reaching a critical mass is a common *proximate cause* (see Chapter 1) of a tipping point. But the *root cause* of why a tipping point has been reached is often found in **network effects**, where the value of a *network* grows with each addition to it (the *effect*). Think of a social network—each person who joins makes the service more enticing because there are then more people to reach.

U.S. Same-Sex Marriage Support

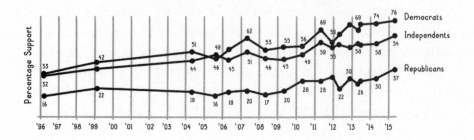

The concept of a network is wider, however, encompassing any system where things (often referred to as *nodes*) can interact. For example, you need enough uranium atoms ("nodes") in the "network" of a nuclear bomb such that when one decays, it can rapidly interact with another, instead of dissipating harmlessly. To use another example from everyday life, the telephone isn't a useful device if there is no one else to call. But as each person gets a phone, the number of possible connections grows proportionally to the square of the number of phones (nodes). Two phones can make only one connection, five can make ten, and twelve can make sixty-six.

Network Effects

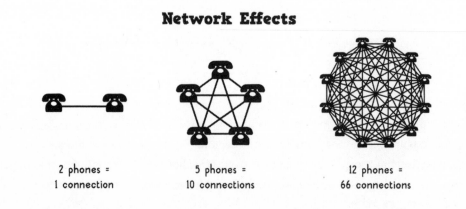

This relationship, known as **Metcalfe's law**, is named after Robert Metcalfe, the co-inventor of the networking technology Ethernet. It describes the nonlinear growth in network value when nodes are connected to one another. His law oversimplifies reality since it assumes that every node (or telephone in this case) has the same value to the network and that every node may want to contact every other, but nevertheless it serves as a decent model. Having a million telephones on the phone network is much more than twice as valuable as having five hundred thousand. And knowing that *everyone* is connected is extremely valuable, which explains why Facebook has such a strong network effect.

Critical mass occurs when there are enough nodes present to make a network useful. Amazingly, the fax machine was invented in the 1840s, but people didn't regularly use it until the 1970s, when there were enough fax machines to reach critical mass. The modern equivalent is internet messaging services: they need to reach critical mass within a community to be useful. Once they pass this tipping point, they can rapidly make their way into the mainstream.

Network effects have value beyond communication, however. Many modern systems gain network effects by simply being able to process more data. For example, speech recognition improves when more voices are added. Other systems gain advantages by being able to provide more liquidity or selection based on the volume or breadth of participants. Think of how more goods are available on Etsy and eBay when more people are participating on those sites.

Network effects apply to person-to-person connections within a community as well. Being part of the right alumni network can help you find the right job or get you answers quickly to esoteric questions. Any time you have nodes in a system participating in some kind of exchange, such as for information or currency, you have the potential for network effects.

Once an idea or technology reaches critical mass, whether through network effects or otherwise, it has gained a lot of inertia, and often has a lot of momentum as well. In the fax example, after a hundred years of struggling for adoption, once fax technology passed the critical mass point, it became embedded in society for the long term. The lesson here is, when you know that the concept of critical mass applies to your endeavor, you want to pay special attention to it.

Just as we suggested questions to ask about tipping points, there are similar questions you can ask about critical mass and network effects: What is the critical mass point for this idea or technology? What needs to happen for it to reach critical mass? Are there network effects or other catalysts that can make reaching critical mass happen sooner? Can I reorganize the system so that critical mass can be reached in a sub-community sooner?

It's important to note that these critical mass models apply in both positive and negative scenarios. Harmful ideas and technologies can also reach critical mass and spread quickly through societies. Historical examples abound, from fascism to institutional racism and other forms of discrimination.

For negative or positive, modern communication systems have made it much easier for ideas to reach critical mass. In Chapter 1 we explored how people are in *echo chambers* online, which make it easier for insular points of view to persist. In addition, ad targeting can find the individuals most susceptible to a message, both by targeting the people who are most inclined to believe it and by experimenting with different ad variations until the most manipulative method is discovered. In this manner, conspiracy theories and scams can thrive.

When discovering the atomic critical mass, Otto Frisch narrowly avoided a catastrophic chain reaction, known more generally as a **cascading failure**, where a *failure* in one piece of a system can trigger a chain reaction of failure that *cascades* through the entire system. Major blackouts on our electric grid are usually the result of cascading failure: overload in one area triggers overload in adjacent areas, triggering further overload in more adjacent areas, and so on.

The 2007/2008 financial crisis is another example of a cascading failure, where a failure in subprime mortgages ultimately led to failures in major financial institutions. In biological systems, the decimation of one species can lead to the decimation of others, as their absence cascades through the food chain. This occurs often when one species almost exclusively feeds on another, such as pandas and bamboo or koalas and eucalyptus leaves. Or think about how many species depend on coral reefs for their survival: when the reef disappears, so do most of the organisms that rely on it.

It's not all bad, though; these are natural laws that can be used for good or bad. The nuclear critical mass can be used for relatively safe, essentially unlimited nuclear energy, or the nuclear critical mass could be the delivery mechanism of a catastrophic nuclear winter. In any case, these mental models are playing an increasing role in society as we get more and more connected. As technologies and ideas spread, you will be better prepared for them if you can spot and analyze these models—how S curves unfold, where tipping points occur, how network effects are utilized. And if you are trying to gain mainstream adoption and long-term inertia for a new idea or technology, you will want to understand how these models directly relate to your strategy.

ORDER OUT OF CHAOS

Many global systems, including the economy and weather, are known as chaotic systems. That means that while you can guess which way they are trending, it's impossible to precisely predict their overall long-term state. You can't know how a particular company or person in the economy will fare over time or exactly when and where an extreme weather event will occur. You can only say that it seems like the unemployment rate is moving down or that hurricane season is coming up.

Mathematician Edward Lorenz is famous for studying such chaotic systems, pioneering a branch of mathematics called chaos theory. He introduced a metaphor known as the **butterfly effect** to explain the concept that chaotic systems are extremely sensitive to small perturbations or changes in initial conditions. He illustrated this concept by saying that the path of a tornado could be affected by a *butterfly* flapping its wings weeks before, sending air particles on a slightly different path than they would have otherwise traveled, which then gets amplified over time and ultimately results in a different path for the tornado. This metaphor has been popularized in many forms of entertainment, including by Jeff Goldblum's character in the 1993 movie *Jurassic Park* and in the 2004 movie *The Butterfly Effect*, starring Ashton Kutcher.

The fact that you are surrounded by chaotic systems is a key reason why adaptability is so important to your success. While it is a good idea to plan ahead, you cannot accurately predict the circumstances you will face. No one plans to lose their spouse at a young age, or to graduate from college during an economic downturn. You must continuously adapt to what life throws at you.

Unlike an air particle, though, you have free will and can actively navigate the world. This means you have the potential to increase the probability of a successful outcome for yourself. You can at least attempt to *turn lemons into lemonade* by using these chaotic systems to your advantage. For example, some studies show that businesses started during a recession actually do better over time, and research by the Kauffman Foundation, summarized in "The Economic Future Just Happened" in 2009, found that the majority of Fortune 500 companies were started during tough economic times.

We're sure you can point to times in your history when a small change led to a big effect in your life. It's the "what if" game. *What if* you hadn't gone to that event that led to meeting your spouse? *What if* you had moved into that other apartment? *What if* you had struck up a relationship with a different teacher or mentor? That's the butterfly effect at the most personal level.

One way to more systematically take advantage of the butterfly effect is using the super model of **luck surface area**, coined by entrepreneur Jason Roberts. You may recall from geometry that the surface area of an object is how much *area* the *surface* of an object covers. In the same way that it is a lot easier to catch a fish if you *cast a wide net*, your personal luck surface area will increase as you interact with more people in more diverse situations.

If you want greater luck surface area, you need to relax your rules for how you engage with the world. For example, you might put yourself in more unfamiliar situations: instead of spending the bulk of your time in your house or office, you might socialize more or take a class. As a result, you will *make your own luck* by meeting more people and finding more opportunities. Thinking of the butterfly effect, you are increasing your chances of influencing a tornado, such as forming a new partnership that ultimately blossoms into a large, positive outcome.

You obviously have to be judicious about which events to attend, or you will constantly be running to different places without getting any focused work done. However, saying no to everything also has a negative consequence—it reduces your luck surface area too much. A happy medium has you attending occasional events that expose you to people who can help you advance your goals. Say no often so you can say yes when you might make some new meaningful connections.

Your luck surface area relates to the natural concept of **entropy**, which measures the amount of disorder in a system. In a clean room where there is a rule for where everything goes—socks in the sock drawer, shirts on hangers, etc.—there are not many possible configurations for everything in the room because of these strict rules. The maximum amount of entropy in this arrangement is small. If you relax those rules, for example by allowing clothes to go on the floor, there are suddenly many more possible configurations for everything in the room. The amount of possible disorderliness, the maximum entropy level possible for the room, has gone up significantly.

"Cleaning goes against entropy
and the natural order."

In this context, increasing your luck surface area means increasing your personal maximum entropy, by increasing the possible number of situations you put yourself in. Your life will be a bit less orderly, but disorder in moderation can be a good thing. Of course, as we have seen so far, too much of a good thing can also be a bad thing. Too much entropy is just chaos.

We refer to our kids as entropy machines because they create disorder very quickly. They don't follow rules for where their belongings go in their rooms, so the maximum possible entropy for their rooms is very high. Almost anything can go almost anywhere and ultimately their rooms can get pretty close to this maximum, resulting in a big mess. As entropy increases, things become more randomly arranged. If left to continue forever, this eventually leads to an evenly distributed system, a completely randomly arranged system—clothes and toys anywhere and everywhere!

In a closed system, like our kids' rooms, entropy doesn't just decrease on its own. Russian playwright Anton Chekhov put it like this: "Only entropy comes easy." If our kids don't make an effort to clean up, the room just gets messier and messier. The natural increase of entropy over time in a closed system is known as the *second law of thermodynamics*. Thermodynamics is the study of heat. If you consider our universe as the biggest closed system, this law leads to a plausible end state of our universe as a homogenous gas, evenly distributed everywhere, commonly known as the *heat death of the universe*.

On a more practical level, the second law serves as a reminder that orderliness needs to be maintained, lest it be slowly chipped away by disorder. This natural progression is based on the reality that most orderliness doesn't happen naturally. Broken eggs don't spontaneously mend themselves. In boiling water, an ice cube melts and never re-forms as ice. If you take a puzzle apart and shake up the pieces, it isn't going to miraculously put itself back together again.

You must continually put energy back into systems to maintain their desired orderly states. If you never put energy into straightening up your workspace, it will get ever messier. The same is true for relationships. To keep the same level of trust with people, you need to keep building on it.

In Chapter 3, we discussed ways to proactively organize your time in order to spend this limited resource wisely, such as by using the *Eisenhower Decision Matrix*. Seen through the lens of entropy, your time, if left unmanaged, will start to go to random, largely reactionary activities. You will get pulled into the chaotic systems that surround you. Instead, you need to manage your time so that it is in a state of lower entropy.

When you are able to make time for important activities, you are more easily able to adapt to your changing environment because you have the ability to allocate time to a particular important activity when needed.

To apply the Eisenhower Decision Matrix usefully, though, you need to assess properly what is an important activity and what is not. Given the butterfly effect and the fact that you must interact with chaotic systems like the economy, making these determinations can be challenging. This is especially true when deciding how and when to pursue new ideas, where an unexpected encounter can reveal new and important information.

To make these determinations, you must therefore seek to understand and simplify chaotic systems like the economy so that you can successfully navigate them. All the mental models in this book are in service of that general goal. You can also develop your own models, such as by making your own **2 × 2 matrices** like the Eisenhower Decision Matrix. Below is one we made up relating specifically to helping you determine what events you might want to attend.

	Low-cost events	High-cost events
High-impact events	Attend	Maybe attend
Low-impact events	Maybe attend	Ignore

You can use this 2 × 2 matrix to help you categorize events as either high or low impact and high or low cost (time, money, etc.). You want to attend high-impact, low-cost events, and ignore low-impact, high-cost events. The other two quadrants are more nuanced. If there is a high-impact, high-cost event, such as a conference far from where you live, it may be worth going to depending on the specifics of the event and your particular situation: do you have the time and money to go? Similarly, if there is a low-impact event down the hall that will take only an hour of your time, it might be worth attending because the cost is so low.

These 2 × 2 matrices draw on a concept from physics called **polarity**, which describes a feature that has only two possible values. A magnet has a north and south *pole*. An electric charge can be positive or negative.

Polarity is useful because it helps you categorize things into one of two states: good or bad, useful or not useful, high-leverage or low-leverage, etc. When you mix two group-ings together, you get the 2 × 2 matrix. These visualizations are powerful because you can distill complicated ideas into a simple diagram and gain insights in the process.

While 2 × 2 matrices can be illuminating, they can also be misleading because most things don't fall squarely into binary or even discrete states. Instead they fall along a con-tinuum. For example, if you're considering ways to make extra money across a set of pos-sible activities, you don't just want to know if you will make any money with each; you want to know how much, and how difficult it will be to generate new income from each activity. Winning the lottery will be significantly different from finding money on the ground or getting a part-time job. One simple way visually to introduce this type of com-plexity is through a *scatter plot* on top of a 2 × 2 matrix, which visualizes the relative values of what you are analyzing.

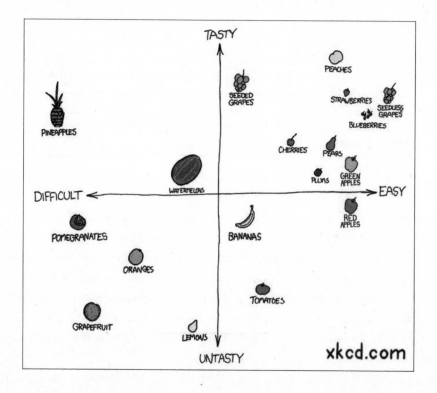

While polarity can be useful, when making comparisons you must be careful to avoid the **black-and-white fallacy**—thinking that things fall neatly into two groups when they do not. When making decisions, you usually have more than two options. It's not all *black* and *white.* Practically, whenever you are presented with a decision with two options, try to think of more.

People are susceptible to the black-and-white fallacy because of the natural tendency to create *us versus them* framings, thinking that the only two options are ones that either benefit themselves at the expense of "others," or vice versa. This tendency arises because you often associate identity and self-esteem with group membership, thereafter creating **in-group favoritism** and, conversely, **out-group bias**. Social psychologists Henri Tajfel and John Turner established research in this area, published as "The Social Identity Theory of Intergroup Behavior" in *Political Psychology* in 2013, that has since been corroborated many times. It showed that with the tiniest of associations, even completely arbitrary ones (like defining groups based on coin tosses), people will favor their "group."

Outside the lab, this tendency toward in-group favoritism often fosters false beliefs that transactions are **zero-sum**, meaning that if your group gains, then the other group must lose, so that the *sum* of gains and losses is *zero*. However, most situations, including most negotiations, are not zero-sum. Instead, most have the potential to be **win-win** situations, where both parties can actually end up better off, or *win*. How is this possible? It's

"Which 'win' is ours? Because the one on the left
looks bigger."

because most negotiations don't include just one term, such as price, but instead involve many terms, such as quality, respect, timing, control, risk, and on and on.

In other words, there are usually several dimensions underlying a negotiation, and each party will value these dimensions differently. This opens up the possibility for a *give-and-take* where you *give* things you value less and *take* things you value more. As a result, both parties can end up better than they were before, getting things they wanted more and giving things they wanted less.

In fact, this give-and-take is the basis for most economic transactions! Otherwise, without misinformation, misunderstanding, or duress, people wouldn't make all these transactions. Zero-sum is the exception, not the rule.

Black-and-white and zero-sum thinking simply do not provide enough possible options, just having two. Recognizing that there are more options and dimensions can be desirable in many situations, such as business deals. The more terms of the deal you consider, the more possible arrangements of deal terms there are. If managed properly, this increases the likelihood of a successful deal for both sides, of finding that win-win state.

You can go too far, though. For example, in a complex business negotiation, you cannot discuss every word in the contract or else discussions will take forever, and you'll never get a deal done. You must instead choose thoughtfully which words are worth discussing and which are not.

More generally, you must continually try to strike the right balance between order and chaos as you interact with your environment. If you let the chaos subsume you, then you will not make progress in any particular direction. But if you are too ordered, then you will not be able to adapt to changing circumstances and will not have enough luck surface area to improve your chances of success.

You want to be somewhere in the middle of order and chaos, where you are intentionally raising your personal entropy enough to expose yourself to interesting opportunities and you are flexible and resilient enough to react to new conditions and paradigms that emerge.

If you study the biographies of successful people, you will notice a pattern: luck plays a significant role in success. However, if you look deeper, you will notice that most also had a broad luck surface area. Yes, they were in the right place at the right time, but they made the effort to be in a right place. If it wasn't that particular place and time, there might have been another. Maybe it wouldn't have resulted in the same degree of success, but they probably would have still been successful.

Another pattern: many of the most influential figures (Bill Gates, Martin Luther

King Jr., etc.) were at the center of major adoptions of ideas or technologies that swept through society via the critical mass models described earlier. In some cases, they created the new idea or technology, but more often they were the ones who brought the ideas or technologies into the mainstream. They created momentum and ultimately inertia by guiding the ideas and technologies through the technology adoption life cycle.

With deeper understanding of these models, you should be able to more easily adapt to the major changes that will come in your lifetime. You should also be able to spot them coming from afar and participate in them, as if you were catching a wave and having it glide you safely to shore. Being adaptable like this helps you in good times and bad. On the positive side, you can make better decisions with your life and career; on the negative side, you can be more resilient when setbacks and unfortunate events occur, and even help limit their negative effects.

KEY TAKEAWAYS

■ Adopt an experimental mindset, looking for opportunities to run experiments and apply the **scientific method** wherever possible.

■ Respect **inertia**: create or join healthy **flywheels**; avoid **strategy taxes** and trying to enact change in high-inertia situations unless you have a tactical advantage such as discovery of a **catalyst** and a lot of **potential energy**.

■ When enacting change, think deeply about how to reach **critical mass** and how you will navigate the **technology adoption life cycle**.

■ Use **forcing functions** to grease the wheels for change.

■ Actively cultivate your **luck surface area** and put in work needed to not be subsumed by **entropy**.

■ When faced with what appears to be a **zero-sum** or **black-and-white** situation, look for additional options and ultimately for a **win-win**.

Lies, Damned Lies, and Statistics

DATA, NUMBERS, AND STATISTICS now have an everyday role in most professional careers, not just in engineering and science. Increasingly, organizations of all kinds are making data-driven decisions. Every field has people studying ways to do it better. Consider K–12 education: What is the most effective way to teach kids to read? How much homework should students be getting? What time of day should school start?

The same is increasingly true in everyday life: What is the best diet? How much exercise is good enough? How safe is this car compared with that one?

Unfortunately, there often aren't straightforward answers to these types of questions. Instead, there are usually conflicting messages on almost every topic: for nutrition, medicine, government policy (environmental regulation, healthcare, etc.), and the list goes on and on.

For any issue, you can find people on both sides with "numbers" to back up their position. This leads many people to feel that data can be too easily manipulated to support whatever story someone wants to tell, hence the title of this chapter. Similarly, even if people aren't intentionally trying to mislead you, study results are often accidentally misinterpreted, or the studies themselves can suffer from design flaws.

However, the answer is not to dismiss all statistics or data-driven evidence as non-sense, leaving you to base decisions solely on opinions and guesses. Instead, you must use mental models to a get a deeper understanding of an issue, including its underlying research, enabling you to determine what information is credible.

You can also use data from your life and business to derive new insights. Insights based on true patterns, such as those found in market trends, customer behavior, and natural occurrences, can form the basis for major companies and scientific breakthroughs. They can also provide insight in everyday life.

As an example, consider being a first-time parent. Lucky parents have a baby who goes to sleep easily and sleeps through the night at one month old. The rest of us have to hear all the advice: use a rocker, swaddle them, let them cry it out, don't let them cry it out, co-sleep, change the baby's diet, change the mother's diet, and on and on.

Our older son never wanted to be put down, but our pediatrician nevertheless advised us to put him down when he was sleepy but still awake. That always led to him screaming the minute he was set down. If he wasn't deeply asleep, he would just rouse himself and start crying. The first few nights of this were harrowing, with each of us taking turns staying awake and holding him while he slept; he may have slept on his own for an hour a night.

HOW I FEEL

trying to put down my baby and have her stay sleeping.

We had to find another way. Through experimentation and collecting our own data over the first few weeks (see *scientific method* in Chapter 4), we discovered that our son liked a tight swaddle and would fall asleep in an electric swing, preferably on the highest setting. When he grew out of the swaddle, we feared that we were going back to square one. Luckily, he quickly adapted, and before he turned one, he could easily be put down and sleep straight through the night.

When we had our second son, we thought of ourselves as baby-care professionals. We had our magic swing and we thought we were all set. And then, per *Murphy's law* (see Chapter 2), baby number two hated the swing. We circled back through all the advice, and after a few days, we tried to set him down when he was sleepy but awake (per our pediatrician's original advice). Lo and behold, he put himself to sleep!

Like babies and their sleep procedures, many aspects of life have inherent variability and cannot be predicted with certainty. Will it rain today? Which funds should you invest your retirement money in? Who are the best players to draft for your fantasy football team?

Despite this uncertainty, you still have to make a lot of choices, from decisions about your health to deciding whom to vote for to taking a risk with a new project at work. This chapter is about helping you think about wading through such uncertainty in the context of decision making. What advice should you listen to and why?

Probability and statistics are the branches of mathematics that give us the most useful mental models for these tasks. As French mathematician Pierre-Simon Laplace wrote in his 1812 book *Théorie Analytique des Probabilités*: "The most important questions of life are indeed, for the most part, really only problems of probability."

We will discuss the useful mental models from the fields of probability and statistics along with common traps to avoid. While many of the basic concepts of probability are fairly intuitive, your *intuition* often fails you (as we've seen throughout this book).

Yes, that means some of this chapter is a bit mathematical. However, we believe that an understanding of these concepts is needed for you to understand the statistical claims that you encounter on a daily basis, and to start to make your own. We've tried to include only the level of detail that is really needed to start to appreciate these concepts. And, as always, we've included plenty of examples to help you grasp them.

TO BELIEVE OR NOT BELIEVE

It is human nature to use past experience and observation to guide decision making, and evolutionarily this makes sense. If you watched someone get sick after they ate a certain food or get hurt by behaving a certain way around an animal, it follows that you should not copy that behavior. Unfortunately, this shortcut doesn't always result in good thinking. For example:

> We had a big snowstorm this year; so much for global warming.

> My grandfather lived to his eighties and smoked a pack a day for his whole life, so I don't believe that smoking causes cancer.

> I have heard several news reports about children being harmed. It is so much more dangerous to be a child these days.

> I got a runny nose and cough after I took the flu vaccine, and I think it was caused by the vaccine.

These are all examples of drawing incorrect conclusions using **anecdotal evidence**, informally collected *evidence* from personal *anecdotes*. You run into trouble when you make generalizations based on anecdotal evidence or weigh it more heavily than scientific evidence. Unfortunately, as Michael Shermer, founder of the Skeptics Society, points out in his 2011 book *The Believing Brain*, "Anecdotal thinking comes naturally, science requires training."

One issue with anecdotal evidence is that it is often not representative of a full range of experiences. People are more inclined to share out-of-the-ordinary stories. For instance, people are more likely to write a review when they had a terrible experience or an amazing experience. As a result, the only takeaway from an anecdote is that a single event may have occurred.

If you hear an anecdote about someone who smoked and escaped lung cancer, that only proves you are not guaranteed to get lung cancer if you smoke. However, based solely on this anecdote, you cannot draw a conclusion on the chances that an average smoker will get cancer or the relative likelihood of smokers getting lung cancer compared with

OH, YOU HAVE ANECDOTAL EVIDENCE?

THAT COMPLETELY OUTWEIGHS MY FACTS, STUDIES, AND STATISTICS.

nonsmokers. If everyone who ever smoked got lung cancer and everyone who didn't smoke never got lung cancer, the data would be a lot more convincing. Unfortunately, the real world is rarely that simple.

You may have heard anecdotes about people who happened to get cold and flu symptoms around the time that they got the flu vaccine and blame their illness on the vaccine. Just because two events happened in succession, or are *correlated*, doesn't mean that the first actually *caused* the second. Statisticians use the phrase **correlation does not imply causation** to describe this fallacy.

xkcd.com

What is often overlooked when this fallacy arises is a **confounding factor**, a third, possibly non-obvious *factor* that influences both the assumed cause and the observed effect, *confounding* the ability to draw a correct conclusion. In the case of the flu vaccine, the cold and flu season is that confounding factor. People get the flu vaccine during the time of year when they are more likely to get sick, whether they have received the vaccine or not. Most likely the symptoms people are experiencing are from a common cold, which the flu vaccine does not protect against.

In other instances, a correlation can occur by random chance. It's easier than ever to test the correlation between all sorts of information, so many spurious correlations are bound to be discovered. In fact, there is a hilarious site (and book) called *Spurious Correlations*, chock-full of these silly results. The graph below shows one such correlation, between cheese consumption and deaths due to bedsheet tanglings.

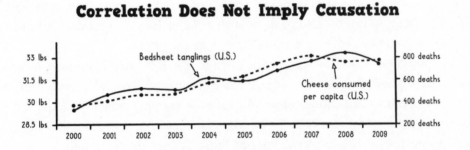

Correlation Does Not Imply Causation

One time when Lauren was in high school, she started feeling like a cold was coming on, and her dad told her to drink plenty of fluids to help her get better. She proceeded to drink half a case of raspberry Snapple that day, and, surprisingly, the next day she felt a lot better! Was this clear evidence that raspberry Snapple is a miracle cure for the common cold? No. She probably just experienced a coincidental recovery due to the body's natural healing ability after also drinking a whole bunch of raspberry Snapple.

Or maybe she wasn't sick at all; maybe she was just randomly having a bad day, followed by a more regular day. Many purveyors of homeopathic "treatments" include similar anecdotal reports of coincidental recoveries in advertisements for their products. What is not mentioned is what would have happened if there were no "treatment." After all, even when you are sick, your symptoms will vary day by day. You should require more credible data, such as a thorough scientific experiment, before you believe any medical claims on behalf of a product.

If you set out to collect or evaluate scientific evidence based on an experiment, the first step is to define or understand its **hypothesis**, the proposed explanation for the effect being studied (e.g., drinking Snapple can reduce the length of the common cold). Defining a hypothesis up front helps to avoid the **Texas sharpshooter fallacy**. This model is named after a joke about a person who comes upon a barn with targets drawn on the side and bullet holes in the middle of each target. He is amazed at the shooter's accuracy, only to find that the targets were drawn around the bullet holes *after* the shots were fired. A similar concept is the *moving target*, where the goal of an experiment is changed to support a desired outcome after seeing the results.

One method to consider, often referred to as the gold standard in experimental design, is the **randomized controlled experiment**, where participants are *randomly* assigned to two groups, and then results from the *experimental* group (who receive a treatment) are compared with the results from the *control* group (who do not). This setup isn't limited to medicine; it can be used in fields such as advertising and product development. (We will walk through a detailed example in a later section.)

A popular version of this experimental design is **A/B testing**, where user behavior is compared between version A (the experimental group) and version B (the control group) of a site or product, which may differ in page flow, wording, imagery, colors, etc. Such experiments must be carefully designed to isolate the one factor you are studying. The simplest way to do this is to change just one thing between the two groups.

Ideally, experiments are also *blinded*, so that participants don't know which group they are in, preventing their conscious and unconscious bias from influencing the results. The classic example is a blind taste test, which ensures that people's brand affinities don't influence their choice.

To take the idea of blinding one step further, the people administering the experiment or analyzing the experiment can also remain unaware of which group the participants are in. This additional blinding helps reduce the impact of **observer-expectancy bias** (also called *experimenter bias*), where the cognitive *biases* of the researchers, or *observers*, may cause them to influence the outcome in the direction they *expected*.

Unfortunately, experimenter blinding doesn't completely prevent observer-expectancy bias, because researchers can still bias results in the preparation and analysis of a study, such as by engaging in selective background reading, choosing hypotheses based on preconceived notions, and selectively reporting results.

In medicine, researchers go to great lengths to achieve properly blinded trials. In 2014, the *British Medical Journal* (*BMJ*) published a review by Karolina Wartolowska et al. of fifty-three studies that compared an actual surgical intervention with a "sham" surgery, "including the scenario when a scope was inserted and nothing was done but patients were sedated or under general anesthesia and could not distinguish whether or not they underwent the actual surgery."

These fake surgeries are an example of a *placebo*, something that the control participants receive that looks and feels like what the experimental participants receive, but in reality is supposed to have no effect. Interestingly, just the act of receiving something that you expect to have a positive effect can actually create one, called the **placebo effect**.

While placebos have little effect on some things, like healing a broken bone, the placebo effect can bring about observed benefits for numerous ailments. The *BMJ* review reported that in 74 percent of the trials, patients receiving the fake surgeries saw some improvement in their symptoms, and in 51 percent of the trials, they improved about as much as the recipients of actual surgeries.

For some conditions, there is even evidence to suggest that the placebo effect isn't purely a figment of the imagination. As an example, placebo "pain relievers" can produce brain activity consistent with the activity produced by actual pain-relieving drugs. For all the parents out there, this is why "kissing a boo-boo" actually can help make it better. Similarly, anticipation of side effects can also result in real negative effects, even with fake treatments, a phenomenon known as the *nocebo effect*.

One of the hardest things about designing a solid experiment is defining its *endpoint*, the metric that is used to evaluate the hypothesis. Ideally, the endpoint is an objective metric, something that can be easily measured and consistently interpreted. Some examples of objective metrics include whether someone bought a product, is still alive, or clicked a button on a website.

However, when the concept that researchers are interested in studying isn't clearly observable or measurable, they must use a **proxy** endpoint (also called a *surrogate endpoint* or *marker*), a measure expected to be closely correlated to the endpoint they would measure if they could. A proxy essentially means a stand-in for something else. Other uses of this mental model include the proxy vote (e.g., absentee ballot) and proxy war (e.g., current conflicts in Yemen and Syria are a proxy war between Iran and Saudi Arabia).

While there is no one objective measure of the quality of a university, every year *U.S. News and World Report* tries to rank schools against one another using a proxy metric that is a composite of objective measures, such as graduation rates and admission data, along with more subjective measures, such as academic reputation. Other examples of common proxy metrics include the body mass index (BMI), used to measure obesity, and

IQ, used to measure intelligence. Proxy metrics are more prone to criticism because they are indirect measures, and all three of these examples have been criticized significantly.

As an example of why this criticism can be valid, consider abnormal heart rhythms (ventricular arrhythmias) that can cause sudden death. Anti-arrhythmic drugs have been developed that prevent ventricular arrhythmias, and so it would seem obvious that these drugs would be expected to prevent sudden death in the patients who take them. But use of these drugs actually leads to a significant *increase* in sudden death in patients with asymptomatic ventricular arrhythmias after a heart attack. For these patients, the reduced post-treatment rate of ventricular arrhythmias is not indicative of improved survival and is therefore not a good proxy metric.

However, despite the complications that arise when conducting well-run experiments, collecting real scientific evidence beats anecdotal evidence hands down because you can draw believable conclusions. Yes, you have to watch out for spurious correlations and subtle biases (more on that in the next section), but in the end you have results that can really advance your thinking.

HIDDEN BIAS

In the last section, we mentioned a few things to watch out for when reviewing or conducting experiments, such as observer-expectancy bias and confounding factors. There are a few more of these subtle concepts to be wary of.

First, sometimes it is not ethical or practical to randomly assign people to different experimental groups. For example, if researchers wanted to study the effect of smoking during pregnancy, it wouldn't be right to make nonsmoking pregnant women start smoking. The smokers in the study would therefore be those who *selected* to continue smoking, which can introduce a *bias* called **selection bias**.

With selection bias, there is no guarantee that the study has isolated smoking to be the only difference between these groups. So if there is a difference detected at the end of the study, it cannot be easily determined how much smoking contributed to this difference. For instance, women who choose to continue smoking during their pregnancy against the advice of doctors may similarly make other medically questionable choices, which could drive adverse outcomes.

Selection bias can also occur when a sample is selected that is not representative of the

broader population of interest, as with online reviews. If the group studied isn't representative, then the results may not be applicable overall.

Essentially, you must be really careful when drawing conclusions based on nonrandom experiments. The *Dilbert* cartoon above pokes fun at the selection bias inherent in a lot of the studies reported in the news.

A similar selection bias occurs with parents and school choice for their kids. Parents understandably want to give their kids a leg up and will often move or pay to send their kids to "better schools." However, is the school better because there are better teachers or because the students are better prepared due to their parents' financial means and interest in education? Selection bias likely explains some significant portion of these schools' better test scores and college admissions.

Another type of selection bias, common to surveys, is **nonresponse bias**, which occurs when a subset of people don't participate in an experiment after they are selected for it, e.g., they fail to *respond* to the survey. If the reason for not responding is related to the topic of the survey, the results will end up biased.

For instance, let's suppose your company wants to understand whether it has a problem with employee motivation. Like many companies, you might choose to study this potential problem via an employee engagement survey. Employees missing the survey due to a scheduled vacation would be random and not likely to introduce bias, but employees not filling it out due to apathy would be nonrandom and would likely bias the results. That's because the latter group is made up of disengaged employees, and by not participating, their disengagement is not being captured.

Surveys like this also do not usually account for the opinions of former employees, which can create another bias in the results called **survivorship bias**. Unhappy employees may have chosen to leave the company, but you cannot capture their opinions when you survey only current employees. Results are therefore biased based on measuring just the population that *survived*, in this case the employees remaining at the company.

Do these biases invalidate this survey methodology? Not necessarily. Almost every methodology has drawbacks, and bias of one form or another is often unavoidable. You should just be aware of all the potential issues in a study and consider them when drawing conclusions. For example, knowing about the survivorship bias in remaining employees, you could examine the data from exit interviews to see whether motivation issues were mentioned by departing employees. You could even try to survey them too.

A few other examples can further illustrate how subtle survivorship bias can be. In World War II, naval researchers conducted a study of damaged aircraft that returned from missions, so that they could make suggestions as to how to bolster aircraft defenses for future missions. Looking at where these planes had been hit, they concluded that areas where they had taken the most damage should receive extra armor.

However, statistician Abraham Wald noted that the study sampled only planes that had survived missions, and not the many planes that had been shot down. He therefore theorized the opposite conclusion, which turned out to be correct: that the areas with holes represented areas where aircraft could be shot and still return safely, whereas the areas without holes probably contained areas that, if hit, would cause the planes to go down.

Similarly, if you look at tech CEOs like Bill Gates and Mark Zuckerberg, you might conclude that dropping out of school to pursue your dreams is a fine idea. However, you'd be thinking only of the people that "survived." You're missing all the dropouts who did

Survivorship Bias

not make it to the top. Architecture presents a more everyday example: Old buildings generally seem to be more beautiful than their modern counterparts. Those buildings, though, are the ones that have survived the ages; there were slews of ugly ones from those time periods that have already been torn down.

When you critically evaluate a study (or conduct one yourself), you need to ask yourself: Who is missing from the sample population? What could be making this sample population nonrandom relative to the underlying population? For example, if you want to grow your company's customer base, you shouldn't just sample existing customers; that sample doesn't account for the probably much larger population of potential customers. This much larger potential customer base may behave very differently from your existing customer base (as is the case with early adopters versus the early majority, which we described in Chapter 4).

One more type of bias that can be inadvertently introduced is **response bias**. While nonresponse bias is introduced when certain types of people do not respond, for those who do respond, various cognitive *biases* can cause them to deviate from accurate or truthful *responses*. For example, in the employee engagement survey, people may lie (by omission or otherwise) for fear of reprisal.

"I'm taking a survey. Do you prefer to be growled or barked at?"

In general, survey results can be influenced by response bias in a number of ways, including the following:

- How questions are worded, e.g., leading or loaded questions
- The order of questions, where earlier questions can influence later ones
- Poor or inaccurate memory of respondents
- Difficulty representing feelings in a number, such as one-to-ten ratings
- Respondents reporting things that reflect well on themselves

It's worth trying to account for all of these subtle biases (selection bias, nonresponse bias, response bias, survivorship bias), because after you do so, you can be even more sure of your conclusions.

BE WARY OF THE "LAW" OF SMALL NUMBERS

When you interpret data, you should watch out for a basic mistake that causes all sorts of trouble: overstating results from a sample that is too small. Even in a well-run experiment (like a political poll), you cannot expect to get a good estimate based on a small sample. This fallacy is sometimes referred to as the *law of small numbers*, and this section explores it in more detail. The name is derived from a valid statistical concept called the **law of large numbers**, which states that the *larger* the sample, the closer your average result is expected to be to the true average.

The figure below shows this in action. Each line represents a different series of coin flips and shows how the percentage of heads changes from the first to the five hun-

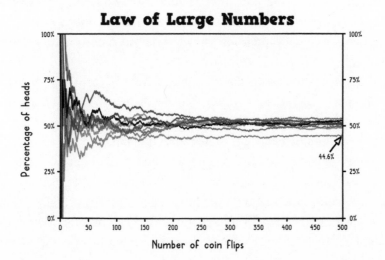

Law of Large Numbers

dredth flip for each series. Note how the curves may deviate quite a bit from the 50 percent mark in the beginning, but start converging closer and closer toward 50 percent as the number of flips increases. But even out to five hundred flips, some of the values are still a fair bit away from 50 percent.

The speed of convergence for a given experiment depends on the situation. We will explain in a later section how you know when you have a large enough sample. For now, we want to focus on what can go wrong if your sample is too small.

First, consider the **gambler's fallacy**, named after roulette players who believe that a streak of reds or blacks from a roulette wheel is more likely to end than to continue with the next spin. Suppose you see ten blacks in a row. Those who fall victim to this fallacy expect the next spin to have a higher chance of coming up red, when in fact the underlying probability of each spin hasn't changed. For this fallacy to be true, there would have to be some kind of corrective force in the roulette wheel that is bringing the results closer to parity. That's simply not the case.

It's sometimes called the *Monte Carlo fallacy* because in a widely cited case in August 18, 1913, a casino in Monte Carlo had an improbable run of twenty-six blacks! There is only a 1 in 137 million chance of this happening in any twenty-six-ball sequence. However, all other twenty-six-spin sequences are equally rare; they just aren't all as memorable.

The gambler's fallacy applies anywhere there is a sequence of decisions, including those by judges, loan officers, and even baseball umpires. In a University of Chicago review of refugee asylum cases from 1985 to 2013, published in the *Quarterly Journal of Economics* as "Decision-Making Under the Gambler's Fallacy: Evidence from Asylum Judges, Loan Officers, and Baseball Umpires," judges were less likely to approve an asylum case if they had approved the last two. It also explains that uncomfortable feeling you might have gotten as a student when you saw that you had chosen answer B four times in a row on a multiple-choice test.

Random data often contains streaks and clusters. Are you surprised to learn that there is a 50 percent chance of getting a run of four heads in a row during any twenty-flip sequence? Streaks like this are often erroneously interpreted as evidence of nonrandom behavior, a failure of intuition called the **clustering illusion**.

Look at the pair of pictures on the next page. Which is randomly generated?

These pictures come from psychologist Steven Pinker's book *The Better Angels of Our Nature*. The left picture—the one with the obvious clusters—is actually the one that is truly random. The right picture—the one that intuitively seems more random—is not; it is a depiction of the positions of glowworms on the ceiling of a cave in Waitomo, New

Clustering Illusion

Zealand. The glowworms intentionally space themselves apart from one another in the competition for food.

In World War II, Londoners sought to find a pattern to the bombings of their city by the Germans. Some became convinced that certain areas were being targeted and others were being spared, leading to conspiracy theories about German sympathizers in certain neighborhoods that didn't get hit. However, statistical analysis showed that there was no evidence to support claims that the bombings were nonrandom.

The improbable should not be confused with the impossible. If enough chances are taken, even rare events are expected to happen. Some people do win the lottery and some people do get struck by lightning. A one-in-a-million event happens quite frequently on a planet with seven billion people.

In the U.S., public health officials are asked to investigate more than one thousand suspected cancer clusters each year. While historically there have been notable cancer clusters caused by exposure to industrial toxins, the vast majority of the cases reported are due to random chance. There are more than 400,000 businesses with fifty or more employees; that's a lot of opportunities for a handful of people to receive the same unfortunate diagnosis.

Knowing the gambler's fallacy, you shouldn't always expect short-term results to match long-term expectations. The inverse is also true: you shouldn't base long-term expectations on a small set of short-term results.

You might be familiar with the phrase *sophomore slump*, which describes scenarios such as when a band gets rave reviews for their first album and the second one isn't as well received, or when a baseball player has a fantastic rookie season but the next year his batting average is not that impressive. In these situations, you may assume there must be some psychological explanation, such as caving under the pressure of success. But in most cases, the true cause is purely mathematical, explained through a model called **regression to the mean**.

Mean is just another word for *average*, and regression to the mean explains why extreme events are usually followed by something more typical, *regressing* closer to the expected mean. For instance, a runner is not expected to follow a record-breaking race with another record-breaking time; a slightly less impressive performance would be expected. That's because a repeat of a rare result is equally as rare as its first occurrence, such that it shouldn't be expected the next time.

The takeaway is that you should never assume that a result based on a small set of observations is typical. It may not be representative of either another small set of observations or a much larger set of observations. Like anecdotal evidence, a small sample tells you very little beyond that what happened was within the range of possible outcomes. While first impressions can be accurate, you should treat them with skepticism. More data will help you distinguish what is likely from what is an anomaly.

THE BELL CURVE

When you are dealing with a lot of data, you can use graphs and summary statistics to combat the feeling of *information overload* (see Chapter 2). The term *statistics* is actually just the name for numbers used to summarize a dataset. (It also refers to the mathematical process by which those numbers are generated.) Graphs and summary statistics succinctly communicate facts about the dataset.

You use summary statistics all the time without even realizing it. If someone asked you, "What is the temperature of a healthy person?" you'd likely say it was 98.6 degrees Fahrenheit or 37 degrees Celsius. That's actually a summary statistic called the **mean**, which, as we just explained, is another word for *average*.

You probably don't even remember when you first learned that fact, and it's even more likely you have no idea where that number comes from. A nineteenth-century German physician, Dr. Carl Wunderlich, diligently collected and analyzed more than a million armpit temperatures from twenty-five thousand patients to calculate that statistic (yes, that's a lot of armpits).

Yet 98.6 degrees Fahrenheit isn't some magical temperature. First of all, more recent data indicates a lower mean, closer to 98.2 degrees. Second, you may have noticed from taking your own temperature or that of a family member that "normal" temperatures vary from this mean. In fact, women are slightly warmer than men on average, and temperatures of up to 99.9°F (37.7°C) are still considered normal. Third, people's temperatures also naturally change throughout the day, moving up on average by 0.9°F (0.5°C) from morning to night.

Just saying a healthy temperature is 98.6°F doesn't account for all of this nuance. That's why a range of summary statistics and graphs are often used on a case-by-case basis to summarize data. The mean (average or expected value) measures *central tendency*, or where the values tend to be *centered*. Two other popular summary statistics that measure central tendency are the **median** (middle value that splits the data into two halves) and the **mode** (the most frequent result). These statistics help describe what a "typical" number might look like for a given set of data.

For body temperature, though, just reporting the central tendency, such as the mean, can at times be too simplistic. This brings us to the second common set of summary statistics, those that measure *dispersion*, or how far the data is spread out.

The simplest dispersion statistics report ranges. For body temperature, that could be specifying the range of values considered normal, e.g., minimum to maximum reported values from healthy people, as in the graph below (called a *histogram*).

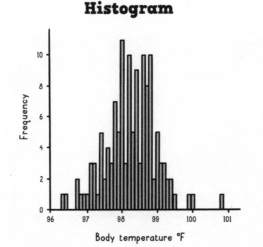

Histogram

Body temperature °F

The graph on the previous page depicts the frequencies of 130 different body temperatures derived from a study of healthy adults. A histogram like this one is a simple way that you can summarize data visually: group the values into buckets, count how many data points are in each bucket, and make a vertical bar graph of the buckets.

Before reporting a range, you might first look for *outliers*, those data points that don't seem to fit with the rest of the data. These are the data points set apart in the histogram, such as the one at 100.8°F. Perhaps a sick person sneaked into the dataset. As a result, you might report a normal temperature range of 96.3°F to 100.0°F. Of course, with more data, you could produce a more accurate range.

In this dataset, central tendency statistics are quite similar because the distribution of the data is fairly symmetric, with just one peak in the middle. As a result, the mean is 98.25°F, the median is 98.3°F, and the mode is 98°F. In other scenarios, though, these three summary statistics may be quite different.

To illustrate this, consider another histogram, below, showing the distribution of U.S. household income in 2016. This dataset also has one peak, at $20,000–$24,999, but it is asymmetric, *skewing* to the right. (All incomes above $200,000 are grouped into one bar; had this not been the case, the graph would have a long tail stretching much farther to the right.)

Unlike for the body temperatures, the median income of $59,039 is very different from the mean income of $83,143. Whenever the data is skewed in one direction like this, the mean gets pulled away from the median and toward the skew, swayed by the extreme values.

Also, a minimum–maximum range is less informative here. A better summary of the dispersion in this case might be an *interquartile range* specifying the 25th percentile to the

Distribution of U.S. Household Income (2016)

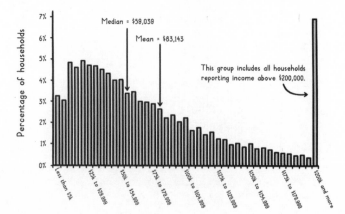

75th percentile of the data, which captures the middle 50 percent of incomes, from $27,300 to $102,350.

The most common statistical measures of dispersion, though, are the **variance** and the **standard deviation** (the latter usually denoted by the Greek letter σ, sigma). They are both measures of how far the numbers in a dataset tend to vary from its mean. The following figure shows how you calculate them for a set of data.

Variance & Standard Deviation

Number of observations: n=5.

Observations: 5, 10, 15, 20, 25

Sample mean: (5+10+15+20+25)/5 = 75/5 = 15

Data point deviations from sample mean, squared:

$(5-15)^2=(-10)^2=100$ $(15-15)^2=(0)^2=0$ $(25-15)^2=(10)^2=100$

$(10-15)^2=(-5)^2=25$ $(20-15)^2=(5)^2=25$

Sample variance: (100+25+0+25+100)/(n-1)=250/(5-1)=250/4=62.5

Sample standard deviation (σ): $\sqrt{(\text{variance})}=\sqrt{(62.5)}=7.9$

Because the standard deviation is just the square root of the variance, if you know one, then you can easily calculate the other. Higher values for each indicate that it is more common to see data points further from the mean, as shown in the targets below.

Variance

Low variance   High variance

The body temperature dataset depicted earlier has a standard deviation of 0.73°F. Slightly more than two-thirds of its values fall within one standard deviation from its mean (97.52°F to 98.98°F) and 95 percent within two standard deviations (96.79°F to 99.71°F). As you'll see, this pattern is commonplace for many datasets consisting of measurements (e.g., heights, blood pressure, standardized tests).

Histograms of these types of datasets have similar bell-curve shapes with a cluster of values in the middle, close to the mean, and fewer and fewer results as you go further away from the mean. When a set of data has this type of shape, it is often suggested that it comes from a **normal distribution**.

The normal distribution is a special type of **probability distribution**, a mathematical function that describes how the *probabilities* for all possible outcomes of a random phenomenon are *distributed*. For example, if you take a random person's temperature, getting any particular temperature has a certain probability, with the mean of 98.2°F being the most probable and values further away being less and less probable. Given that a probability distribution describes all the possible outcomes, all probabilities in a given distribution add up to 100 percent (or 1).

To understand this better, let's consider another example. As mentioned above, people's heights also roughly follow a normal distribution. Below is a graphical representation of the distribution of men's and women's heights based on data from the U.S. Centers for Disease Control and Prevention. The distributions both have the typical bell-curve shape, even though the men's and women's heights have different means.

Normal Distribution

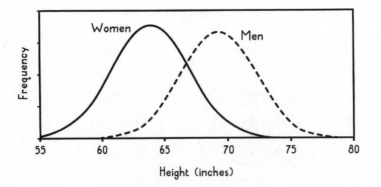

In normal distributions like these (and as we saw with the body temperatures), approximately 68 percent of all values should fall within one standard deviation of the mean, about 95 percent within two, and nearly all (99.7 percent) within three. In this manner, a normal distribution can be uniquely described by just its mean and standard deviation. Because so many phenomena can be described by the normal distribution, knowing these facts is particularly useful.

Normal Distribution Standard Deviations

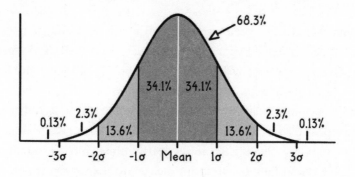

So, if you stopped a random woman on the street, you could use these facts to form a likely guess for her height. A guess of around five feet four inches (162 centimeters) would be best, as that's the mean. Additionally, you could, with about two-to-one odds, guess that she will have a height between five feet one inch and five feet seven inches. That's because the standard deviation of women's heights is slightly less than three inches, so about two-thirds of women's heights will fall within that range (within one standard deviation of the mean). By contrast, women shorter than four feet ten inches or taller than five feet ten inches make up less than about 5 percent of all women (outside two standard deviations from the mean).

There are many other common probability distributions besides the normal distribu-

Probability Distributions

Log-normal distribution

Applies to phenomena that follow a power law relationship, such as wealth, the sizes of cities, and insurance losses.

Poisson distribution

Applies to independent and random events that occur in an interval of time or space, such as lightning strikes or numbers of murders in a city.

Exponential distribution

Applies to the timing of events, such as the survival of people and products, service times, and radioactive particle decay.

tion that are useful across a variety of circumstances. A few are depicted in the figure on the previous page.

We called this section "The Bell Curve," however, because the normal distribution is especially useful due to one of the handiest results in all of statistics, called the **central limit theorem**. This theorem states that when numbers are drawn from the same distribution and then are averaged, this resulting average approximately follows a normal distribution. This is the case even if the numbers originally came from a completely different distribution.

To appreciate what this theorem means and why it is so useful, consider the familiar opinion poll that determines an approval rating, such as for the U.S. Congress. Each person is asked whether they approve of Congress or not. That means the individual data points are each just a yes or a no.

This type of data looks nothing like a normal distribution, as each data point can take only one of two possible values. Binary data like this is often analyzed using a different probability distribution, called the Bernoulli distribution, which represents the result of a single yes/no-type experiment or question, such as from a survey or poll. This distribution is useful in a wide variety of situations, such as analyzing advertising campaigns (whether someone purchased or not), clinical trials (responded to treatment or not), and A/B testing (clicked or not).

The estimated approval rating is just an average of all of the different individual answers (1 for approval and 0 otherwise). For example, if 1,000 people were polled and 240 approved, then the approval rating would be 24.0 percent. The central limit theorem tells us that this statistical average (sample mean) is approximately normally distributed (assuming enough people participate in the survey). The figure on the next page illustrates how this works visually with the Bernoulli distribution and two others that also initially look nothing like the normal distribution.

The middle column shows how the distribution of the sample mean from a Bernoulli distribution, made up of a series of ones and zeros, ends up looking like a bell curve. The first row depicts a distribution with a 75 percent chance of disapproval (the spike at 0 on the left) and a 25 percent chance of approval (the spike at 1 on the right). This 25 percent chance is based on the approval rating across the whole country, if you polled everyone. Each person in a poll comes from this population distribution.

When you take a poll, you get only an estimate of the overall approval rating (like the 24 percent approval rating estimate mentioned earlier). When you do that, you are taking a sample from the entire population (e.g., asking one thousand people) and averaging the

Central Limit Theorem

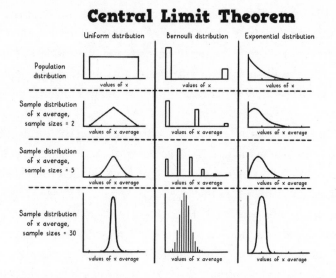

	Uniform distribution	Bernoulli distribution	Exponential distribution
Population distribution	values of x	values of x	values of x
Sample distribution of x average, sample sizes = 2	values of x average	values of x average	values of x average
Sample distribution of x average, sample sizes = 5	values of x average	values of x average	values of x average
Sample distribution of x average, sample sizes = 30	values of x average	values of x average	values of x average

results to calculate the estimate. This sample mean has a distribution itself, called the sample distribution, which describes the chances of getting each possible approval rating from the sample. You can think of this distribution as the result of plotting the different approval ratings (sample means) obtained from many, many polls.

The second row shows a plot of this sample distribution for an approval rating based on polling two randomly selected people. This plot looks different from the original distribution, but still nothing like a normal distribution, as it can have only three outcomes: two approvals (the spike at 1), two disapprovals (the spike at 0), or one approval and one disapproval (the spike at 0.5).

If you base the polls on asking five people, the sample distribution starts to look a bit more like a bell shape with six possible outcomes (third row). With thirty people (thirty-one outcomes, depicted in the fourth row), it starts to look a lot like the characteristic bell-curve shape of the normal distribution.

As you ask more and more people, the sample distribution becomes more and more like a normal distribution, with a mean of 25 percent, the true approval rating from the population distribution. Just as in the case of body temperatures or heights, while this mean is the most likely value obtained by the poll, values close to it are also likely, such as 24 percent. Values further and further away are less and less likely, with probabilities following the normal distribution.

How much less likely, exactly? It depends on how many people you ask. The more people you ask, the tighter the distribution. To convey this information, polls like this usually report a *margin of error*. An article describing the poll results might include something like "Congress has a 24 percent approval rating with a margin of error of ±3 percent." The "±3 percent" is the margin of error, but where this margin of error comes from or what it really means is rarely explained. With knowledge of the above mental models, you now can know!

The margin of error is really a type of **confidence interval**, an estimated range of numbers that you think may include the true value of the parameter you are studying, e.g., the approval rating. This range has a corresponding *confidence level*, which quantifies the *level* of *confidence* you have that the true value of parameter is in the range you estimated. For example, a confidence level of 95 percent tells you that if you ran the poll many times and calculated many confidence intervals (one for each poll), on average 95 percent of them would include the true approval rating (i.e., 25 percent).

Most media reports don't mention the confidence level used to calculate their margin of error, but it is usually safe to assume they used 95 percent. Research publications, by contrast, are usually more explicit in stating what confidence levels they used to represent the uncertainty in their estimates (again typically, though not always, 95 percent).

For the approval-rating scenario, the range is calculated using the fact that the central limit theorem tells us that the sample mean is approximately normally distributed, so we should expect 95 percent of possible values to be found within two standard deviations of the true mean (i.e., the real approval rating).

The part that hasn't been explained yet is that the standard deviation of this distribution, also called the *standard error*, is not the same as the sample standard deviation calculation from earlier. However, these two values are directly related. In particular, the standard error is the same as the standard deviation for the sample, divided by the square root of the sample size. This means that if you want to reduce the margin of error by a factor of two, you need to increase the sample size by a factor of four. For a yes/no poll like the approval rating, a margin of error of 10 percent is achieved with just 96 people, 5 percent at 384 people, 3 percent at 1,067 people, and 2 percent at 2,401. Since the margin of error is an expression of how confident the pollsters are in their estimate, it makes sense that it is directly related to the size of the sample group.

The illustration on the next page shows how confidence intervals work for repeated experiments. It depicts one hundred 95 percent confidence intervals for the probability of flipping heads. Each was calculated from an experiment that involved simulating flipping a fair coin one hundred times. These confidence intervals are represented graphically in the figure by **error bars**, which are a visual way to display a measure of uncertainty for an estimate.

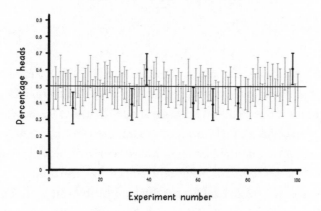

95% Confidence Intervals from 100 Fair Coin Flips

Experiment Repeated 100 Times

Error bars are not always confidence intervals; they could be derived from other types of error calculations too. On an error bar, the dot in the middle is the parameter estimate, in this case the sample mean, and the lines at the end indicate the top and bottom of the range, in this case the confidence interval.

The error bars in the plot vary due to what was seen in the different experiments, but they each span a range of about twenty percentage points, which corresponds to the ±10 percent mentioned above (with a sample size of one hundred flips). Given the 95 percent confidence level, you would expect ninety-five of these confidence intervals to include the true mean of 50 percent. In this case, ninety-three of the intervals included 50 percent. (The seven intervals that didn't are highlighted in black.)

Confidence intervals like these are often used as estimates of reasonable values for a parameter, such as the probability of getting heads. However, as you just saw, the true value of the parameter (in this case 50 percent) is sometimes outside a given confidence interval. The lesson here is, you should know that a confidence interval is not the definitive range for all possible values, and the true value is not guaranteed to be included in the interval.

One thing that really bothers us is when statistics are reported in the media without error bars or confidence intervals. Always remember to look for them when reading reports and to include them in your own work. Without an error estimate, you have no idea how confident to be in that number—is the true value likely really close to it, or could it be really far away from it? The confidence interval tells you that!

IT DEPENDS

As you saw in the last section, the average woman's height is five feet four inches. If you had to guess the height of a random stranger, but you didn't know for a fact that they were a woman, five feet four inches wouldn't be a great guess because the average man is closer to five feet nine inches, and so something in the middle would be better. But if you had the additional information that the person was a woman, then five feet four inches would be the best guess. The additional information changes the probability.

This is an example of a model called **conditional probability**, the *probability* of one thing happening under the *condition* that something else also happened. Conditional probability allows us to better estimate probabilities by using this additional information.

Conditional probabilities are common in everyday life. For example, home insurance rates are tailored to the differing conditional probabilities of insurance claims (e.g., premiums are higher in coastal Florida, where hurricane damage is more likely, relative to where we live in Pennsylvania). Similarly, genetic testing can tell you if you are at higher risk for certain diseases; women with abnormal BRCA1 or BRCA2 genes have up to an 80 percent risk of developing breast cancer by age ninety.

Conditional probability is denoted with a | symbol. For example, the probability (P) that you will get breast cancer by age ninety given that you are a woman with a BRCA mutation would be denoted as P(breast cancer by ninety | woman with BRCA mutation).

Some people find conditional probabilities confusing. They mix up the probability that an event A will happen given a condition that event B happened—$P(A|B)$—with the probability that an event B will happen given the condition that event A happened—$P(B|A)$. This is known as the *inverse fallacy*, whereby people think that $P(A|B)$ and $P(B|A)$ must have similar probabilities. While you just saw that P(breast cancer by ninety | woman with BRCA mutation) is about 80 percent, by contrast *P*(woman with BRCA mutation | breast cancer by ninety) is only 5 to 10 percent, because many other people develop breast cancer who do not have these mutations.

Let's walk through a longer example to see this fallacy in action. Suppose the police pull someone over at random at a drunk-driving checkpoint and administer a Breathalyzer test that indicates they are drunk. Further, suppose the test is wrong on average 5 percent of the time, saying that a sober person is drunk. What is the probability that this person is wrongly accused of drunk driving?

Your first inclination might be to say 5 percent. However, you have been given the probability that the test says someone is drunk given they are sober, or *P*(Test=drunk | Person=sober) = 5 percent. But what you have been asked for is the probability that the person is sober given that the test says they are drunk, or *P*(Person=sober | Test=drunk). These are not the same probabilities!

What you haven't considered is how the results depend on the *base rate* of the percentage of drunk drivers. Consider the scenario where everyone makes the right decision, and no one ever drives drunk. In this case the probability that a person is sober is 100 percent, regardless of what the Breathalyzer test results say. When a probability calculation fails to account for the *base rate* (like the base rate of drunk drivers), the mistake that is made is called the **base rate fallacy**.

Let's consider a more realistic base rate, where one in a thousand drivers is drunk, meaning that there is a small chance (0.1 percent) that a person the police randomly pull over is drunk. And since we know one in twenty tests will be wrong (the tests will be wrong 5 percent of the time), the police will most likely go through a lot of wrong tests before they find a person who was actually drunk-driving.

In fact, if the police stop a thousand people, they would on average conduct nearly fifty wrong tests along their way to finding one actual drunk driver. So there is approximately only a 2 percent chance that a failed Breathalyzer in this scenario indicates that the person is actually drunk. Alternatively, this can be stated as a 98 percent chance that the person is sober. That's way, way more than 5 percent!

So, *P*(A|B) does not equal *P*(B|A), but how are they related? There is a very useful result in probability called **Bayes' theorem**, which tells us the relationship between these two conditional probabilities. On the next page, you will see how Bayes' theorem relates these probabilities and how, in the drunk-driving example, Bayes' theorem could be applied to calculate the 2 percent result.

Bayes' Theorem

$$P(A|B) = \frac{P(B|A)\,P(A)}{P(B)}$$

Probability of event A
given occurrence of event B

Base Rate Fallacy

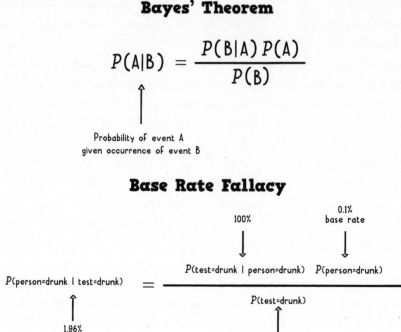

$$P(\text{person=drunk} \mid \text{test=drunk}) = \frac{P(\text{test=drunk} \mid \text{person=drunk})\;P(\text{person=drunk})}{P(\text{test=drunk})}$$

100%

0.1%
base rate

1.96%

5.095%
(true positives—0.1%*100% +
false positives—99.9%*5%)

Now that you know about Bayes' theorem, you should also know that there are two schools of thought in statistics, based on different ways to think about probability: **Frequentist** and **Bayesian**. Most studies you hear about in the news are based on frequentist statistics, which relies on and requires many observations of an event before it can make reliable statistical determinations. Frequentists view probability as fundamentally tied to the *frequency* of events.

By observing the frequency of results over a large sample (e.g., asking a large number of people if they approve of Congress), frequentists estimate an unknown quantity. If there are very few data points, however, they can't say much of anything, since the confidence intervals they can calculate will be extremely large. In their view, probability without observations makes no sense.

Bayesians, by contrast, allow probabilistic judgments about any situation, regardless of whether any observations have yet occurred. To do this, Bayesians begin by bringing related evidence to statistical determinations. For example, picking a penny up off the street, you'd probably initially estimate a fifty-fifty chance that it would come up heads if you flipped it, even if you'd never observed a flip of that particular coin before. In Bayesian statistics, you can bring such knowledge of base rates to a problem. In frequentist statistics, you cannot.

Many people find this Bayesian way of looking at probability more intuitive because it is similar to how your beliefs naturally evolve. In everyday life, you aren't starting from scratch every time, as you would in frequentist statistics. For instance, on policy issues, your starting point is what you currently know on that topic—what Bayesians call a *prior*—and then when you get new data, you (hopefully) update your prior based on the new information. The same is true for relationships, with your starting point being your previous experiences with that person; a strong prior would be a lifelong relationship, whereas a weak prior would be just a first impression.

You saw in the last section that frequentist statistics produce confidence intervals. These statistics tell you that if you ran an experiment many times (e.g., the one-hundred-coin-flips example we presented), the confidence intervals calculated should contain the parameter you are studying (e.g., 50 percent probability of getting heads) to the level of confidence specified (e.g., 95 percent of the time). To many people's dismay, a confidence interval does not say there is a 95 percent chance of the true value of the parameter being in the interval. By contrast, Bayesian statistics analogously produces *credible intervals*, which do say that; credible intervals specify the current best estimated range for the probability of the parameter. As such, this Bayesian way of doing things is again more intuitive.

In practice, though, both approaches yield very similar conclusions, and as more data becomes available, they should converge on the same conclusion. That's because they are both trying to estimate the same underlying truth. Historically, the frequentist viewpoint has been more popular, in large part because Bayesian analysis is often computationally challenging. However, modern computing power is quickly reducing this challenge.

Bayesians contend that by choosing a strong prior, they can start closer to the truth, allowing them to converge on the final result faster, with fewer observations. As observations are expensive in both time and money, this reduction can be attractive. However, there is a flip side: it is also possible that Bayesians' prior beliefs are actually doing the opposite, starting them further from the truth. This can happen if they have a strong belief that is based on *confirmation bias* (see Chapter 1) or another cognitive mistake (e.g., an unjustified strong prior). In this case, the Bayesian approach may take longer to converge on the truth because the frequentist view (starting from scratch) is actually closer to the truth at the start.

The takeaway is that two ways of approaching statistics exist, and you should be aware that, done right, both approaches are valid. Some people are hard-core ideologues who pledge allegiance to one philosophy versus the other, whereas pragmatists (like us) use whichever methodology works best for the situation. And more commonly, remember not to confuse a conditional probability with its inverse: $P(A|B)$ is not equal to $P(B|A)$. You now know that these probabilities are related by Bayes' theorem, which takes into account relevant base rates.

RIGHT OR WRONG?

So far you have learned that you shouldn't base your decisions on anecdotes and that small samples cannot reliably tell you what will happen in larger populations. You might be wondering, then: How much data is enough data to be sure of my conclusions? Deciding the *sample size*, the total number of data points collected, is a balancing act. On one side, the more information you collect, the better your estimates will be, and the more sure you can be of your conclusions. On the other side is the fact that gathering more data takes more time and more money, and potentially puts more participants at risk. So, how do you know what the right sample size is? That's what we cover in this section.

Even with the best experimental design, sometimes you get a fluke result that leads you to draw the wrong conclusions. A higher sample size will give you more confidence that a positive result is not just a fluke and will also give you a greater chance of detecting a positive result.

Consider a typical polling situation, such as measuring public support for an upcoming referendum, e.g., marijuana legalization. Suppose that the referendum ultimately fails, but the pollsters had randomly selected as their respondents people who were more in favor of it when compared with the whole population. This situation could result in a **false positive**: *falsely* giving a *positive* result when it really wasn't true (like the wrong Breathalyzer test). Conversely, suppose the referendum ultimately succeeds, but the pollsters had randomly selected people less in favor of it when compared with the whole population. This situation could result in a **false negative**: *falsely* giving a *negative* result when it really *was* true.

As another example, consider a mammogram, a medical test used in the diagnosis of breast cancer. You might think a test like this has two possible results: positive or negative. But really a mammogram has four possible outcomes, depicted in the following table. The

Possible Test Outcomes

Results of mammogram

	Evidence of cancer	No evidence of cancer
Patient has breast cancer	True positive	False negative
Patient does not have breast cancer	False positive	True negative

two possible outcomes you immediately think of are when the test is right, the true positive and the true negative; the other two outcomes occur when the test is wrong, the false positive and the false negative.

These error models occur well beyond statistics, in any system where judgments are made. Your email spam filter is a good example. Recently our spam filters flagged an email with photos of our new niece as spam (false positive). And actual spam messages still occasionally make it through our spam filters (false negatives).

Because making each type of error has consequences, systems need to be designed with these consequences in mind. That is, you have to make decisions on the trade-off between the different types of error, recognizing that some errors are inevitable. For instance, the U.S. legal system is supposed to require proof beyond a reasonable doubt for criminal convictions. This is a conscious trade-off favoring false negatives (letting criminals go free) over false positives (wrongly convicting people of crimes).

In statistics, a false positive is also known as a *type I error* and a false negative is also called a *type II error*. When designing an experiment, scientists get to decide on the probability of each type of error they are willing to tolerate. The most common false positive rate chosen is 5 percent. (This rate is also denoted by the Greek letter α, alpha, which is equal to 100 minus the confidence level. This is why you typically see people say a confidence level of 95 percent.) That means that, on average, if your hypothesis is false, one in twenty experiments (5 percent) will get a false positive result.

Regardless of the sample size of your experiment, you can always choose the false positive error rate. It doesn't have to be 5 percent; you could choose 1 percent or even 0.1 percent. The catch is that, for a given sample size, when you do set such a low false positive rate, you increase your false negative error rate, possibly failing to detect a real result. This is where the sample size selection comes in.

Once you set your false positive rate, you then determine what sample size you need in order to detect a real result with a high enough probability. This value, called the **power** of the experiment, is typically selected to be an 80 to 90 percent chance of detection, with a corresponding false negative error rate of 10 to 20 percent. (This rate is also denoted by the Greek letter β, beta, which is equal to 100 minus the power.) Researchers say their study is *powered* at 80 percent.

Statistical Testing

	Nothing to detect	Something to detect
Detected effect	False positive rate (%) aka type I error rate, alpha (α) or significance level Typical rate: 5%	Power (%) 100 - False negative rate Typical level: 80%–90%
Did not detect effect	Confidence level (%) 100 - False positive rate Typical level: 95%	False negative rate (%) aka type II error rate or beta (β) Typical rate: 10%–20%

Let's consider an example to illustrate how all these models work together. Suppose a company wants to prove that its new sleep meditation app is working. Their background research shows that half of the time, the average person falls asleep within ten minutes.

The app developers think that their app can improve this rate, helping more people fall asleep in less than ten minutes.

The developers plan a study in a sleep lab to test their theory. The test group will use their app and the control group will just go to sleep without it. (A real study might have a slightly more complicated design, but this simple design will let us better explain the statistical models.) The statistical setup behind most experiments (including this one) starts with a hypothesis that there is no difference between the groups, called the **null hypothesis**. If the developers collect sufficient evidence to reject this hypothesis, then they will conclude that their app really does help people fall asleep faster.

That is, the app developers plan to observe both groups and then calculate the percentage of people who fall asleep within ten minutes for each group. If they see enough of a difference between the two percentages, they will conclude that the results are not compatible with the null hypothesis, which would mean their app is likely really working.

The developers also need to specify an *alternative hypothesis*, which describes the smallest meaningful change they think could occur between the two groups, e.g., 15 percent more people will fall asleep within ten minutes. This is the real result they want their study to confirm and have an 80 percent chance to detect (corresponding to a false negative rate of 20 percent).

This alternative hypothesis is needed to determine the sample size. The smaller the difference in the alternative hypothesis, the more people will be needed to detect it. With the experimental setup described, a sample size of 268 participants is required.

All of these models come together visually in the figure on the next page.

First, look at the bell curves. (Due to the central limit theorem, we can assume that our differences will be approximately normally distributed.) The curve on the left is for the results under the null hypothesis: that there is no real difference between the two groups. That's why this left bell curve is centered on 0 percent. Even so, some of the time they'd measure a higher or lower difference than zero due to random chance, with larger differences being less likely. That is, due to the underlying variability, even if the app has no real effect, they might still measure differences between the two groups because of the variable times it takes for people to fall asleep.

The other bell curve (on the right) represents the alternative hypothesis that the app developers hope to be true: that there is a 15 percent increase in the percentage of people who fall asleep within ten minutes using the app as compared with people not using the app. Again, even if this hypothesis were true, due to variability, some of the time they'd

Statistical Significance

Alpha: 5%   Beta: 20%   Sample size: 268

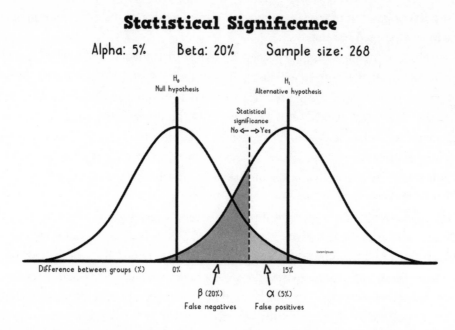

still measure less than a 15 percent increase, and some of the time more than a 15 percent increase. That's why the right bell curve is centered on 15 percent.

The dotted line represents the threshold for **statistical significance**. All values larger than this threshold (to the right) would result in rejection of the null hypothesis because differences this large are very unlikely to have occurred if the null hypothesis were true. In fact, they would occur with less than a 5 percent chance—the false positive rate initially set by the developers.

The final measure commonly used to declare whether a result is statistically significant is called the **p-value**, which is formally defined as the *probability* of obtaining a result equal to or more extreme than what was observed, assuming the null hypothesis was true. Essentially, if the *p*-value is smaller than the selected false positive rate (5 percent), then you would say that the result is statistically significant. *P*-values are commonly used in study reports to communicate such significance.

For example, a *p*-value of 0.01 would mean that a difference equal to or larger than the one observed would happen only 1 percent of the time if the app had no effect. This value corresponds to a value on the figure in the extreme tail of the left bell curve and close to the middle of the right bell curve. This placement indicates that the result is more consistent with the alternative hypothesis, that the app has an effect of 15 percent.

Now, notice how these two curves overlap, showing that some differences between the two groups are consistent with both hypotheses (under both bell curves simultaneously). These gray areas show where the two types of error can occur. The light gray area is the false positive region and the dark gray area is the false negative region.

A false positive would occur when a large difference is measured between the two groups (like one with a *p*-value of 0.01), but in reality, the app does nothing. This could happen if the no-app group randomly had trouble falling asleep and the app group randomly had an easy time.

Alternatively, a false negative would occur when the app really does help people fall asleep faster, but the difference observed is too small to be statistically significant. If the study is 80 percent powered, which is typical, this false negative scenario would occur 20 percent of the time.

Assuming the sample size remains fixed, lowering the chance of making a false positive error is equivalent to moving the dotted line to the right, shrinking the light gray area. When you do so, though, the chance of making a false negative error grows (depicted in the following figure as compared with the original).

If you want to reduce one of the error rates without increasing the other, you need to

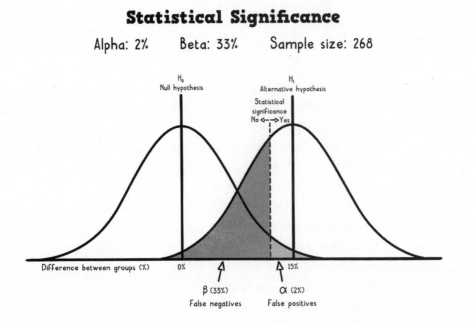

Statistical Significance

Alpha: 2%   Beta: 33%   Sample size: 268

H_0
Null hypothesis

H_1
Alternative hypothesis

Statistical
significance
No ←--→ Yes

Difference between groups (%)   0%   15%

β (33%)
False negatives

α (2%)
False positives

increase the sample size. When that happens, each of the bell curves becomes narrower (see the figure below, again as compared to the original).

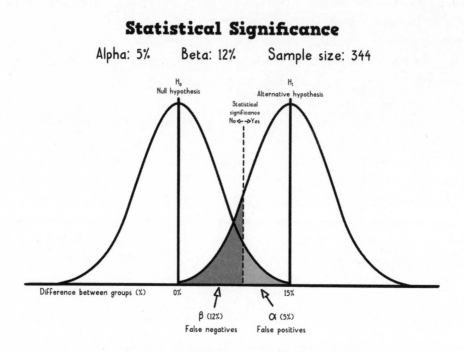

Statistical Significance

Alpha: 5%   Beta: 12%   Sample size: 344

Increasing the sample size and narrowing the bell curves decreases the overlap between the two curves, shrinking the total gray area in the process. This is of course attractive because there is less chance of making an error; however, as we noted in the beginning of this section, there are many reasons why it may not be practical to increase the sample size (time, money, risk to participants, etc.).

The table on the next page illustrates how sample size varies for different limits on the error rates for the sleep app study. You will see that if error rates are decreased, the sample size must be increased.

The sample size values in the following table are all dependent on the selected alternative hypothesis of a 15 percent difference. The sample sizes would all further increase if the developers wanted to detect a smaller difference and would all decrease if they wanted to detect only a larger difference.

Researchers often feel pressure to use a smaller sample size in order to save time and money, which can make choosing a larger difference for the alternative hypothesis ap-

Sample Size Varies with Power and Significance

Alpha	Confidence level	Beta	Power	Sample size
10%	90%	20%	80%	196
10%	90%	10%	90%	284
5%	95%	30%	70%	204
5%	95%	20%	80%	268
5%	95%	10%	90%	370
1%	99%	20%	80%	434
1%	99%	10%	90%	562

pealing. But such a choice comes at a high risk. For instance, the developers can reduce their sample size to just 62 (from 268) if they change the alternative hypothesis to a 30 percent increase between the two groups (up from 15 percent).

However, if the true difference the app makes is really only 15 percent, with this smaller sample size they will be able to detect this smaller difference only 32 percent of the time! That's down from 80 percent originally and means that two-thirds of the time they'd get a false negative, failing to detect the 15 percent difference. As a result, ideally any experiment should be designed to detect the smallest meaningful difference.

One final note on *p*-values and statistical significance: Most statisticians caution against overreliance on *p*-values in interpreting the results of a study. Failing to find a significant result (a sufficiently small *p*-value) is not the same as having confidence that there is no effect. *The absence of evidence is not the evidence of absence.* Similarly, even though the study may have achieved a low *p*-value, it might not be a replicable result, which we will explore in the final section.

Statistical significance should not be confused with scientific, human, or economic significance. Even the most minuscule effects can be detected as statistically significant if the sample size is large enough. For example, with enough people in the sleep study, you could potentially detect a 1 percent difference between the two groups, but is that meaningful to any customers? No.

Alternatively, more emphasis could be placed on the difference measured in a study along with its corresponding confidence interval. For the app study, while the customers want to know that they have better chances of falling asleep with the app than without, they also want to know how much better. The developers might even want to increase the sample size in order to be able to guarantee a certain margin of error in their estimates.

Further, the American Statistical Association stressed in *The American Statistician* in 2016 that "scientific conclusions and business or policy decisions should not be based only on whether a p-value passes a specific threshold." Focusing too much on the p-value encourages black-and-white thinking and compresses the wealth of information that comes out of a study into just one number. Such a singular focus can make you overlook possible suboptimal choices in a study's design (e.g., sample size) or biases that could have crept in (e.g., selection bias).

WILL IT REPLICATE?

By now you should know that some experimental results are just flukes. In order to be sure a study result isn't a fluke, it needs to be replicated. Interestingly, in some fields, such as psychology, there has been a concerted effort to replicate positive results, but those efforts have found that fewer than 50 percent of positive results can be replicated.

That rate is low, and this problem is aptly positive results the **replication crisis**. This final section offers some models to explain how this happens, and how you can nevertheless gain more confidence in a research area.

Replication efforts are an attempt to distinguish between false positive and true positive results. Consider the chances of replication in each of these two groups. A false positive is expected to replicate—that is, a second false positive is expected to occur in a repetition of the study—only 5 percent of the time. On the other hand, a true positive is expected to replicate 80 to 90 percent of the time, depending on the power of the replication study. For the sake of argument, let's assume this is 80 percent as we did in the last section.

Using those numbers, a replication rate of 50 percent requires about 60 percent of the studies to have been true positives and 40 percent of them to have been false positives. To see this, consider 100 studies: If 60 were true positives, we would expect 48 of those to replicate (80 percent of 60). Of the remaining 40 false positives, 2 would replicate (5 percent of 40) for a total of 50. The replication rate would then be 50 per 100 studies, or 50 percent.

So, under this scenario, about a fourth of the failed replications (12 of 50) are explained

Replication Crisis

Re-test 100 Studies

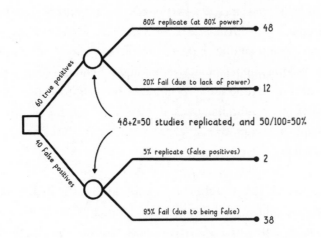

80% replicate (at 80% power) — 48

20% fail (due to lack of power) — 12

60 true positives

48+2=50 studies replicated, and 50/100=50%

40 false positives

5% replicate (false positives) — 2

95% fail (due to being false) — 38

by a lack of power in the replication efforts. These are real results that would likely be replicated successfully either if an additional replication study were done or if the original replication study had a higher sample size.

The rest of the results that failed to replicate should have never been positive results in the first place. Many of these original studies probably underestimated their type I error rate, increasing their chances of being a false positive. That's because when a study is designed for a 5 percent chance of a false positive, that chance applies only to one statistical test, but very rarely is only one statistical test conducted.

The act of running additional tests to look for statistically significant results has many names, including **data dredging**, fishing, and *p-hacking* (trying to *hack* your data looking for small enough *p*-values). Often this is done with the best of intentions, as seeing data from an experiment can be illuminating, spurring a researcher to form new hypotheses. The temptation to test these additional hypotheses is strong, since the data needed to analyze them has already been collected. The trouble comes in, though, when a researcher overstates results that arise from these additional tests.

The *XKCD* cartoon on page 171 illustrates how data dredging can play out: when no statistically significant relationship was found between jelly beans and acne, the scientists proceeded to dredge through twenty-one subgroups until one with a sufficiently low *p*-value was found, resulting in the headline "Green Jelly Beans Linked to Acne!"

Each time another statistical test was done, the chance of forming an erroneous conclusion continued to grow above 5 percent. To see this, suppose you had a twenty-sided die. The chances of making a mistake on the first test would be the same as the chances of rolling a one. Each additional test run would be another roll of the die, each with another one-in-twenty chance of rolling a one. After twenty-one rolls (matching the twenty-one jelly bean colors in the comic), there is about a two-thirds chance that a one is rolled at least once, i.e., that there was at least one erroneous result.

If this type of data dredging happens routinely enough, then you can see why a large number of studies in the set to be replicated might have been originally false positives. In other words, in this set of one hundred studies, the base rate of false positives is likely much larger than 5 percent, and so another large part of the replication crisis can likely be explained as a base rate fallacy.

Unfortunately, studies are much, much more likely to be published if they show statistically significant results, which causes **publication bias**. Studies that fail to find statistically significant results are still scientifically meaningful, but both researchers and *publications* have a *bias* against them for a variety of reasons. For example, there are only so many pages in a publication, and given the choice, publications would rather publish studies with significant findings over ones with none. That's because successful studies are more likely to attract attention from media and other researchers. Additionally, studies showing significant results are more likely to contribute to the careers of the researchers, where publication is often a requirement to advance.

Therefore, there is a strong incentive to find significant results from experiments. In the cartoon, even though the original hypothesis didn't show a significant result, the experiment was "salvaged" and eventually published because a secondary hypothesis was found that did show a significant result. The publication of false positives like this directly contributes to the replication crisis and can delay scientific progress by influencing future research toward these false hypotheses. And the fact that negative results aren't always reported can also lead to different people testing the same negative hypotheses over and over again because no one knows other people have tried them.

There are also many other reasons a study might not be replicable, including the various biases we've discussed in previous sections (e.g., selection bias, survivorship bias, etc.), which could have crept into the results. Another reason is that, by chance, the original study might have showcased a seemingly impressive effect, when in reality the effect is much more modest (regression to the mean). If this is the case, then the replication

xkcd.com

study probably does not have a large enough sample size (isn't sufficiently powered) to detect the small effect, resulting in a failed replication of the study.

There are ways to overcome these issues, such as the following:

- Using lower *p*-values to properly account for false positive error in the original study, across all the tests that are conducted
- Using a larger sample size in a replication study to be able to detect a smaller effect size
- Specifying statistical tests to run ahead of time to avoid *p*-hacking

Nevertheless, as a result of the replication crisis and the reasons that underlie it, you should be skeptical of any isolated study, especially when you don't know how the data was gathered and analyzed. More broadly, when you interpret a claim, it is important to evaluate critically any data that backs up that claim: Is it from an isolated study or is there a body of research behind the claim? If so, how were the studies designed? Have all biases been accounted for in the designs and analyses? And so on.

Many times, this investigation will require some digging. Media sources can draw false conclusions and rarely provide the necessary details to allow you to understand the full design of an experiment and evaluate its quality, so you will usually need to consult the original scientific publication. Nearly all journals require a full section describing the statistical design of a study, but given the word constraints of a typical journal article, details are sometimes left out. Look for longer versions or related presentations on research websites. Researchers are also generally willing to answer questions about their research.

In the ideal scenario, you would be able to find a body of research made up of many studies, which would eliminate doubts as to whether a certain result was a chance occurrence. If you are lucky, someone has already published a **systematic review** about your research question. Systematic reviews are an organized way to evaluate a research question using the whole body of research on a certain topic. They define a detailed and comprehensive (*systematic*) plan for *reviewing* study results in an area, including identifying and finding relevant studies in order to remove bias from the process.

Some but not all systematic reviews include **meta-analyses**, which use statistical techniques to combine data from several studies into one analysis. The data-driven reporting site FiveThirtyEight is a good example; it conducts meta-analyses across polling data to better predict political outcomes.

There are advantages to meta-analyses, as combining data from multiple studies can increase the precision and accuracy of estimates, but they also have their drawbacks. For example, it is problematic to combine data across studies where the designs or sample populations vary too much. They also cannot eliminate biases from the original studies themselves. Further, both systematic reviews and meta-analyses can be compromised by publication bias because they can include only results that are publicly available.

Whenever we are looking at the validity of a claim, we first look to see whether a thorough systematic review has been conducted, and if so, we start there. After all, systematic reviews and meta-analyses are commonly used by policy makers in decision making, e.g., in developing medical guidelines.

If one thing is clear from this chapter, it's probably that designing good experiments is tough! We hope you've also gathered that probability and statistics are useful tools for better understanding problems that involve uncertainty. However, as this section should also make clear, statistics is not a magical cure for uncertainty. As statistician Andrew Gelman suggested in *The American Statistician* in 2016, we must "move toward a greater acceptance of uncertainty and embracing of variation."

More generally, keep in mind that while statistics can help you obtain confident predictions across a variety of circumstances, it cannot accurately predict what will occur in an individual event. For instance, you may know that the average summer day is sunny and warm at your favorite beach spot, but that is no guarantee that it won't be rainy or unseasonably cool the week you plan to take off from work.

Similarly, medical research tells you that your risk of getting lung cancer increases if you smoke, and while you can estimate the confidence interval that an average smoker will get lung cancer in their lifetime, probability and statistics can't tell you what specifically will happen for any one individual smoker.

While probability and statistics aren't magic, they do help you better describe your confidence around the likelihood of various outcomes. There are certainly lots of pitfalls to watch out for, but we hope you also take away the fact that research and data are more useful for navigating uncertainty than hunches and opinions.

- Avoid succumbing to the **gambler's fallacy** or the **base rate fallacy**.

- **Anecdotal evidence** and correlations you see in data are good **hypothesis** generators, but **correlation does not imply causation**—you still need to rely on well-designed experiments to draw strong conclusions.

- Look for tried-and-true experimental designs, such as **randomized controlled experiments** or **A/B testing**, that show **statistical significance**.

- The **normal distribution** is particularly useful in experimental analysis due to the **central limit theorem**. Recall that in a normal distribution, about 68 percent of values fall within one standard deviation, and 95 percent within two.

- Any isolated experiment can result in a **false positive** or a **false negative** and can also be biased by myriad factors, most commonly **selection bias**, **response bias**, and **survivorship bias**.

- Replication increases confidence in results, so start by looking for a **systematic review** and/or **meta-analysis** when researching an area.

- Always keep in mind that when dealing with uncertainty, the values you see reported or calculate yourself are uncertain themselves, and that you should seek out and report values with **error bars**!

Decisions, Decisions

IF YOU COULD KNOW HOW your decisions would turn out, decision making would be so easy! It is hard because you have to make decisions with imperfect information.

Suppose you are thinking of making a career move. You have a variety of next steps to consider:

- You could look for the same job you're doing now, though with some better attributes (compensation, location, mission of organization, etc.).
- You could try to move up the professional ladder at your current job.
- You could move to a similar organization at a higher position.
- You could switch careers altogether, starting by going back to school.

There are certainly more options. When you dig into them all, the array of choices seems endless. And you won't be able to try any of them out completely before you commit to one. Such is life.

How do you make sense of it all? The go-to framework for most people in situations like this is the **pro-con list**, where you *list* all the positive things that could happen if the decision was made (the *pros*), weighing them against the negative things that could happen (the *cons*).

"I don't believe in pressuring my children. When the time is right, they'll arrive at the default choice and go to law school."

While useful in some simple cases, this basic pro-con methodology has significant shortcomings. First, the list presumes there are only two options, when as you just saw there are usually many more. Second, it presents all pros and cons as if they had equal weight. Third, a pro-con list treats each item independently, whereas these factors are often interrelated. A fourth problem is that since the pros are often more obvious than the cons, this disparity can lead to a **grass-is-greener mentality**, causing you *mentally* to accentuate the positives (e.g., *greener grass*) and overlook the negatives.

As an example, in 2000, Gabriel finished school and began a career as an entrepreneur. Early on, at times, he considered switching to a career in venture capital, where he would fund and support companies instead of starting his own. When he initially made a pro-con list, this seemed like a great idea. There were many pros (the chance to work with founders changing the world, the potential for extremely high compensation, the opportunity to work on startups in a high-leverage way without the risk and stress of being the founder, etc.) and no obvious cons.

However, there were several cons that he just didn't fully appreciate or just didn't know about yet (the relentless socializing involved—not good for a major introvert—the burden of having to constantly say no to people, the difficulty of breaking into the field, the fact that much of your time is spent with struggling companies, etc.). While certainly a great career for some who get the opportunity, venture capital was not a good fit for Gabriel, even if he didn't realize it at first. With more time and experience, the full picture has become clear (the grass isn't greener, at least for him), and he has no plans to make that career change.

This anecdote is meant to illustrate that it is inherently difficult to create a complete pro-con list when your experience is limited. Other mental models in this chapter will help you approach situations like these with more objectivity and skepticism, so you can uncover the complete picture faster and make sense of what to do about it.

You've probably heard the phrase *If all you have is a hammer, everything looks like a nail.* This phrase is called **Maslow's hammer** and is derived from this longer passage by psychologist Abraham Maslow in his 1966 book *The Psychology of Science*:

> I remember seeing an elaborate and complicated automatic washing machine for automobiles that did a beautiful job of washing them. But it could do only that, and everything else that got into its clutches was treated as if it were an automobile to be washed. I suppose it is tempting, if the only tool you have is a hammer, to treat everything as if it were a nail.

The hammer of decision-making models is the pro-con list; useful in some instances, but not the optimal tool for every decision. Luckily, there are other decision-making models to help you efficiently discover and evaluate your options and their consequences across a variety of situations. As some decisions are complex and consequential, they demand more complicated mental models. In simpler cases, applying these sophisticated models would be overkill. It is best, however, to be aware of the range of mental models available so that you can pick the right tool for any situation.

WEIGHING THE COSTS AND BENEFITS

One simple approach to improving the pro-con list is to add some numbers to it. Go through each of your pros and cons and put a score of −10 to 10 next to it, indicating how much that item is worth to you relative to the others (negatives for cons and positives for pros). When considering a new job, perhaps location is much more important to you than a salary adjustment? If so, location would get a higher score.

Scoring in this way helps you overcome some of the pro-con list deficiencies. Now each item isn't treated equally anymore. You can also group multiple items together into one score if they are interrelated. And you can now more easily compare multiple options:

simply add up all the pros and cons for each option (e.g., job offers) and see which one comes out on top.

This method is a simple type of **cost-benefit analysis**, a natural extension of the pro-con list that works well as a drop-in replacement in many situations. This powerful mental model helps you more systematically and quantitatively *analyze* the *benefits* (pros) and *costs* (cons) across an array of options.

For simple situations, the scoring approach just outlined works well. In the rest of this section, we explain how to think about cost-benefit analysis in more complicated situations, introducing a few other mental models you will need to do so. Even if you don't use sophisticated cost-benefit analysis yourself, you will want to understand how it works because this method is often used by governments and organizations to make critical decisions. (Math warning: because numbers are involved, there is a bit of arithmetic needed.)

The first change when you get more sophisticated is that instead of putting relative scores next to each item (e.g., −10 to 10), you start by putting explicit dollar values next to them (e.g., −$100, +$5,000, etc.). Now when you add up the costs and benefits, you will end up with an estimate of that option's worth to you in dollars.

For example, when considering the option of buying a house, you would start by writing down what you would need to pay out now (your down payment, inspection, closing costs), what you would expect to pay over time (your mortgage payments, home improvements, taxes . . . the list goes on), and what you expect to get back when you sell the house. When you add those together, you can estimate how much you stand to gain (or lose) in the long term.

As with pro-con lists, it is still hard to account for every cost and benefit in a cost-benefit analysis. However, it is important to note that this model works well only if you are thorough, because you will use that final number to make decisions. One useful tactic is to talk to people who have made similar decisions and ask them to point out costs or benefits that you may have missed. For instance, by talking to other homeowners, you might learn about maintenance costs you didn't fully consider (like how often things break, removing dead trees, etc.). Longtime homeowners can easily rattle off this hidden litany of costs (said with experience!).

When writing down costs and benefits, you will find that some are intangible. Continuing the house example, when you buy a house, you might have some anxiety around keeping it up to date, and that anxiety can be an additional "cost." Conversely, there may be intangible benefits to owning a home, such as not having to deal with a landlord. In a cost-benefit analysis, when faced with intangibles like these, you still want to assign dollar values to them, even if they are just rough estimates of how much they are worth to you. Doing so will help you create a fair quantitative comparison between the courses of action you are considering.

Writing down dollar values for intangible costs and benefits can seem strange—how do you know what it's worth to you to not have to deal with a landlord? But if you think about it, this is no different than scoring a pro-con list. In the scoring method, if the extra amount you'd have to pay monthly rated a −10 (out of 10) and landlord avoidance rated a +1 (out of 10), then you have a quick way to start an estimate: just take the extra payment amount and divide it by 10. Say the excess monthly payments are expected to be $1,000 per month; then you could estimate it is worth $100 per month to avoid a landlord. Of course, you can pick any numbers that make sense to you.

You can get hung up here because it can feel arbitrary to write down specific values for things that you don't know exactly. However, you should know that doing so truly helps your analysis. The reason is that you really do have some sense for how valuable things are and putting that (even inexact) sense into your analysis will improve your results. And, as we will see in a moment, there is a method for testing how much these values are influencing your results.

So far, you've moved from scoring to dollar values. Next, you graduate to a spreadsheet! Instead of a column of costs and a column of benefits, now you want to arrange the costs and benefits on a timeline. Give each item its own row, and each column in the timeline will now list the cost or benefit created by that item in a given year. So, the first column holds all the costs and benefits you expect this year (in year 0), the next column in year 1, then year 2, and so on. The row for a $2,000-per-month mortgage payment would look like −$24,000, −$24,000, −$24,000, for as many years as the life of the mortgage.

The reason it is important to lay out the costs and benefits over time in this manner (in addition to increased clarity) is that benefits you get today are worth more than those same benefits later. There are three reasons for this that are important to appreciate, so please excuse the tangent; back to the cost-benefit analysis in a minute.

First, if you receive money (or another benefit) today, you can use it immediately. This opens up opportunities for you that you wouldn't otherwise have. For instance, you could invest those funds right now and be receiving a return on that money via a different investment, or you could use the funds for additional education, investing in yourself. (See *opportunity cost of capital* in Chapter 3.)

Second, most economies have some level of **inflation**, which describes how, over time, prices tend to increase, or *inflate*. As a result, your money will have less purchasing power in the future than it does today. When we were younger, the standard price for a slice of pizza was one dollar; now a slice will run you upward of three dollars! That's inflation.

Because of inflation, if you get one hundred dollars ten years from now, you won't be able to buy as much as you could if you had the same amount of money today. Consequently, you don't want to regard an amount of money in ten years as the equivalent amount of money available today.

Third, the future is uncertain, and so there is risk that your predicted benefits and costs will change. For instance, benefits that depend on currencies, stock markets, and interest rates will fluctuate in value, and the further you go into the future, the harder they are to predict.

Now back to cost-benefit analysis. As you recall, you have a spreadsheet that lays out current and future costs and benefits across time. To account for the differences in value between current and future benefits, you use a mental model we introduced back in Chapter 3: the *discount rate*. You simply *discount* future benefits (and costs) when comparing them to today. Let's walk through an example to show you how it works.

Cost-benefit analysis is arguably most straightforward with simple investments, so let's use one. Bonds are a common investment option, which operate like a loan: you invest (loan) money today and expect to get back more money in the future when the bond matures (is due). Suppose you invest $50,000 in a bond, which you expect to return $100,000 in ten years. Feel free to make a spreadsheet and follow along.

Cost-Benefit Analysis

	Time line						
	Year 0	Year 1	Year 2	Year 3	Year 4	...	Year 10
Costs	$(50,000)	-	-	-	-	...	-
Benefits	-	-	-	-	-	...	$100,000
Discounted (6%)	$55,839					...	
Net benefit	$5,839					...	

The only cost today (year 0) is $50,000, to purchase the bond. The only benefit in the future (year 10) is $100,000, what you get back when the bond matures. However, as noted, that benefit is not actually worth $100,000 in today's dollars. You need to discount this future benefit back to what it is worth today.

Using a discount rate of 6 percent (relatively appropriate for this situation—more on that in a bit), you can use a *net present value* calculation (again see Chapter 3 if you need a refresher) to translate the benefit of $100,000 in ten years into today's dollars given the 6 percent discount rate. The formula is $100,000/1.06^{10}$ and you get the result of $55,839.

That's all you need for a relatively sophisticated cost-benefit analysis right there! To finish the analysis, just add up all the discounted costs and benefits in today's dollars. You have the discounted benefit of $55,839 minus the initial cost of $50,000, netting you $5,839.

You want the net benefit to be positive or else the deal isn't worth doing, since you'd end up worse off (in today's dollars). In this case, the net benefit is positive, so the investment is worth considering among your other options.

A central challenge with cost-benefit analysis is that this end result is sensitive to the chosen discount rate. One way to show this sensitivity is through a **sensitivity analysis**, which is a useful method to *analyze* how *sensitive* a model is to its input parameters. Using the $50,000 bond example, let's run a sensitivity analysis on the discount rate. To do so, you just vary the discount rate and calculate the net benefit for each variation.

Sensitivity Analysis

Discount rate	Net benefit
0%	$50,000
2%	$32,035
4%	$17,556
6%	**$5,839**
8%	−$3,680
10%	−$11,446
12%	−$17,803
14%	−$23,026
16%	−$27,332

Notice how a seemingly small difference in the discount rate can represent a huge difference in the net benefit. That is, the net benefit is very sensitive to the discount rate.

While the net benefit is positive at a 6 percent discount rate, it is three times more positive at 4 percent, and it is negative at 8 percent. That's because at higher discount rates, the future benefit is discounted more. Eventually, it is discounted so much that the net benefit drops into negative territory.

Running a sensitivity analysis like this can give you an idea of a range of net benefits you can expect under reasonable discount rates. You should similarly run a sensitivity analysis on any input parameter about which you are uncertain so that you can tell how much it influences the outcome.

Recall how earlier we discussed the difficulties around putting dollar values to intangible costs and benefits, such as how much not having a landlord is worth. You could use sensitivity analysis to test how much that input parameter matters to the outcome, and how a range of reasonable values would directly influence the outcome.

In general, sensitivity analysis can help you quickly uncover the key drivers in your spreadsheet inputs and show you where you may need to spend more time to develop higher accuracy in your assumptions. Sensitivity analysis is also common in statistics, and we actually already presented another one in Chapter 5 when we showcased how sample size is sensitive to *alpha* and *beta* when designing experiments.

Given that the discount rate is always a key driver in cost-benefit analyses, figuring out a reasonable range for the discount rate is paramount. To do so, consider again the factors that underlie the discount rate: inflation (that the purchasing power of money can change over time), uncertainty (that benefits may or may not actually occur), and opportunity cost of capital (that you could do other things with your money). Since these factors are situationally dependent, there is unfortunately no standard answer for what discount rate to use for any given situation.

Governments typically use rates close to their interest rates, which normally move with inflation rates. Large corporations use sophisticated methods that account for their rates of borrowing money and the return on investment seen from previous projects, together resulting in a rate that is usually significantly higher than government interest rates. New businesses, which are highly speculative, should be using much higher discount rates still, since it costs them a lot to borrow money and they are often in a race against time before they run out of money or get eaten by competitors. Thus, the range of acceptable rates can vary widely, from close to the inflation rate all the way up to 50 percent or higher in an extremely high-risk/high-reward situation.

One decent approach is to use the rate at which you can borrow money. You would want your investment returns to be higher than this rate or else you shouldn't be borrow-

Investment Management

"I don't know, Jack. This 'magic beans' startup
sounds kind of risky."

ing money to invest. Note that this rate would typically have the inflation rate already built into it, since credit rates move with interest rates, which typically move with inflation. That is, people loaning you money also want to be protected from inflation, and so they usually build an expected inflation rate into their lending rates.

As investments can look very different based on different discount rates, there are many open debates about which discount rates are most appropriate to use in differing situations, especially when it comes to government programs. Different discount rates can favor one program over another, and so there can be a lot of pressure from different lobbying groups to choose a particular rate.

Another problem occurs in situations where the costs or benefits are expected to persist far into the future, such as with climate change mitigation. Because the effects of the discount rate compound over time, even rather small rates discount far-future effects close to zero. This has the effect of not valuing the consequences to future generations, and some economists think that is unfair and potentially immoral.

Even with this central issue around discount rate, cost-benefit analysis is an incredibly valuable model to frame a more quantitative discussion around how to proceed with a decision. As such, many governments mandate its use when evaluating policy options. In 1981, U.S. President Ronald Reagan signed Executive Order 12291, which mandated that "regulatory action shall not be undertaken unless the potential benefits to society from the regulation outweigh the potential costs to society." This language has been tweaked by subsequent U.S. presidents, though the central idea of it continues to drive policy, with the U.S. federal government conducting cost-benefit analyses for most significant proposed regulatory actions.

One final issue with cost-benefit analysis to keep in mind is the trickiness of comparing two options that have different time horizons. To illustrate this trap, let's compare our theoretical bond investment from earlier to another bond investment. Our bond investment from before cost $50,000 and returned $100,000 in ten years, which at a 6 percent discount rate resulted in a net benefit in today's dollars of $5,839.

Our new investment will also be a $50,000 bond investment, though instead of returning $100,000 in ten years, it pays back $75,000 in just six years. The cost today (year 0) for this second bond is again –$50,000. Using the same 6 percent discount rate, the $75,000 benefit six years from now discounted back to today's dollars would be worth $52,872, for a net benefit of $2,872 ($52,872 – $50,000). This net benefit is less than the net benefit of the first bond investment opportunity of $5,839 and so it seems the first bond is a better investment.

However, if you purchased the second bond, your $75,000 would be freed up after six years, leaving you four more years to invest that money in another way. If you were able to invest that money in a new investment at a high enough rate, this second bond is potentially more attractive in the end. When making a comparison, you therefore must consider what could happen over the same time frame.

In other words, cost-benefit analysis is only as good as the numbers you put into it. In computer science, there is a model describing this phenomenon: **garbage in, garbage out**. If your estimates of costs and benefits are highly inaccurate, your timelines don't line up, or your discount rate is poorly reasoned (*garbage in*), then your net result will be similarly flawed (*garbage out*).

On the other hand, if you take great care to make accurate estimates and perform relevant sensitivity analyses, then cost-benefit analysis can be a first-rate model for framing a decision-making process, and is in most cases a desirable replacement for a pro-con list. Next time you make a pro-con list, at least consider the scoring method to turn it into a simple cost-benefit analysis.

TAMING COMPLEXITY

When you can list out your options for a decision, and their costs and benefits are relatively clear, then cost-benefit analysis is a good starting point for approaching the decision. However, in many cases, your options and their associated costs and benefits are not very clear. Sometimes there is too much uncertainty in potential outcomes; other times, the situation can be so complex that it becomes difficult even to understand your options in the first place. In either case, you'll need to use some other mental models to navigate such complexity.

Consider a relatively common situation that homeowners face: the expensive repair. Suppose you want to repair your pool equipment before the summer swimming season. You get bids from two contractors. One bid is from your usual dependable pool service, but it seems high at $2,500. The second bid comes in at a lower cost of $2,000, though this contractor is a team of one, you don't have a history with them, and they also seem like they might be a little out of their depth.

As such, you get the impression that there is only a 50 percent chance that this contractor will finish at the quoted cost in a timely manner (in one week). If not, you estimate the following scenarios:

- A 25 percent chance that they will be one week late at an extra cost of $250 for the extra labor
- A 20 percent chance that they will be two weeks late at an extra cost of $500
- A 5 percent chance that they will not only take longer than three weeks to complete

the job, but also that some of their work will need to be redone, totaling extra costs of $1,000

This situation (multiple bids with timing/quality concerns) is very common, but because of the uncertainty introduced in the outcome, it's a bit too complex to analyze easily with just cost-benefit analysis. Luckily, there is another straightforward mental model you can use to make sense of all these potential outcomes: the **decision tree**. It's a diagram that looks like a *tree* (drawn on its side), and helps you analyze *decisions* with uncertain outcomes. The branches (often denoted by squares) are decision points and the leaves represent different possible outcomes (often using open circles to denote chance points). A decision tree that represents this pool situation could look like the figure below.

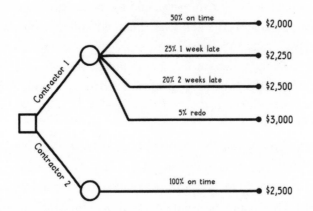

The first square represents your choice between the two contractors, and then the open circles further branch out to the different possible outcomes for each of those choices. The leaves with the closed circles list the resulting costs for each outcome, and their probabilities are listed on each line. (This is a simple *probability distribution* [see Chapter 5], which describes how all the probabilities are distributed across the possible outcomes. Each group of probabilities sums to 100 percent, representing all the possible outcomes for that choice.)

You can now use your probability estimates to get an **expected value** for each contractor, by multiplying through each potential outcome's probability with its cost, and then summing them all up. This resulting summed *value* is what you would *expect* to pay on average for each contractor, given all the potential outcomes.

The expected value for your usual contractor (Contractor 2 in the decision tree) is just $2,500, since there is only one possible outcome. The expected value for the new contractor (Contractor 1 in the decision tree) is the sum of the multiplications across their four possible outcomes: $1,000 + $562.50 + $500 + $150 = $2,212.50. Even though the new contractor has an outcome that might cost you $3,000, the expected value you'd pay is still less than you'd pay your usual contractor.

Expected Value

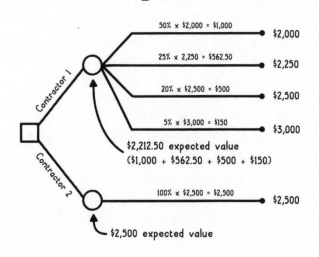

What this means is that if these probabilities are accurate, and you could run the scenario one hundred times in the real world where you pick the new contractor each time, your average payment to them would be expected to be $2,212.50. That's because half the time you'd pay only $2,000, and the other half, more. You'd never pay exactly $2,212.50, since that isn't a possible outcome, but overall your payments would average out to that expected value over many iterations.

If you find this confusing, the following example might be helpful. In 2015, U.S. mothers had 2.4 kids on average. Does any particular mother have exactly 2.4 kids? We hope not. Some have one child, some two, some three, and so on, and it all averages out to 2.4. Likewise, the various contractor payment outcomes and their probabilities add up to the expected value payment amount, even though you never pay that exact amount.

In any case, from this lens of the decision tree and the resulting expected values, you might rationally choose the new contractor, even with all their potential issues. That's because your expected outlay is lower with that contractor.

Of course, this result could change with different probabilities and/or potential outcome payments. For example, if you thought that, instead of a 5 percent chance for a $3,000 bill, there was a 50 percent chance you could end in this highest outcome, then the expected value for the new contractor would become higher than your usual contractor's bid. Remember that you can always run a sensitivity analysis on any inputs that you think might significantly influence the decision, as we discussed in the last section. Here you would vary the probabilities and/or potential outcome payments and see how the expected values change accordingly.

Additionally, consider another way the decision could change. Suppose you've already scheduled a pool party a few weeks out. Now, if the lower-bid contractor pushes into that second week, you're going to be faced with a lot of anxiety about your party. You will have to put pressure on the contractor to get the job done, and you might even have to bring in reinforcements to help finish the job at a much higher cost. That's a lot of extra hassle.

To a wealthier person who associates a high opportunity cost with their time, all this extra anxiety and hassle may be valued at an extra $1,000 worth of cost, even if you aren't paying that $1,000 directly to the contractor. Accounting for this possible extra burden would move up the two-week-late outcome from $2,500 (previously a $500 overrun) to $3,500 (now a $1,500 overrun).

Similarly, if this new contractor really messes up the job and you do have to bring in your regular contractor to do most everything over again on short notice, it will cost you the extra $1,000 in anxiety and hassle, as well as literally more payment to the other contractor. So, that small 5 percent chance of a $3,000 outcome might end up costing the equivalent of an extra $2,000, moving it to $5,000 in total.

By using these increased values in your decision tree, you can effectively "price in" the extra costs. Because these new values include more than the exact cost you'd have to pay out, they are called **utility values**, which reflect your total relative preferences across the various scenarios. We already saw this idea in the last section when we discussed putting a price to the preference of not having a landlord. This is the mental model that encapsulates the concept.

Utility values can be disconnected from actual prices in that you can value something more than something else, even though it costs the same on the open market. Think about your favorite band—it's worth more to you to see them in concert than another band that offers their concerts at the same price, simply because you like them more. You would get more utility out of that concert because of your preference. In the pool case, the stress involved with scrambling to fix the pool before your party is an extra cost of lost utility in addition to the actual cost you would have to pay out to the contractors.

In terms of the decision tree, the outcome values for the leaves can become the utility values, incorporating all the costs and benefits (tangible and intangible) into one number for each possible outcome. If you do that, then the conclusion now results in a flipped decision to use your usual contractor (Contractor 2 in the decision tree below).

Utility Values

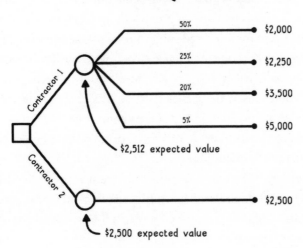

However, note that it is still a really close decision, as both contractors now have almost the same expected value! This closeness illustrates the power of probabilistic outcomes. Even though the new contractor is now associated with much higher potential "costs," 50 percent of the time you'd still expect to pay them a much smaller amount. This lower cost drives the expected value down a lot because it happens so frequently.

Just as in cost-benefit analysis and scoring pro-con lists, we recommend using utility values whenever possible because they paint a fuller picture of your underlying preferences, and therefore should result in more satisfactory decisions. In fact, more broadly, there is a philosophy called **utilitarianism** that expresses the view that the most ethical decision is the one that creates the most *utility* for all involved.

Utilitarianism as a philosophy has various drawbacks, though. Primarily, decisions involving multiple people that increase overall utility can seem quite unfair when that utility is not equally distributed among the people involved (e.g., income inequality despite rising standards of living). Also, utility values can be hard to estimate. Nevertheless, utilitarianism is a useful philosophical model to be aware of, if only to consider what decision would increase overall utility the most.

In any case, decision trees will help you start to make sense of what to do in situations with an array of diverse, probabilistic outcomes. Think about health insurance—should you go for a higher-deductible plan with lower payments or a lower-deductible plan with higher payments? It depends on your expected level of care, and whether you can afford the lower-probability scenario where you will need to pay out a high deductible. (Note that the answer isn't obvious, because with the lower-deductible plan you are making higher monthly premium payments. This increase in premiums could be viewed as paying out a portion of your deductible each month.) You can examine this scenario and others like it via a decision tree, accounting for your preferences along with the actual costs.

Decision trees are especially useful to help you think about unlikely but severely impactful events. Consider more closely the scenario where you have a medical incident that requires you to pay out your full deductible. For some people, that amount of outlay could equate to bankruptcy, and so the true cost of this event occurring to them is much, much higher than the actual cost of the deductible.

As a result, if you were in this situation, you would want to make the loss in utility value for this scenario extremely high to reflect your desire to avoid bankruptcy. Doing so would likely push you into a higher-premium plan with a lower deductible (that you can still afford), and more assurance that you would avoid bankruptcy. In other words, if there is a chance of financial ruin, you might want to avoid that plan even though on average it would lead to a better financial outcome.

One thing to watch out for in this type of analysis is the possibility of **black swan events**, which are extreme, consequential events (that end in things like financial ruin), but which have significantly higher probabilities than you might initially expect. The name is derived from the false belief, held for many centuries in Europe and other places, that black swans did not exist, when in fact they were (and still are) common birds in Australia.

As applied to decision tree analysis, a conservative approach would be to increase your probability estimates of low-probability but highly impactful scenarios like the bankruptcy one. This revision would account for the fact that the scenario might represent a black swan event, and that you might therefore be wrong about its probability.

One reason that the probability of black swan events may be miscalculated relates to the *normal distribution* (see Chapter 5), which is the bell-curve-shaped probability distribution that explains the frequency of many natural phenomena (e.g., people's heights). In a normal distribution, rare events occur on the tails of the distribution (e.g., really tall or short people), far from the middle of the bell curve. Black swan events, though, often come from **fat-tailed distributions**, which literally have *fatter tails*, meaning that events way out from the middle have a much higher probability when compared with a normal distribution.

Fat-Tailed Distribution

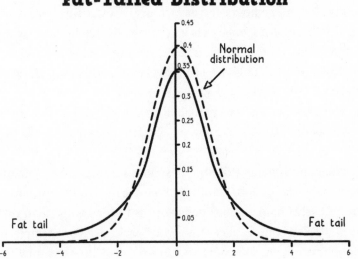

There are many naturally occurring fat-tailed distributions as well, and sometimes people just incorrectly assume they are dealing with a normal distribution when in fact they are dealing with a distribution with a fatter tail, and that means that events in the tail occur with higher probability. In practice, these are distributions where some of the biggest outliers happen more often than you would expect from a normal distribution, such as occurs with insurance payouts, or in the U.S. income distribution (see the *histogram* in Chapter 5).

Another reason why you might miscalculate the probability of a black swan event is that you misunderstand the reasons for its occurrence. This can happen when you think a situation should come from one distribution, but multiple are really involved. For example, there are genetic reasons (e.g., dwarfism and Marfan syndrome) why there might be many more shorter or taller people than you would expect from just a regular normal distribution, which doesn't account for these rarer genetic variations.

A third reason is that you may underestimate the possibility and impact of *cascading failures* (see Chapter 4). As you recall, in a cascading-failure scenario, parts of the system are correlated: if one part falters, the next part falters, and so on. The 2007/2008 financial crisis is an example, where the failure of mortgage-backed securities cascaded all the way to the banks and associated insurance companies.

Our climate presents another example. The term *one-hundred-year flood*, denotes a flood that has a 1 percent chance of occurring in any given year. Unfortunately, climate change is raising the probability of the occurrence of what was once considered a one-hundred-year flood, and it no longer has a 1 percent chance in many areas. The dice are loaded. Houston, Texas, for example, has had three so-called five-hundred-year floods in the last three years! The probabilities of these events clearly need to be adjusted as the cascading effects of climate change continue to unfold.

To better determine the outcome probabilities in highly complex systems like banking or climate, you may first have to take a step back and try to make sense of the whole system before you can even try to create a decision tree or cost-benefit analysis for a particular subset or situation. **Systems thinking** describes this act, when you attempt to *think* about the entire *system* at once. By thinking about the overall system, you are more likely to understand and account for subtle interactions between components that could otherwise lead to unintended consequences from your decisions. For example, when thinking about making an investment, you might start to appreciate how seemingly unrelated parts of the economy might affect its outcome.

Some systems are fairly simple and you can picture the whole system in your head. Others are so complex that it is too challenging simultaneously to hold all the interlocking pieces in your head. One solution is literally to diagram the system visually. Drawing diagrams can help you get a better sense of complex systems and how the parts of the system interact with one another.

Techniques for how to effectively diagram complex systems are beyond the scope of this book, but know that there are many techniques that you can learn, including *causal loop diagrams* (which showcase feedback *loops* in a system) and *stock and flow diagrams* (which showcase how things accumulate and *flow* in a system). Gabriel's master's thesis involved diagraming the email spam system. The picture on the next page is one of his causal loop diagrams—you aren't meant to understand this diagram; it's just an example

Email Spam Causal Loop Diagram

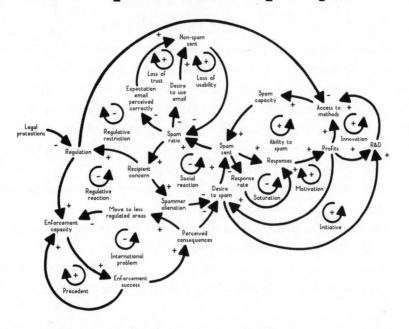

of what these things can end up looking like. Just know now that it was really helpful in gaining a much better understanding of this complex system.

As a further step, you can use software to imitate the system, called a *simulation*. In fact, software exists that allows you to compose a diagram of a system on your screen and then immediately turn it into a working simulation. (Two such programs that do this online are Insight Maker and True-World.) In the process, you can set initial conditions, and then see how the system unfolds over time.

Simulations help you more deeply understand a complex system and lead to better predictions of black swans and other events. Simulations can also help you identify how a system will adjust when faced with changing conditions. **Chatelier's principle**, named after French chemist Henri-Louis Le Chatelier, states that when any chemical system at equilibrium is subject to a change in conditions, such as a shift in temperature, volume, or pressure, it readjusts itself into a new equilibrium state and usually partially counteracts the change.

For example, if someone hands you a box to carry, you don't immediately topple over; you instead shift your weight distribution to account for the new weight. Or in economics, if a new tax is introduced, tax revenues from that tax end up being lower in the long run than one would expect under current conditions because people adjust their behavior to avoid the tax.

If this sounds like a familiar concept, it's because Chatelier's principle is similar to the mental model *homeostasis* (see Chapter 4), which comes from biology: recall how your body automatically shivers and sweats in response to external conditions in order to regulate its internal temperature. Chatelier's principle doesn't necessarily mean the system will regulate around a predetermined value, but that it will react to externally imposed conditions, and usually in a way that partially counteracts the external stimulus. You can see the principle in action in real time with simulations because they allow you to calculate how your simulated system will adjust to various changes.

A related mental model that also arises in dynamic systems and simulations is **hysteresis**, which describes how a system's current state can be dependent on its history. Hysteresis is also a naturally occurring phenomenon, with examples across most scientific disciplines. In physics, when you magnetize a material in one direction, such as by holding a magnet to another piece of metal, the metal does not fully demagnetize after you remove the magnet. In biology, the T cells that help power your immune system, once activated, thereafter require a lower threshold to reactivate. Hysteresis describes how both the metal and the T cells partially remember their states, such that what happened previously can impact what will happen next.

Again, this may already seem like a familiar concept, because it is similar to the mental model of *path dependence* (see Chapter 2), which more generally describes how choices have consequences in terms of limiting what you can do in the future. Hysteresis is one type of path dependence, as applied to systems.

In engineering systems, for example, it is useful to build some hysteresis into the system to avoid rapid changes. Modern thermostats do this by allowing for a range of temperatures around the set point: if you want to maintain 70 degrees Fahrenheit, a thermostat might be set to turn the heater on when the temperature drops to 68 degrees and back off when it hits 72 degrees. In this way, it isn't kicking on and off constantly. Similarly, on websites, designers and developers often build in a lag for when you move your mouse off page elements like menus. They build their programs to remember that you were on the menu so that when you move off, it doesn't abruptly go away, which can appear jarring to the eye.

You can use all these mental models around visualizing complex systems and simulating them to help you better assess potential outcomes and their associated probabilities. Then you can feed these results into a more straightforward decision model like a decision tree or cost-benefit analysis.

A particular type of simulation that can be especially useful in this way is a **Monte Carlo simulation**. Like *critical mass* (see Chapter 4), this is a model that emerged during the Manhattan Project in Los Alamos in the run-up to the discovery of the atomic bomb. Physicist Stanislaw Ulam was struggling with using traditional mathematics to determine how far neutrons would travel through various materials and came up with this new method after playing solitaire (yes, the card game). In his words, quoted in *Los Alamos Science*:

> The first thoughts and attempts I made to practice [the Monte Carlo method] were suggested by a question which occurred to me in 1946 as I was convalescing from an illness and playing solitaires. The question was what are the chances that a Canfield solitaire laid out with 52 cards will come out successfully? After spending a lot of time trying to estimate them by pure combinatorial calculations, I wondered whether a more practical method than "abstract thinking" might not be to lay it out say one hundred times and simply observe and count the number of successful plays.

A Monte Carlo simulation is actually many simulations run independently, with random initial conditions or other uses of random numbers within the simulation itself. By running a simulation of a system many times, you can begin to understand how probable different outcomes really are. Think of it as a dynamic sensitivity analysis.

Monte Carlo simulations are used in nearly every branch of science. But they are useful outside science as well. For example, venture capitalists often use Monte Carlo simulations to determine how much capital to reserve for future financings. When a venture fund invests in a company, that company, if successful, will probably raise more money in the future, and the fund will often want to participate in some of those future financings to maintain its ownership percentage. How much money should it reserve for a company? Not all companies are successful, and different companies raise different amounts, so the answer is not straightforward at the time of the initial investment. Many funds use Monte Carlo simulations to understand how much they ought to reserve, given their current fund history and the estimates of company success and size of potential financings.

More generally, making the effort to understand complex systems better through systems thinking—whether it be by using diagrams, running simulations, or employing other mental models—not only helps you get a broad picture of the system and its range of outcomes, but also can help you become aware of the best possible outcomes. Without such knowledge, you can get stuck chasing a **local optimum** solution, which is an admittedly good solution, but not the best one.

If you can, you want to work toward that best solution, which would be the **global optimum**. Think of rolling hills: the top of a nice nearby hill would be a good success (local optimum), though in the distance there is a much bigger hill that would be a much better success (global optimum). You want to be on that bigger hill. But first you have to have a full view of the system to know the bigger hill exists.

Local vs. Global Optimum

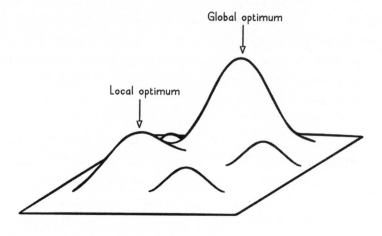

BEWARE OF UNKNOWN UNKNOWNS

In 1955, psychologists Joseph Luft and Harrington Ingham originated the concept of **unknown unknowns**, which was made popular by former U.S. Secretary of Defense Donald Rumsfeld at a news briefing on February 12, 2002, with this exchange:

> Jim Miklaszewski: In regard to Iraq, weapons of mass destruction, and terrorists, is there any evidence to indicate that Iraq has attempted to or is willing to supply terrorists with weapons of mass destruction? Because there are reports that there is no evidence of a direct link between Baghdad and some of these terrorist organizations.
>
> Rumsfeld: Reports that say that something hasn't happened are always inter-

esting to me, because as we know, there are known knowns; there are things we know we know. We also know there are known unknowns; that is to say we know there are some things we do not know. But there are also unknown unknowns—the ones we don't know we don't know. And if one looks throughout the history of our country and other free countries, it is the latter category that tend to be the difficult ones.

The context and evasiveness of the exchange aside, the underlying model is useful in decision making. When faced with a decision, you can use a handy *2 × 2 matrix* (see Chapter 4) as a starting point to envision these four categories of things you know and don't know.

Knowns & Unknowns

	Known	Unknown
Known	What you know you know	What you know you don't know
Unknown	What you don't know you know	What you don't know you don't know

This model is particularly effective when thinking more systematically about risks, such as risks to a project's success. Each category deserves its own attention and process:

- *Known knowns:* These might be risks to someone else, but not to you since you already know how to deal with them based on your previous experience. For example, a project might require a technological solution, but you already know what that solution is and how to implement it; you just need to execute that known plan.

- *Known unknowns:* These are also known risks to the project, but because of some uncertainty, it isn't exactly clear how they will be resolved. An example is the risk of relying on a third party: until you engage with them directly, it is unknown how they will react. You can turn some of these into known knowns by doing *de-risking* exercises (see Chapter 1), getting rid of the uncertainty.
- *Unknown knowns:* These are the risks you're not thinking about, but for which there exist clear mitigation plans. For example, your project might involve starting to do business in Europe over the summer, but you don't yet know they don't do much business in August. An adviser with more experience can help identify these risks from the start and turn these into known knowns. That way they will not take you by surprise later on and potentially throw off your project.
- *Unknown unknowns:* These are the least obvious risks, which require a concerted effort to uncover. For example, maybe something elsewhere in the organization or in the industry could dramatically change this project (like budget cuts or an acquisition or new product announcement). Even if you identify an unknown unknown (turning it into a known unknown), you still remain unsure of its likelihood or consequences. You must then still do de-risking exercises to finally turn it into a known known.

As you can see, you enumerate items in each of the four categories, and then work to make them all known knowns. This model is about giving yourself more complete knowledge of a situation. It's similar to systems thinking, from the last section, in that you are attempting to get a full picture of the system so you can make better decisions.

As a personal example, consider having a new baby. From reading all the books, you know the first few weeks will be harrowing, you'll want to take some time off work, you'll need to buy a car seat, crib, diapers, etc.—these are the known knowns. You also know that how your baby might sleep and eat (or not) can be an issue, but until the baby is born, their proclivities remain uncertain—they are known unknowns. You might not yet know that swaddling a baby is a thing, but you'll be shown how soon enough by a nurse or family member, turning this unknown known into a known known. And then there are things that no one knows yet or is even thinking about, such as whether your child could have a learning disability.

A related model that can help you uncover unknown unknowns is **scenario analysis** (also known as *scenario planning*), which is a method for thinking about possible futures more deeply. It gets its name because it involves *analyzing* different *scenarios* that might unfold. That sounds simple enough, but it is deceptively complicated in practice. That's

"Well he certainly does a very thorough risk analysis."

because thinking up possible future scenarios is a really challenging exercise, and thinking through their likelihoods and consequences is even more so.

Governments and large corporations have dedicated staff for scenario analysis. They are continually thinking up and writing reports about what the world could look like in the future and how their citizenry or shareholders might fare under those scenarios. Many academics, especially in political science, urban planning, economics, and related fields, similarly engage in prognosticating about the future. And of course, science fiction is essentially an entire literary genre dedicated to scenario analysis.

To do scenario analysis well, you must conjure plausible yet distinct futures, ultimately considering several possible scenarios. This process is difficult because you tend to latch onto your first thoughts (see *anchoring* in Chapter 1), which usually depict a direct extrapolation of your current trajectory (the present), without challenging your own assumptions.

One technique to ensure that you do challenge your assumptions is to list major events that could transpire (e.g., stock market crash, government regulation, major industry merger, etc.) and then trace their possible effects back to your situation. Some may have little to no effect, whereas others might form the basis for a scenario you should consider deeply.

Another technique for thinking more broadly about possible future scenarios is the **thought experiment**, literally an *experiment* that occurs just in your *thoughts*, i.e., not in the physical world. The most famous thought experiment is probably "Schrödinger's cat," named after Austrian physicist Erwin Schrödinger, who thought it up in 1935 to explore the implications of different interpretations of the physics of quantum mechanics. From his 1935 paper "The Present Situation in Quantum Mechanics":

> A cat is penned up in a steel chamber, along with the following device (which must be secured against direct interference by the cat): in a Geiger counter, there is a tiny bit of radioactive substance, so small, that perhaps in the course of the hour one of the atoms decays, but also, with equal probability, perhaps none; if it happens, the counter tube discharges and through a relay releases a hammer that shatters a small flask of hydrocyanic acid. If one has left this entire system to itself for an hour, one would say that the cat still lives if meanwhile no atom has decayed. The first atomic decay would have poisoned it.

So, you have a cat in a box, and if a radioactive atom decayed in the last hour, it would have killed the cat. This thought experiment poses some seemingly unanswerable questions: Until you observe the cat by opening the box, is it alive or dead, or in an in-between state, as certain interpretations of quantum mechanics would suggest? And what exactly happens when you open the box?

Schrödinger's Cat Thought Experiment

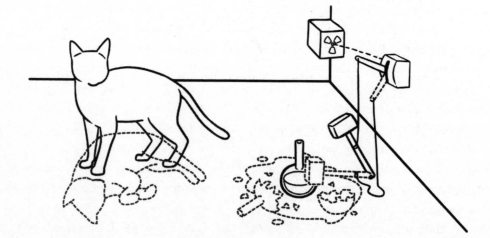

Answers to this thought experiment are beyond the scope of this book and were argued over for decades after it was posed. Therein lies the power of the thought experiment.

Thought experiments are particularly useful in scenario analysis. Posing questions that start with "What would happen if . . ." is a good practice in this way: What would happen if life expectancy jumped forty years? What would happen if a well-funded competitor copied our product? What would happen if I switched careers?

These types of what-if questions can also be applied to the past, in what is called **counterfactual thinking**, which means *thinking* about the past by imagining that the past was different, *counter* to the *facts* of what actually occurred. You've probably seen this model in books and movies about scenarios such as what would have happened if Germany had won World War II (e.g., Philip K. Dick's *The Man in the High Castle*). Examples from your own life can help you improve your decision making when you think through the possible consequences of your past decisions. What if I had taken that job? What if I had gone to that other school? What if I hadn't done that side project?

When reconsidering your past decisions, though, it is important not only to think of the positive consequences that might have occurred if you had made a different life choice. The *butterfly effect* (see Chapter 4) reminds us that one small change can have ripple effects, so when considering a counterfactual scenario, it is important to remember that if you change one thing, it is unlikely that everything else would stay the same.

Posing what-if questions can nevertheless help you think more creatively, coming up with scenarios that diverge from your intuition. More generally, this technique is one of many associated with **lateral thinking**, a type of *thinking* that helps you move *laterally* from one idea to another, as opposed to critical thinking, which is more about judging an idea in front of you. Lateral thinking is *thinking outside the box*.

Another helpful lateral-thinking technique involves adding some randomness when you are generating ideas. For example, you can choose an object at random from your surroundings or a noun from the dictionary and try to associate it in some way with your current idea list, laterally forming new offshoot ideas in the process.

No matter what techniques you use, however, it is extremely difficult to perform scenario analysis alone. Seeking outside input produces better results, as different people with different perspectives bring new ideas to the table.

It is therefore tempting to involve multiple people in brainstorming sessions from the get-go. However, studies show this is not the right approach because of **groupthink**, a bias that emerges because *groups* tend to *think* in harmony. Within group settings, members often strive for consensus, avoiding conflict, controversial issues, or even alternative solutions once it seems a solution is already favored by the group.

The **bandwagon effect** describes the phenomenon whereby consensus can take hold quickly, as other group members "hop on the *bandwagon*" as an idea gains popularity. More generally, it describes people's tendency to take social cues and follow the decisions of others. In this way, the probability of a person adopting an idea increases the more other people have already done so.

In some cases, this is rational behavior, as when you follow the bandwagon and adopt a product based on well-researched reviews from owners of the product. In other cases, though, fads and trends can be based on little substance.

"Put me down for whoever comes out ahead in your poll."

Groupthink is terrible for scenario analysis and can have much wider implications, leading to bad group decision making in general if not actively managed. There are many ways to manage groupthink, though, including setting a culture of questioning assumptions, making sure to evaluate all ideas critically, establishing *a Devil's advocate position* (see Chapter 1), actively recruiting people with differing opinions, reducing leadership's influence on group recommendations, and splitting the group into independent subgroups.

It is this last recommendation that is particularly relevant for scenario analysis, as it forms the basis for **divergent thinking**, where you actively try to get *thinking* to *diverge* in order to discover multiple possible solutions, as opposed to **convergent thinking**, where you actively try to get *thinking* to *converge* on one solution. One tactic is to meet once without brainstorming at all, just to go over the goal of the scenario analysis. Then send everyone off individually or in small groups. You could give them a prompt to react to, such as survey data, or have them come up with their own thought experiments and scenario ideas from scratch (divergent thinking). Finally, you bring everyone back together to go over all the proposed scenarios in order to narrow them down to just a few scenarios to explore further (convergent thinking).

It is additionally likely that people close to you, such as those within your organization, share similar cultural traits, and therefore you should look beyond your normal contacts and venture outside your organization to get as much lateral and divergent thinking as you can. One way to do so is actively to seek out people from different backgrounds to participate. Another way, easily enabled by the internet, is to **crowdsource** ideas, where you seek (*source*) ideas quite literally from anyone who would like to participate (the *crowd*).

Crowdsourcing has been effective across a wide array of situations, from soliciting tips in journalism, to garnering contributions to Wikipedia, to solving the real-world problems of companies and governments. For example, Netflix held a contest in 2009 in which crowdsourced researchers beat Netflix's own recommendation algorithms.

Crowdsourcing can help you get a sense of what a wide array of people think about a topic, which can inform your future decision making, updating your prior beliefs (see *Bayesian statistics* in Chapter 5). It can also help you uncover unknown unknowns and unknown knowns as you get feedback from people with previous experiences you might not have had.

In James Surowiecki's book *The Wisdom of Crowds*, he examines situations where input from crowds can be particularly effective. It opens with a story about how the crowd at a county fair in 1906, attended by statistician Francis Galton, correctly guessed the weight of an ox. Almost eight hundred people participated, each individually guessing, and the average weight guessed was 1,197 pounds—exactly the weight of the ox, to the pound! While you cannot expect similar results in all situations, Surowiecki explains the key conditions in which you can expect good results from crowdsourcing:

"I WASN'T COPYING OFF OTHERS. I WAS JUST CROWDSOURCING THE ANSWERS."

- *Diversity of opinion:* Crowdsourcing works well when it draws on different people's private information based on their individual knowledge and experiences.
- *Independence:* People need to be able to express their opinions without influence from others, avoiding groupthink.
- *Aggregation:* The entity doing the crowdsourcing needs to be able to combine the diverse opinions in such a way as to arrive at a collective decision.

If you can design a system with these properties, then you can draw on the *collective intelligence* of the crowd. This allows you to glean the useful bits of information that might be hidden among a group of diverse participants. In the ox example, a butcher may notice something different than a farmer would and different yet than a vet would. All this knowledge was captured in the collective weight guessed. A more modern example of making use of collective intelligence would be an audience poll as done on the television show *Who Wants to Be a Millionaire?*

In general, drawing on collective intelligence makes sense when the group's collective pool of knowledge is greater than what you could otherwise get access to; this helps you arrive at a more intelligent decision than you would arrive at on your own. "The crowd" can help systematically think through various scenarios, get new data and ideas, or simply help improve existing ideas.

One direct application of crowdsourcing to scenario analysis is the use of a **prediction market**, which is like a stock market for predictions. In a simple formulation of this concept, the price of each stock can range between $0 and $1 and represents the market's current probability of an event taking place, such as whether a certain candidate will be elected. For example, a price of $0.59 would represent a 59 percent probability that the candidate would be elected.

If you think the probability is significantly higher than 59 percent, then you could buy a yes share at that price. Alternatively, if you think the probability is significantly lower than 59 percent, then you could buy a no share at that price. If the candidate actually gets elected, then the market pays out holders of yes predictions at $1 per share, and if they are not elected, then those yes shares become worthless. Conversely, if the candidate doesn't get elected, then the market pays out holders of the no predictions at $1 per share and the yes shares become worthless.

If more people are making yes predictions than no predications, then the price of the stock rises, and vice versa. By looking at the current prices in the prediction market, you can get a sense of what the market thinks will happen, based on how people are betting (buying shares). Many big companies operate similar prediction markets internally, where employees can predict the outcome of things like sales forecasts and marketing campaigns.

Several larger public prediction markets also exist, such as PredictIt, which focuses on political predictions in the manner described above. While this market has successfully predicted many election outcomes across the world, in 2016 it failed to correctly predict both the election of Donald Trump and the UK's Brexit vote. Retrospective analysis showed that diversity of opinion seemed lacking and that participants in the prediction market likely didn't have enough direct contact with Trump or Brexit supporters. In addition, predictors were not operating fully independently, instead being influenced by the initial outsized odds against Trump and Brexit.

Another project, called the Good Judgment Project, crowdsources predictions for world events. Its co-creator, Philip E. Tetlock, studied thousands of participants and discovered **superforecasters**, people who make excellent *forecasts*, repeatedly. He found that these superforecasters consistently beat the world's leading intelligence services in their predictions of world events, even though they lack classified intelligence that these services have access to!

In a book entitled *Superforecasting*, Tetlock examines characteristics that lead superforecasters to make such accurate predictions. As it happens, these are good characteristics to cultivate in general:

- *Intelligence:* Brainpower is crucial, especially the ability to enter a new domain and get up to speed quickly.
- *Domain expertise:* While you can learn about a particular domain on the fly, the more you learn about it, the more it helps.
- *Practice:* Good forecasting is apparently a skill you can hone and get better at over time.
- *Working in teams:* Groups of people can outperform individuals as long as they avoid groupthink.
- *Open-mindedness:* People who are willing to challenge their beliefs tend to make better predictions.
- *Training in past probabilities:* People who looked at probabilities of similar situations in the past were better able to assess the current probability, avoiding the *base rate fallacy* (see Chapter 5).

- *Taking time:* The more time people took to make the prediction, the better they did.
- *Revising predictions:* Forecasters who continually revised their predictions based on new information successfully avoided *confirmation bias* (see Chapter 1).

Using prediction markets and the techniques of superforecasters can help you improve your scenario analysis by making it more accurate and focusing it on the events that are actually more likely to occur. As we've seen in Chapters 2 and 4, many unpredictable changes will inevitably occur; however, by spending time with these mental models, you can be better prepared for these changes. Even if you cannot predict exactly what will happen, you may envision similar scenarios and your preparation for those scenarios will help you.

In this chapter as a whole, we've seen an array of decision models that surpass the simple pro-con list that we started with. When you've arrived at a decision using one or more of these mental models, a good final step is to produce a **business case**, a document that outlines the reasoning behind your decision.

This process is a form of *arguing from first principles* (see Chapter 1). You are laying out your premises (principles) and explaining how they add up to your conclusion (decision). You are making your *case*. Taking this explicit step will help you identify holes in your decision-making process. In addition, a business case provides a jumping-off point to discuss the decision with your colleagues.

A business case can range from very short and informal (a few paragraphs) to extremely detailed and formal (a massive report) and is often accompanied by a presentation. In its final form it is used to convince others (or yourself!) that the decision is the right one. By using the mental models from this chapter, you can put together compelling business cases to help you and your organization make excellent decisions.

And it's not just for business. We started this chapter by discussing a potential career change. Knowing what you know now, you can approach that same problem in a much better way. For example, you could do scenario analysis to better uncover and imagine how different possible career futures could unfold. You could then more systematically analyze the seemingly best possible career paths more numerically through cost-benefit analysis, or using a decision tree if some of the choices are more probabilistic in nature. Then, in the end, you can put all of it together into a succinct business case to lay out the argument for your next career move.

- When tempted to use a **pro-con list**, consider upgrading to a **cost-benefit analysis** or **decision tree** as appropriate.

- When making any quantitative assessment, run a **sensitivity analysis** across inputs to uncover key drivers and appreciate where you may need to seek greater accuracy in your assumptions. Pay close attention to any **discount rate** used.

- Beware of **black swan events** and **unknown unknowns**. Use **systems thinking** and **scenario analysis** to more systematically uncover them and assess their impact.

- For really complex systems or decision spaces, consider **simulations** to help you better assess what may happen under different scenarios.

- Watch out for blind spots that arise from **groupthink**. Consider **divergent** and **lateral thinking** techniques when working with groups, including seeking more diverse points of view.

- Strive to understand the **global optimum** in any system and look for decisions that move you closer to it.

Dealing with Conflict

IN ADVERSARIAL SITUATIONS, nearly every one of your choices directly or indirectly affects other people, and these effects can play a large role in how a conflict turns out. In the words of English poet John Donne, "No man is an island."

In Chapter 6, we discussed mental models that help you with making decisions. In this chapter we will give you more models to help with decision making, with a focus on guiding you through adversarial situations.

As an example, consider the **arms race**. The term was originally used to describe a *race* between two or more countries to accumulate weapons for a potential *armed* conflict. It can also be used more broadly to describe any type of escalating competition. Think of the Cold War between the U.S. and Russia after World War II, where both countries kept accumulating more and more sophisticated nuclear weapons. And that's not even the only arms race from the Cold War: both countries also intensely competed for dominance of the Olympics (medal race) and space exploration (space race).

Arms races are prevalent in our society. For example, many employers in the U.S. have increasingly required college or even more advanced degrees as a condition of employment, even though many of these jobs don't use the knowledge acquired from these degrees.

Arms Race

Growing Educational Demand for Employment

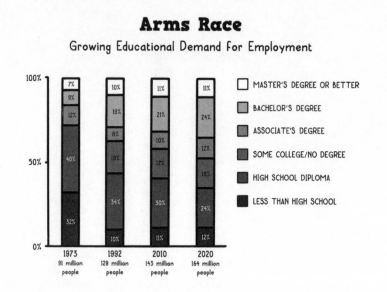

And getting these degrees is increasingly more expensive as the result of another arms race, in which colleges spend more and more on making their campuses feel like resorts. Stereotypical cinder-block dorm rooms with a mini-fridge and a communal bathroom down the hall are being replaced with apartment-style suites that come with stainless-steel appliances and private bathrooms. And, according to *The New York Times,* some schools have even been building "lazy rivers" like the ones at amusement parks! This arms race has directly contributed to the cost of U.S. higher education going sky high.

Getting into an arms race is not beneficial to anyone involved. There is usually no clear end to the race, as all sides continually eat up resources that could be spent more usefully elsewhere. Think about how much better it would be if the money spent on making campuses luxurious was instead invested in better teaching and other areas that directly impact the quality and accessibility of a college education.

Unfortunately, situations like this are common in everyday personal life too: many people go into considerable debt trying to keep up with their social circles (or circles they aspire to belong to) by buying bigger houses, fancier cars, and designer clothes, and by sending their kids to expensive private schools. The phrase *keeping up with the Joneses* describes this phenomenon and comes from the name of a comic strip that followed the McGinis family, who were fixated on matching the lifestyle of their neighbors, the Joneses.

"Oh great. The Joneses replaced
their bird bath with a hot tub."

Based on what you know about us so far, you might not be surprised to find out that we send our sons to engineering camps in the summer. Last year, the closest offering for one of these camps was at a private school on the Philadelphia Main Line, a highly affluent region. When Lauren was waiting to pick up one of our sons, she overheard a group of campers arguing over which of their families owned the most Teslas. While comparisons of social status are not uncommon, it was disheartening to see elementary school–aged children engage in this kind of discussion, especially one so extreme.

As an individual, avoiding an arms race means not getting sucked into keeping up with the Joneses. You want to use your income on things that make you fulfilled (such as on family vacations or on classes that interest you), rather than on unfulfilling status symbols.

As an organization, avoiding an arms race means differentiating yourself from the competition instead of pursuing a one-upmanship strategy on features or deals, which can eat away at your profit margins. By focusing on your unique value proposition, you can devote more resources to improving and communicating it rather than to keeping up with your competition. The satirical publication *The Onion* famously parodied the corporate arms race between razor blade manufacturers, as depicted on the next page.

⌀ the ONION®

Fuck Everything, We're Doing Five Blades

 James M. Kilts, CEO and President, The Gillette Company
2/18/04 3:00pm

In the rest of this chapter, we explore mental models to help you analyze and better deal with conflicts like arms races. We hope that after reading it, you will be equipped to emerge from any adversarial situation with the best outcome for yourself.

PLAYING THE GAME

Game theory is the study of strategy and decision making in adversarial situations, and it provides several foundational mental models to help you think critically about conflict. *Game* in this context refers to a simplified version of a conflict, in which players engage in an artificial scenario with well-defined rules and quantifiable outcomes, much like a board game.

In most familiar games—chess, poker, baseball, Monopoly, etc.—there are usually winners and losers. However, game theorists recognize that in real-life conflicts there isn't always a clear winner or a clear loser. In fact, sometimes everyone playing the game can win and other times everyone can lose.

The most famous "game" from game theory is called the **prisoner's dilemma**. It can be used to illustrate useful game-theory concepts and can also be adapted to many life situations, including the arms race.

Here's the setup: Suppose two criminals are captured and put in jail, each in their own cell with no way to communicate. The prosecutor doesn't have enough evidence to convict either one for a major crime but does have enough to convict both for minor infractions. However, if the prosecutor could get one of the prisoners to turn on their co-conspirator, the other one could be put away for the major crime. So the prosecutor offers each prisoner the same deal: the first one who betrays their partner walks free now, and anyone who stays silent goes to prison.

In game theory, diagrams can help you study your options. One example is called a *payoff matrix*, showing the *payoffs* for possible player choices in *matrix* form (see 2 × 2 *matrix* in Chapter 4). From the prisoner's perspective, the payoff matrix looks like this:

Prisoner's Dilemma

Payoff Matrix: Sentences Received

	B remains silent	B betrays A
A remains silent	1 year, 1 year	10 years, 0 years
A betrays B	0 years, 10 years	5 years, 5 years

Here's where it gets interesting. The simplest formulation of this game assumes that the consequences for the players are only the prison sentences listed, i.e., there is no consideration of real-time negotiation or future retribution. If, as a player, you are acting independently and rationally, the dominant strategy given this formulation and payoff matrix is always to betray your partner: No matter what they do, you're better off betraying, and that's the only way to get off free. If your co-conspirator remains silent, you go from one to zero years by betraying them, and if they betray you too, you go from ten to five years.

The rub is that if your co-conspirator follows the same strategy, you both go away for much longer than if you both just remained silent (five years versus one year). Hence the *dilemma*: do you risk their betrayal, or can you trust their solidarity and emerge with a small sentence?

The dual betrayal with its dual five-year sentences is known as the **Nash equilibrium** of this game, named after mathematician John Nash, one of the pioneers of game theory and the subject of the biopic *A Beautiful Mind*. The Nash equilibrium is a set of player choices for which a change of strategy by any one player would worsen their outcome. In this case, the Nash equilibrium is the strategy of dual betrayals, because if either player instead chose to remain silent, that player would get a longer sentence. To both get a shorter sentence, they'd have to act cooperatively, coordinating their strategies. That coordinated strategy is unstable (i.e., not an equilibrium) because either player could then betray the other to better their outcome.

In any game you play, you want to know whether there is a Nash equilibrium, as that is the most likely outcome unless something is done to change the parameters of the game. For example, the Nash equilibrium for an arms race is choosing a high arms strategy where both parties continue to arm themselves. Here's an example of a payoff matrix for this scenario:

Arms Race

Payoff Matrix: Economic Outcomes

	B disarms	B arms
A disarms	win, win	lose big, win big
A arms	win big, lose big	lose, lose

As you can see, the arms race directly parallels the prisoner's dilemma. Both A and B arming (the lose-lose situation) is the Nash equilibrium, because if either party switched to disarming, they'd be worse off, enabling an even poorer outcome, such as an invasion they couldn't defend against (denoted as "lose big"). The best outcome again results from being cooperative, with both parties agreeing to disarm (the win-win situation), thus opening up the opportunity to spend those resources more productively. That's the arms race equivalent of remaining silent, but it is also an unstable situation, since either side could then better their situation by arming again (and potentially invading the other side, leading to a "win big" outcome).

In both scenarios, a superior outcome is much more likely if everyone involved does not consider the situation as just one turn of the game but, rather, if both sides can continually take turns, running the same game over and over—called an *iterated* or *repeated* game. When we mentioned earlier the possibility of future retribution, this is what we were talking about. What if you have to play the game with the same people again and again?

In an iterated game of prisoner's dilemma, cooperating in a **tit-for-tat** approach usually results in better long-term outcomes than constant betrayal. You can start out cooperating, and thereafter follow suit with what your opponent has recently done. In these situations, you want to wait for your opponent to establish a pattern of bad behavior before you reciprocate in kind. You don't want to destroy a previously fruitful relationship based on one bad choice by your counterpart.

Similarly, cooperation pays off in most long-term life situations where reputation matters. If you are known as a betrayer, people will not want to be your friend or do business with you. On the other hand, if people can trust you based on your repeated good behavior, they will want to make you their ally and collaborate with you.

In any case, analyzing conflicts from a game-theory perspective is a sound approach to help you understand how your situation is likely to play out. You can write out the payoff matrix and use a *decision tree* (see Chapter 6) to diagram different choice scenarios and their potential outcomes, from your perspective. Then you can figure out how you get to your desired outcome.

NUDGE NUDGE WINK WINK

To get to a desired outcome in a game, you may have to influence other players to make the moves *you* want them to make, even if they may not want to make them initially. In these next few sections, we present mental models that can help you do just that. They work well in conflict situations but also in any situation where influence is useful. First, consider six powerful yet subtle influence models that psychologist Robert Cialdini presents in his book *Influence: The Psychology of Persuasion.*

Cialdini recounts a study (since replicated) showing that waiters increase their tips when they give customers small gifts. In the study, a single mint increased tips by 3 percent on average, two mints increased tips by 14 percent, and two mints accompanied by a "For you nice people, here's an extra mint" increased tips by 23 percent.

The mental model this study illustrates is called **reciprocity**, whereby you tend to feel an obligation to return (or *reciprocate*) a favor, whether that favor was invited or not. In many cultures, it is generally expected that people in social relationships will exchange favors like this, such as taking turns driving a carpool or bringing a bottle of wine to a dinner party. *Quid pro quo* (Latin for "something for something") and *I'll scratch your back if you'll scratch mine* are familiar phrases that relate to this model.

Reciprocity also explains why some nonprofits send you free address labels with your name on them along with their donation solicitation letters. It also explains why salespeople give out free concert or sports tickets to potential high-profile clients. Giving someone something, even if they didn't ask for it, significantly increases the chances they will reciprocate.

This natural tendency becomes problematic when it is used to acquire political influence, for example when politicians accept money or favors from lobbyists or others in exchange for later votes. Lobbyists are of course free to financially support candidates holding positions that align with the goals of their group. It becomes a concern when it appears there may be an implicit agreement involved. A 2016 study in the *American Journal of Political Science* showed that even without an understood agreement, though, politicians are more likely to listen to a donor than to another local constituent (see figure).

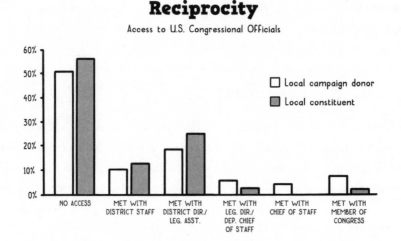

Reciprocity

Access to U.S. Congressional Officials

The second model that Cialdini describes is **commitment**—if you agree (or *commit*) to something, however small, you are more likely to continue to agree later. That's because not being consistent causes psychological discomfort, called *cognitive dissonance* (see Chapter 1).

Commitment explains why websites favor button titles like "I'll sign up later" instead of "No thanks"; the former implies a commitment to sign up at a later time. The sales *foot-in-the-door technique* follows the same principle, where a mattress salesperson tries to get a "small yes" out of you (asking, for instance, "Do you want to sleep better at night?"), since that makes it more likely they'll get to a "big yes" (in answer to "Do you want to buy this mattress?").

Salespeople will also try to find common ground through a model Cialdini calls **liking**. Quite simply, you are more prone to take advice from people you *like*, and you tend to like people who share characteristics with you. That's why they ask you questions such as "Are you a baseball fan?" or "Where did you grow up?" and, after your response, they might tell you, "I'm a Yankees fan too!" or "Oh, my cousin lives there. . . ."

The technique of *mirroring* also follows this model, where you mirror the physical and verbal cues of people you talk to. People tend to do this naturally, but trying to do this more (for example, consciously folding your arms when they fold their arms) can help you gain people's trust. Studies show that the more you mirror, the more you will be perceived as similar.

People want to emulate the people they like and trust. "Global Trust in Advertising," a 2015 Nielsen survey of consumers across sixty different countries, found that 83 percent of people trusted recommendations from their friends and family (people they typically like), a higher rate than any form of advertising studied. This is why word-of-mouth referrals are so important to businesses. Some even base their entire business model on them. Think of the many businesses that have sellers hold sales parties with their friends. This tactic was popularized in modern business with companies like Tupperware (containers), Amway (health and home products), Avon (skin care), and Cutco (knives, which, incidentally, Gabriel sold as a teenager). Recently this business model has become even more popular, including the hundreds of new businesses enabled by social media, such as LuLaRoe (clothing) and Pampered Chef (food products).

A fourth influence model is known as **social proof**, drawing on *social* cues as *proof* that you are making a good decision. You are more likely to do things that you see other people doing, because of your instinct to want to be part of the group (see *in-group favoritism* in Chapter 4). Think of fashion and food trends or "trending" stories and memes online.

Social proof can be effective in encouraging good choices. You have probably seen signs in hotels encouraging you to reuse your towels because it is better for the environment. Cialdini and others hypothesized in the October 2008 *Journal of Consumer Research* that reuse would increase if the signs instead pointed out that most other guests reuse their towels, and they were right. The social proof message increased towel reuse by 25 percent compared to the standard environmental message. Similarly, universities like Sacred Heart University are using social proof to combat binge drinking, informing students that most of their peers do not engage in the dangerous practice.

Unfortunately, social proof is also effective at encouraging bad behavior. Park rangers at Petrified Forest National Park in Arizona are rightly concerned about theft of petrified wood, as it is the central attraction of their park. Researchers compared two mes-

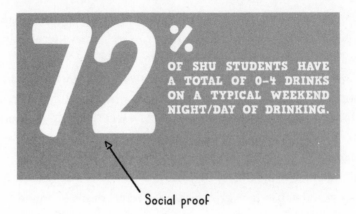

72% OF SHU STUDENTS HAVE A TOTAL OF 0-4 DRINKS ON A TYPICAL WEEKEND NIGHT/DAY OF DRINKING.

Social proof

sages: "Please don't remove the petrified wood from the park, in order to preserve the natural state of the Petrified Forest" and "Many past visitors have removed the petrified wood from the park, changing the natural state of the Petrified Forest." The latter, negatively framed message had the effect of tripling theft! Sadly, this same concept also extends to suicide rates, which have been shown to increase following media reports of suicide.

The form of social proof most prevalent in our society now is arguably social media. With the Russian attempts to influence elections in the U.S. and other countries, social

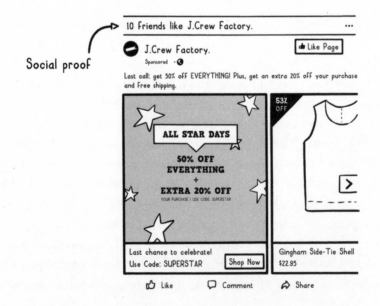

Social proof

10 Friends like J.Crew Factory.

J.Crew Factory.
Sponsored

Last call: get 50% off EVERYTHING! Plus, get an extra 20% off your purchase and free shipping.

ALL STAR DAYS

50% OFF EVERYTHING
+
EXTRA 20% OFF
YOUR PURCHASE | USE CODE: SUPERSTAR

Last chance to celebrate!
Use Code: SUPERSTAR

Shop Now

53% OFF

Gingham Side-Tie Shell
$22.95

Like   Comment   Share

media is playing an increasingly central role in global politics. In more everyday situations, follower counts are used as a proxy for social proof, brands retweet or otherwise show real people using their products, and Facebook advertisements showcase which friends have already "liked" a certain company or product.

Scarcity is another influence model, this one describing how you become more interested in opportunities the less available they are, triggering your *fear of missing out* (*FOMO*). So-called "limited-time offers" and "once-in-a-lifetime opportunities" prey on this fear. These are easy to spot online, such as the travel site that says there are "only 3 rooms left at this price," or the retailer reporting "only 5 left in stock." Scarcity signals also often imply social proof, e.g., this shirt is going to run out because it is so popular.

Scarcity

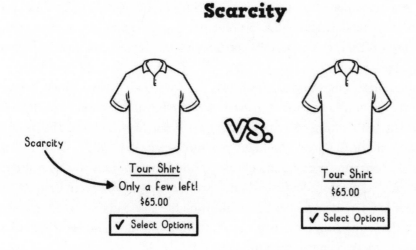

Cialdini's sixth major influence model is **authority**, which describes how you are inclined to follow perceived authority figures. In a series of sensational experiments described in his book *Obedience to Authority,* psychologist Stanley Milgram tested people's willingness to obey instructions from a previously unknown authority figure. Participants were asked to assist an experimenter (the authority figure) in a "learning experiment." They were then asked to give increasingly high electric shocks to "the learner" when they made a mistake. The shocks were fake, but the participant wasn't told that at the time; the learner was really an actor who pretended to feel pain when the "shocks" were sent. This study has been replicated many times, and a *meta-analysis* (see Chapter 5) found that participants were willing to administer *fatal* voltages 28 percent to 91 percent of the time!

In less dramatic settings, authority can still be powerful. Authority explains why celebrity endorsements work, though which types of celebrity endorsements are the most effective changes over time. Nowadays kids are less likely to know Hollywood celebrities and more likely to be influenced by YouTubers or Instagrammers. Similarly, author Michael Ellsberg recounted in *Forbes* magazine how a guest post on author Tim Ferriss's blog translated into significantly more book sales than a prime-time segment about his book on CNN and an op-ed printed in the Sunday edition of *The New York Times*.

Authority also explains why simple changes in wardrobe and accessories can increase the likelihood of getting you to do something. For instance, lab coats were worn in the Milgram experiments to convey authority.

Sometimes people even try to support an argument by appealing to a supposed authority even if that person does not have direct expertise in the relevant area. For example, advocates of extreme dosing of vitamin C cite that Linus Pauling, a two-time Nobel Prize winner, supports their claims, despite the fact that he received his awards in completely unrelated areas.

Authorities are often more knowledgeable of the facts and issues in their area of expertise, but even then, it is important to go back to first principles and evaluate their arguments on merit. In the words of astrophysicist Carl Sagan, from his book *The Demon-Haunted World*: "One of the great commandments of science is, 'Mistrust arguments from authority.' . . . Too many such arguments have proved too painfully wrong. Authorities must prove their contentions like everybody else." (See *paradigm shift* in Chapter 1.)

Similarly, a lack of a certain credential shouldn't be the sole basis for refuting a person's argument either. We firmly believe that any intelligent person could learn about any topic with the right research and enough time.

Cialdini's influence models can be used in many situations, including in adversarial ones where you are trying to persuade others to make certain choices. If you want a crash course on the use of these mental models in real-life just go to a casino, where all of them are used simultaneously to ultimately take your money. Casinos give away a lot of free stuff (reciprocity); they get you to first buy chips with cash (commitment); they try to personalize your experience to your interests (liking); they show you examples of other people who won big (social proof); they constantly present you with offers preying on your fear of missing out (scarcity); and dealers will even give you suboptimal advice (authority). Beware. There is a reason why *the house always wins*!

PERSPECTIVE IS EVERYTHING

Outside of Cialdini's six principles, there are several other mental models you can use for influence in conflict situations (and elsewhere), all of which are related to *framing* (see Chapter 1). Recall how the framing of a concept or situation can change the perception of it, such as how a newspaper headline can frame the same event in dramatically different ways, causing the reader to take away different conclusions. This change in perspective can be used as an effective influence model for good or bad, especially in moments of conflict.

The essay *Common Sense* by Thomas Paine played a critical role in securing American independence from Great Britain and serves as a potent example from history to illustrate the effectiveness of framing. As the American Revolution began in 1776, most American colonists still thought of themselves not as Americans but as Britons, but after Paine's intervention that framing started to reverse.

Despite increasing hostility between the two sides, colonists were holding out hope for a peaceful reconciliation with their home country. However, it had become clear to some, such as Paine, that King George III was never going to grant the colonists the rights they deserved, and that declaring and fighting for independence was the only way to secure those rights. Paine thought that it was wishful thinking to believe that the conflict would somehow resolve itself amicably and favorably for the colonists, without the admittedly severe consequences of war. Paine's genius was in realizing that many more colonists would need to start thinking of themselves as Americans if they were going to secure the rights they sought.

In this context, Paine published *Common Sense*, which made a compelling case for independence in clear, passionate prose. In fact, it was so compelling that it sold more than 500,000 copies in its first year of publication, when the population of the colonies was only 2.5 million—now, that's a bestseller!

Paine made it clear to many colonists that Britain did not really consider them Britons, citing the way Britain had been treating them. He then made the case, from the perspective of a colonist, that uniting with other colonists to fight for independence as newly minted Americans was the only long-term sensible option. *Common Sense* ends like this:

> Under our present denomination of British subjects, we can neither be received nor heard abroad: The custom of all courts is against us, and will be so, until, by an independence, we take rank with other nations.

These proceedings may at first appear strange and difficult; but, like all other steps which we have already passed over, will in a little time become familiar and agreeable; and, until an independence is declared, the Continent will feel itself like a man who continues putting off some unpleasant business from day to day, yet knows it must be done, hates to set about it, wishes it over, and is continually haunted with the thoughts of its necessity.

And it worked. Paine successfully framed the argument in a way that got people to buy into his idea, getting them to start to think of themselves as Americans first, not Britons. This created the necessary support for the United States Declaration of Independence, which was written later that year. In fact, John Adams, the second president of the U.S., wrote that "without the pen of the author of *Common Sense*, the sword of Washington would have been raised in vain."

In conflicts, you may similarly get the outcome you want by winning people over to your point of view. Thomas Paine did this masterfully by building allies when a conflict was unavoidable. Sometimes you may use framing in this way to prevent a direct fight altogether.

There are some more subtle aspects of framing to consider, captured in a few mental models that we explore in the rest of this section. Let's think about a more mundane situation than the American Revolution: getting a babysitter. While mid-career professionals are unlikely to take up babysitting for extra cash, they are likely to babysit for free when a friend is in a pinch. The first scenario is framed from a market perspective ("Would you babysit my kids for fifteen dollars an hour?") and the second is framed from a social perspective ("Can you please do me a favor?"). The difference in the way this situation is framed can be thought of as **social norms versus market norms** and draws on the concept of reciprocity from the previous section.

When you consider something from a *market* perspective (like babysitting for money), you consider it in the context of your own financial situation and its impact on you in an impersonal way ("I can earn sixty dollars, but it may not be worth my time"). In contrast, when you consider something from the *social* perspective (like doing your friend a favor), you consider it in the context of whether it is the right thing to do ("My friend needs my help for four hours, so I am going to help her").

In his book *Predictably Irrational*, economist Dan Ariely offers another illustrative example, of an Israeli daycare center trying to address the problem of parents showing up late to pick up their kids. As the problem became prevalent, the daycare instituted a fine for showing up late. In spite of the fine, this policy actually resulted in *more* late pickups. Ariely explains:

> Before the fine was introduced, the teachers and parents had a social contract, with social norms about being late. Thus, if parents were late—as they occasionally were—they felt guilty about it—and their guilt compelled them to be more prompt in picking up their kids in the future. . . . But once the fine was imposed, the day care center had inadvertently replaced the social norms with market norms. Now that the parents were paying for their tardiness, they interpreted the situation in terms of market norms. In other words, since they were being fined, they could decide for themselves whether to be late or not, and they frequently chose to be late. Needless to say, this was not what the day care center intended.
>
> But the real story only started here. The most interesting part occurred a few weeks later, when the day care center removed the fine. Now the center was back to the social norm. Would the parents also return to the social norm? Would their guilt return as well? Not at all. Once the fine was removed, the behavior of the parents didn't change. They continued to pick up their kids late. In fact, when the fine was removed, there was a slight increase in the number of tardy pickups (after all, both the social norms and the fine had been removed).

You must be careful not to inadvertently replace social norms with market norms, because you may end up eliminating benefits that are hard to bring back (see *irreversible*

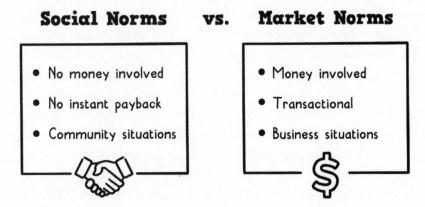

Social Norms vs. Market Norms

- No money involved
- No instant payback
- Community situations

- Money involved
- Transactional
- Business situations

decisions in Chapter 2). Once social norms are undermined, the damage has been done and they are no longer norms. So take pause when you're thinking about introducing monetary incentives into a situation where social norms are the standard.

You may run into similar issues when situations revolve around the perception of fairness. Economists use a game called the **ultimatum game** to study how the perception of fairness affects actions. Here's how it works: The *game* is played by two people. One person receives some money (say $10). This first person offers to split the money with the second person (say $5/$5, $7/$3, $8/$2, or whatever they want). This offer is an *ultimatum,* so the second person only has two choices: to accept or reject the offer. If its accepted, they both keep the offered split, and if rejected, they both get nothing.

The purely logical way to play the ultimatum game is for the first person to offer the minimum (e.g., a $9.99/$0.01 split) and for the second person to accept it, since otherwise they would get nothing, and there is no other negotiation possible. In practice, though, across most cultures, the second person usually rejects offers lower than 30 percent of the total, because of the perceived unfairness of the offer. In these circumstances the second person would rather deny the first person anything, even at the expense of receiving nothing themselves.

It is important that you keep this strong desire for fairness in mind when you make decisions that impact people important to you, such as those in your family (chore distribution, wills, etc.) or your organization (compensation, promotions, etc.). Just like social norms versus market norms, framing can have a substantial effect on the perception of fairness in various situations. Another pair of framings that come up often is **distributive justice** versus **procedural justice**.

Distributive justice frames fairness around how things are being *distributed,* with more equal distributions being perceived as more fair. By contrast, procedural justice frames fairness around adherence to *procedures,* with more transparent and objective procedures being perceived as more fair.

If your rich grandfather leaves his fortune to all his kids equally, that would probably be perceived as fair from a distributive justice perspective. However, if one of the kids was taking care of your grandfather for the last twenty years, then this distribution no longer seems fair from a procedural justice perspective. Many current political debates around topics such as income inequality and affirmative action revolve around these different formulations of justice.

Sometimes this distinction is framed as *fair share versus fair play.* For example, in the U.S., K–12 public education is freely available to all. Because of this educational access, some conclude that everyone has an equal opportunity to become successful. Others believe that the quality of public educational opportunities differs widely depending on where you live, and that education itself doesn't grant access to the best advancement opportunities, which often come through family and social connections. From this latter perspective, *fair play* doesn't really exist, and so there needs to be some corrections to achieve a more *fair share*, such as affirmative action or similar policies. As Martin Luther King Jr. put it in a May 8, 1967, interview with *NBC News*: "It's all right to tell a man to lift himself by his own bootstraps, but it is a cruel jest to say to a bootless man that he ought to lift himself by his own bootstraps."

In any case, perceived unfairness triggers strong emotional reactions. Knowing that, people will try to influence you by framing situations from a fairness perspective. In fact, many arguments try to sway you from rational decision making by pulling at your emotions, including fear, hope, guilt, pride, anger, sadness, and disgust. Influence by manipulation of emotions, whether created by perceived injustice, violation of social norms, or otherwise, is called **appeal to emotion**.

Fear is a particularly strong influencer, and it has its own named model associated with it, **FUD**, which stands for **fear**, **uncertainty**, and **doubt**. FUD is commonly used in marketing ("Our competitor's product is dangerous"), political speeches ("We could suffer dire consequences if this law is passed"), religion (eternal damnation), etc.

A related practice is the use of a **straw man**, where instead of addressing your argument directly, an opponent misrepresents (frames) your argument by associating it with something else (the *straw man*) and tries to make the argument about that instead. For example, suppose you ask your kid to stop playing video games and do his homework, and he replies that you're too strict and never let him do anything. He has tried to move the topic of conversation from doing homework to your general approach to parenting.

In complex subjects where there are a multitude of problems and potential solutions (e.g., climate change, public policy, etc.), it is easy to have two people *talk past each other* when they both set up straw men rather than address each other's points. In these settings it helps to *get on the same page* and clarify exactly what is under *debate*. However, sometimes one side (or both) may be more interested in persuading bystanders than in resolving the debate. In these situations, they could be deliberately putting up a straw man, which can unfortunately be an effective way to frame the argument to their advantage in terms of bystander influence.

Many negative political ads and statements use straw men to take a vote or action out of context. You may be familiar with the National Football League (NFL) controversy regarding the fact that some players kneeled during the national anthem in protest of police brutality against African Americans. Some politicians responded by criticizing the action as disrespectful to the military. Shifting the focus to *how* the players were protesting drew attention away from the underlying issue of *why* they were protesting.

Another related mental model is **ad hominem** (Latin for "to the person"), where the person making the argument is attacked without addressing the central point they made. "Who are you to make this point? You're not an expert on this topic. You're just an amateur." It's essentially *name-calling* and often involves lobbing much more incendiary labels at the other side. Political discourse in recent years in the U.S. is unfortunately littered with this model, and the usual names leveled are so undignified that we don't want to include them in our book.

This model is the flip side of the authority model we examined in the last section. Instead of relying on authority to gain influence, here another's authority is being attacked so that they will lack influence. Again, like straw man and appeal to emotion, these models attempt to frame a situation away from an important issue and toward another that is easier to criticize.

When you are in a conflict, you should consider how its framing is shaping the perception of it by you and others. Take the prisoner's dilemma. The prosecutors have chosen to frame the situation competitively because, for them, the Nash equilibrium with both criminals getting five years is actually the preferred outcome. However, if the criminals can instead frame the situation cooperatively—stick together at all costs—they can vastly improve their outcome.

WHERE'S THE LINE?

In Chapter 3, we advised seeking out *design patterns* that help you more quickly address issues, and watching out for *anti-patterns*, intuitively attractive yet suboptimal solutions. Influence models like those we've been discussing in the past two sections can also be **dark patterns** when they are used to manipulate you for someone else's benefit (like at the casino).

The name comes from websites that organize their sites to keep you in the *dark* through using disguised ads, burying information on hidden costs, or making it really difficult to cancel a subscription or reach support. In short, they use these types of *patterns* to manipulate and confuse you.

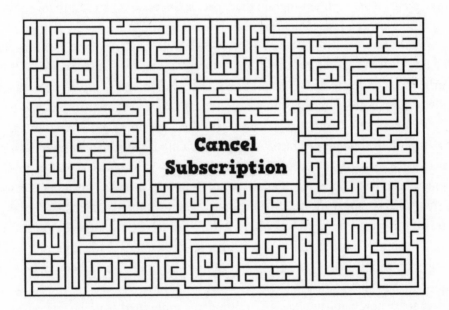

However, this concept is also applicable to everyday life offline as well. And knowing a few specific dark patterns can be helpful in adversarial situations. You're probably familiar with the mythical tale of the **Trojan horse**, a large wooden horse made by the Greeks to win a war against the Trojans. The Greeks couldn't get into the city of Troy, and so they pretended to sail away, leaving behind this supposed parting gift. What the Trojans didn't know is that the Greeks also left a small force of soldiers inside the horse. The Trojans brought the horse into the city, and under the cover of night, the Greek soldiers exited the horse and proceeded to destroy Troy and win the war.

A Trojan horse can refer to anything that persuades you to lower your defenses by seeming harmless or even attractive, like a gift. It often takes the form of a **bait and switch**, such as a malicious computer program that poses as an innocuous and enticing download (the *bait*), but instead does something nefarious, like spying on you (the *switch*).

A familiar example would be an advertised low price for an item (such as a hotel room) that doesn't really exist at that price (after "resort fees" or otherwise). Builders similarly attract buyers to new-construction homes with low list prices that correspond to so-called "builder-grade" finishes that no one really wants. They then proceed to show buyers a model home with more expensive finishes—all upgrades—which in aggregate can easily push the bounds of a buyer's budget. *If it sounds too good to be true, it usually is.*

Spectacular examples of dark patterns can be found in business. Enron, a now bankrupt energy company, once built a fake trading floor at its Houston headquarters to trick Wall Street analysts into believing that Enron was trading much more than it actually was. When the analysts came to Houston for Enron's annual meeting, the Enron executives pretended that there was all this action going on, when in fact it was all a ruse that they had been rehearsing, including having an elaborate array of TVs and computers assembled into a "war room."

Theranos, a now bankrupt healthcare company, committed a similar fraud when putting on demonstrations of its "product" for partners, including executives from Walgreens. Theranos machines were put on display, but according to the U.S. Securities and Exchange Commission, the blood samples collected were actually run on outside lab equipment that Theranos purchased through a shell company.

The Enron and Theranos tactics both exemplify another dark pattern, called a **Potemkin village**, which is something specifically built to convince people that a situation is better than it actually is. The term is derived from a historically questionable tale of a portable village built to impress Empress Catherine II on her 1787 visit to Crimea. Nevertheless, there are certainly real instances of Potemkin villages, including a village built by

North Korea in the 1950s near the DMZ to lure South Korean soldiers to defect, and, terribly, a Nazi-designed concentration camp in World War II fit to show the Red Cross, which actually disguised a way station to Auschwitz.

In film, *The Truman Show* depicts a Potemkin village on a massive scale, where the character Truman Burbank (played by Jim Carrey) resides in an entirely fake town filled with actors as part of a reality TV show. A form of this dark pattern can occur online when a website makes it seem like it has more users or content than it actually does in order to get you to participate. For example, the infamous dating site Ashley Madison (which targets people already in relationships) was found to be sending messages from fake female accounts to lure males in.

The military has employed this model widely, from dummy guns to dummy tanks and even dummy paratroopers. These were used by all sides in World War II and in many other armed conflicts to trick foreign intelligence services. They are also used internally in training exercises. As technology has improved, so have the dummies. Modern dummies can mimic the heat signature of a real tank, even fooling infrared detectors.

People similarly make homes and businesses seem secure by putting up fake security cameras, having lights in their home on timers, or even putting up signs for a security service they don't actually use. A related business practice is known as *vaporware*, where a company announces a product that it actually hasn't made yet to test demand, gauge industry reaction, or give a competitor pause from participating in the same market.

In any conflict situation, you should be on the lookout for dark patterns. While many influence models, such as the ones in this section, are commonly thought of as malicious and are therefore easier to look out for (e.g., bait and switch), others from the previous two sections are subtler. Many are considered more innocuous (e.g., scarcity), but they too can all be used to manipulate you. For example, are the common nonprofit uses of reciprocity techniques (free address labels) or social proof (celebrity endorsements) also dark patterns? In one sense, they might lead you to donate more than you would otherwise. However, it may be a good cause and they aren't tricking you in the same way that a hidden bait-and-switch cost is.

This sliding scale poses an interesting ethical question, one that any organization in business or politics is often faced with: Should you focus on truth and clarity in your promotional materials? Or should you look to influence models to find language that is more persuasive, perhaps due to its emotional appeal? Do the *ends justify the means*? Only you can decide where the line is for you.

THE ONLY WINNING MOVE IS NOT TO PLAY

Considering a conflict through a game-theory lens helps you identify what you have to gain and what you have to lose. We have just looked at models that increase your chances of a good outcome through influencing other players. Now we will consider the same problem from the inverse (see *inverse thinking* in Chapter 1) and explore models that decrease your chances of a bad outcome. Often this means finding a way to avoid the conflict altogether.

At the climax of the classic 1983 movie *WarGames*, World War III seems imminent. An artificial intelligence (known as Joshua) has been put in charge of the U.S. nuclear launch control system. Thinking he has hacked into his favorite game manufacturer, a teenage hacker (played by Matthew Broderick) unwittingly asks Joshua to play a "game" against him called Global Thermonuclear War, setting off a chain of events that has Joshua attempting to launch a real full-scale nuclear attack against Russia.

Through dialogue, the character Professor Falken explains why he created Joshua and this game:

> The whole point was to find a way to practice nuclear war without destroying ourselves. To get the computers to learn from mistakes we couldn't afford to make. Except, I never could get Joshua to learn the most important lesson. . . . Futility. That there's a time when you should just give up.

Professor Falken then draws an analogy to tic-tac-toe, continuing,

> There's no way to win. The game itself is pointless! But back at the war room, they believe you can win a nuclear war. That there can be "acceptable losses."

When all hope seems lost, the teenager recalls this conversation and asks if there is any way to make Joshua play against itself in tic-tac-toe, hoping the computer will learn that any strategy ends in a tie. After learning the futility of playing tic-tac-toe, Joshua proceeds to simulate all the possible strategies for the Global Thermonuclear War game and comes to the same conclusion. He says (in a computer voice):

> A strange game. The only winning move is not to play. How about a nice game of chess?

The reason that there is no winner in Global Thermonuclear War is that both sides have amassed enough weapons to destroy the other side and so any nuclear conflict would quickly escalate to **mutually assured destruction** (**MAD**). As a result, neither side has any incentive to use its weapons offensively or to disarm completely, leading to a stable, albeit tense, peace.

Mutually assured destruction isn't just a military model. A parallel in business is when companies amass large patent portfolios, but generally don't use them on one another for fear of escalating lawsuits that could potentially destabilize all the companies involved. Occasionally you see these suits and countersuits, such as the ones between Apple and Qualcomm (over chip patents), Oracle and Google (over Java patents), and Uber and Google (over autonomous vehicle patents), but these companies often have so many patents (sometimes tens of thousands each) that there could be literally hundreds of suits like these if not for MAD.

There are countless possible destructive outcomes to a conflict besides this arguably most extreme outcome of MAD. Engaging in any direct conflict is dangerous, though, because conflicts are unpredictable and often cause *collateral damage* (see Chapter 2). For example, drawn-out divorce battles can be harmful to the children. That's why it makes sense to consider conflict prevention measures like mediation, or, more generally, *diplomacy* (see *win-win* in Chapter 4 for some related mental models).

If diplomacy by itself doesn't work, though, there is another set of models to turn to, starting with **deterrence**, or using a threat to prevent (*deter*) an action by an adversary. Credible mutually assured destruction makes an excellent deterrent. But even one nuclear blast is so undesirable that simply the possession of a nuclear weapon has proven to be a powerful deterrent. For example, North Korea seemingly developed nuclear weapons to secure its survival as a state, despite being an authoritarian dictatorship with a well-documented history of human rights violations. So far, this tactic is working as a deterrence strategy along with other strategies it pursues, including threats of conventional bombing of South Korea and aligning with China.

The deterrence model can be appropriate when you want to try to prevent another person or organization from taking an action that would be harmful to you or society at large. In the criminal justice system, punishments may be enacted to try to deter future crime (e.g., three-strikes laws). Government regulations are often designed in part to deter unpleasant future economic or societal outcomes (e.g., deposit insurance deterring bank runs). Businesses also take actions to deter new entrants, for example, by using their scale to price goods so low that new firms cannot profitably compete (e.g., Walmart) or lobbying for regulations that benefit them at the expense of competition (e.g., anti–net neutrality laws).

The primary challenge of this model, though, is actually finding an effective deterrent. As we discussed in Chapter 2, things don't always go according to plan. When you want to put a deterrent in place, you must evaluate whether it is truly effective and whether there are any unintended consequences.

For example, what are effective crime deterrents? Research shows that people are more deterred by the certainty they will be caught and convicted than by the specific punishment they might receive. If there is little chance of getting caught, some simply do not care what the punishment is. Further, most people are not even aware of the specific punishments they might face. Financial fraudster Bernie Madoff thought he was never going to be caught and probably never considered the possibility of a 150-year prison sentence.

Additionally, there is evidence to suggest that not only does prison time not reduce repeat offenses, but there is actually a chance that it increases the probability of committing a crime again. The real solution to deterring crime is likely related to the root cause of why people commit specific types of crimes rather than to any particular punishment.

A tactical approach to deterrence is the **carrot-and-stick** model, which uses a promise of a reward (the *carrot*) and at the same time a threat of punishment (the *stick*) to deter behavior. In our household, we sometimes try to deter fighting between our kids using dessert as the carrot and loss of iPad time as the stick. It's a form of *good cop, bad cop*.

What you don't want is for the carrot-stick combination to be too weak such that the rational decision is just to ignore the carrot and deal with the stick. Economic sanctions and corporate fines are hotly debated in terms of efficacy because of this, with the latter often being thought of as more of a *cost of doing business* than a deterrent.

One effective example of the carrot-and-stick approach is Operation Ceasefire, an initiative started in Boston that aims to curtail gang-related violence. The stick part of the program focuses on a message to specific repeat perpetrators of violent crime about the certainty of future enforcement, including a promise that any new violence, especially gun violence, will result in an immediate and intense police response. The carrot part of the program is the offer of help to these same individuals, including money, job training, community support, and one-to-one mentoring in a concerted effort to get them to live productive lives. In the U.S., cities that have implemented this strategy, such as Boston, Chicago, Cincinnati, and Indianapolis, have amazingly reduced their gun homicide rates nearly 25 to 60 percent by assisting only a handful of people.

Unclear on the carrot-and-stick concept

www.betsystreeter.com

A sister mental model to deterrence is **containment**. In global conflicts, containment is an attempt to *contain* the enemy, to prevent its further expansion, be it expanding geographically (e.g., invading a neighboring country), militarily (e.g., obtaining more nuclear weapons), or politically (e.g., spreading an ideology). Containing an ongoing conflict can save you energy and resources. Think of it like treating a cut before it gets infected or removing an early-stage tumor before it metastasizes.

Containment acknowledges that an undesirable occurrence has already happened, that you cannot easily undo it, and so instead you're going to try to stop it from spreading or occurring again in the future. For example, HIV isn't yet easily curable, but if you catch it early, with modern treatments you can usually contain it such that it does not develop into AIDS.

You should apply a containment strategy in situations where you want to stop something bad from spreading, such as a negative rumor or a harmful business practice. For example, Facebook and Twitter probably couldn't have gotten rid of fake news from their platform in the run-up to the 2016 U.S. election, but they could have done a better job at containing it.

These types of situations can get out of hand quickly, so you often first want to **stop the bleeding**, by a *quick and dirty* method if necessary. Once the situation has stabilized, you can take a step back, find the *root cause* (see Chapter 1), and then try to find a more reliable long-term solution. In an emergency medical situation, you may use a tourniquet to stop actual bleeding. The metaphorical equivalent is situationally dependent, but it usually involves doing something fast and definitive, such as issuing a clear apology.

In some cases, the best short-term option might be shutting down the area where the problem exists, kind of like amputating an infected limb to prevent sepsis. In a personal context, that might mean severing a toxic relationship, at least for the time being. In an organizational context, it might mean terminating a project or employee.

Another containment tactic is **quarantine**, the restriction of the movement of people or goods in order to prevent the spread of disease. Your spam folder is a form of quarantine, curbing the impact of suspicious emails. Twitter started dealing with aggressive bots and people by quarantining them behind an additional tap or click so that fewer people see their messages.

A related tactic is **flypaper theory**, which calls for you to deliberately attract enemies to one location where they are more vulnerable, like attracting flies to *flypaper*, usually also directing them far away from your valuable assets. A former commander of U.S. ground forces in Iraq, General Ricardo Sánchez, described the benefits of this strategy in a 2003 CNN interview with regard to preventing terrorism on U.S. soil: "This is what I would call a terrorist magnet, where America, being present here in Iraq, creates a target of opportunity. . . . But this is exactly where we want to fight them. . . . This will prevent the American people from having to go through their attacks back in the United States."

In a computing context, this is known as a *honeypot*, which is used to attract and trap malicious actors for study, in the same way honey lures bears. A honeypot may be a special set of servers set up to look like the core servers where valuable data is stored, but which instead are isolated servers set up specifically to entrap hackers. A sting operation by police where they lure criminals into a place to arrest them could be called an offline honeypot.

Without containment, bad circumstances can spread, possibly leading to a **domino effect**, where more negative consequences unfold in inevitable succession like falling dominoes (see also *cascading failure* in Chapter 4). In the game-theory context, this effect could be a series of player choices that lands you in a bad outcome. Consider an iterated game of prisoner's dilemma. While in each turn it is attractive to betray the other players because you get outsized yields that turn, doing so, especially repeatedly, in most cases leads to everyone else following suit, leaving you and everyone else stuck in the suboptimal Nash equilibrium.

In the Cold War, the primary worry for the West was the spread of communism, and the dominoes were countries that might fall, one after another, which was justification to fight containment wars, as in Korea and Vietnam. The thought was that if Korea and Vietnam fell, then Laos and Cambodia might be next, and more and more countries would fall until all of Asia (even places like India) would eventually be subsumed by communism.

Domino Effect

However, be aware that the domino effect is invoked a lot more than is warranted, because people are generally bad at determining both the likelihood that events might occur and the causal relationship between events. These miscalculations often manifest in three related models, usually fallacious though not always, that you should be on the lookout for.

The first is the **slippery slope argument**: arguing that one small thing leads to an inevitable chain of events and a terrible final outcome (in the eyes of the person making the argument). Here is an example of a common slippery slope argument: "If we allow any gun control, then it will eventually result in the government taking all guns away." This line of reasoning is usually fallacious because there often isn't 100 percent inevitability in each piece of the logical chain.

The second model is **broken windows theory**, which proposes that visible evidence of small crimes, for example *broken windows* in a neighborhood, creates an environment that encourages worse crimes, such as murder. The thinking goes that broken windows are a sign that lawlessness is tolerated, and so there is a perceived need to *hold the line* and prevent a descent into a more chaotic state (see *herd immunity* in Chapter 2).

While interventions associated with broken windows theory are intuitively appealing, it is unclear how effective they are at actually reducing widespread criminal activity relative to alternatives. Related theories often take the form of a contagion metaphor, where something the person doesn't like (e.g., rap music, homosexuality, socialism) is compared to a disease that will spread through society, continually becoming more virulent if left unchecked.

The third model to watch out for is **gateway drug theory**, which makes the claim that one *drug*, such as marijuana, is a *gateway* to more dangerous drug use. However, the evidence for this claim is also murky at best (see *correlation does not imply causation* in Chapter 5). You should question any situation where one of these models arises and analyze its veracity for yourself (see *arguing from first principles* in Chapter 1).

Nevertheless, there are instances when a model like this can be true. Consider how businesses sometimes capture customers through a **loss leader strategy**, where one product is priced low (the gateway drug) to increase demand for complementary products with higher margins. The prototypical example is a supermarket discounting milk to draw in customers, who will almost certainly leave with more items. Similarly, companies sell mobile phones or printers for low prices knowing they will make money up in the

I left Target with only the one item I came to buy

SAID NO ONE EVER

long run through monthly service plans or high ink prices. We have nearly given up on letting our kids download free apps because we anticipate the endless nagging about in-app purchases.

When analyzing these domino-effect situations, write down each step in the logical chain (list each domino) and try to ascribe a realistic probability to each event (the probability that each will fall). Even if not 100 percent in every case, it might be likely that some dominoes might fall. In that case, you need to ask yourself: Is that acceptable? Do I need to engage in more active containment, or can a more *wait-and-see* approach be taken? For example, with gun control, banning assault rifles is extremely unlikely to lead to the government taking away all guns, but it might very well lead to more gun control of other assault-like weapons or add-ons. A 2017 *Politico*/Morning Consult poll found 72 percent of Americans favored both "banning assault-style weapons" and "banning high-capacity magazines."

If you are in no position to meaningfully deter or contain an emerging conflict that you'd like to avoid, **appeasement** may be a necessary evil. This involves *appeasing* opponents by making concessions in order to avoid direct or further conflict with them. The most famous example of appeasement occurred in 1938 when Britain allowed Germany to annex Sudetenland, an important piece of Czechoslovakia, to avoid an armed conflict with Hitler's army. Of course, the conflict Britain sought to avoid happened anyway. And that's the worry with appeasement: you may just be delaying the inevitable.

As a parent, sometimes appeasement is necessary to get through the day. For instance, we tend to bend the rules when we are traveling. Everyone is tired, and much of the time is spent in crowded, cramped hotel rooms or cars. At times like these, our normal diplomacy, deterrence, and containment tactics don't work as smoothly. As a result, the kids often end up with way more snacks and screen time than they would normally get—appeasement tactics that effectively prevent meltdowns and fights.

Deterrence, containment, and appeasement are all strategic mental models to keep you out of costly direct conflict. You want to enlist these models when other conflict-avoidance models have failed and you are still faced with a situation that you think you can't "win," as when engaging would create so much damage it isn't worth it or when you want to preserve your resources for more fruitful engagements (see *opportunity cost* in Chapter 3).

Finally, as Joshua said in *WarGames,* sometimes "the only winning move is not to play." An increasingly common example is conflict with the online troll, someone whose whole game is to irritate people and bait them into arguments they can't win. As a result, the best move is usually not to engage with them (*don't feed the trolls; don't stoop to their level; rise above the fray*), though, as in any situation, you have to assess it on a case-by-case basis, and where reporting mechanisms exist, you should consider them too. Any parent will similarly tell you that you need to *pick your battles*.

CHANGING THE GAME

From a game-theory perspective, deterrence and related models effectively change a game, adjusting how players perceive their payoff matrix and therefore what decisions they make when playing the game. When you practice deterrence through a credible threat, you enumerate a **red line**, which describes a figurative line that, if crossed, would trigger retaliation (see *commitment* in Chapter 3). That threat of retaliation causes other players to reconsider their choices. This line is also referred to as a *line in the sand*, describing a figurative line (drawn in the sand) that you do not intend to be crossed.

When using this strategy, you must give enough notice so that others can adjust their strategies based on your threat. You also have to explain exactly what you intend to do when the red line is crossed. The most severe threat is a so-called **nuclear option**, signaling that you will undertake some kind of extreme action if pressed. For example, North Korea has repeatedly threatened the literal *nuclear* bombing of South Korea if invaded.

Another extreme tactic is a **zero-tolerance policy**, where even a minor infraction results in strict punishment. For example, a zero-tolerance drug policy would have you fired from your job or expelled from school on the first offense, as opposed to a series of punishments that escalate to an extreme measure.

The problem with these tactics is someone can **call your bluff**, challenging you to act on your threat, claim, or policy, and actually prove it is true, *calling* you out. At that point, if you don't follow through on your promise of action, you will lose significant credibility and your opponent's payoff matrix might not change the way you want it to. For that reason, you should be prepared to follow through on whatever deterrence threats you make.

Another common situation to look out for is a **war of attrition**, where a long series of battles depletes both sides' resources, eventually leaving vulnerable the side that starts to run out of resources first. Each battle in a war of attrition hurts everyone involved, so in these situations you want either to have more resources at the start, make sure you are losing resources at a much slower rate than your opponents, or both.

The most famous military example is Germany's invasion of Russia in World War II, the deadliest conflict in human history. Over the course of the invasion, military losses for the Soviets were more than ten million, compared with more than four million for Germany. Russia had significantly more resources, however, and Germany was never able to capture Moscow. This war of attrition accounted for 80 percent of deaths suffered by the German armed forces in all of World War II, depleting their resources enough to open them up to defeat on all fronts.

Big companies often use this strategy against upstarts through various means, such as protracted lawsuits, price wars, marketing campaigns, and other head-to-head face-offs, *bleeding them dry*. In sports, a team may use this strategy if they are more physically fit than the other, such that at the end of the game, the more fit team can push to victory. It's essentially a *waiting game*.

Because a war of attrition is a long-term strategy, it can counterintuitively make sense to lose a battle intentionally, or even many battles, to win the eventual war. The winner of such a battle gets a **hollow victory**, sometimes referred to as an *empty victory* or *Pyrrhic victory*. The latter is named after King Pyrrhus of Epirus, Greece, whose army suffered irreplaceable casualties in defeating the Romans at the Battle of Heraclea, and then ultimately lost the war. In sports and gaming, this scenario is known as a *sacrifice play*. Examples include bunts and sacrifice flies in baseball and intentionally giving up a piece to get better board position in chess.

From the other side, though, if you see that you are going to lose a war of attrition, you need to find a way out or a way to change the game. One way to do that is to engage in **guerrilla warfare**, which focuses your smaller force on nimbler (*guerrilla*) tactics that the unwieldy larger force has trouble reacting to effectively (see *leverage* in Chapter 3). Max Boot, author of *Invisible Armies*, recounted in a 2013 interview on NPR, titled "American Revolution Reinvents Guerrilla Warfare," how the colonists in the American Revolution used guerrilla warfare right from the start of the conflict:

> Well, it first of all comes down to not coming out into the open, where you could be annihilated by the superior firepower of the enemy. The British got a taste of how the Americans would fight on the very first day of the Revolution, with the shot heard around the world, the Battle of Lexington and Concord, where the British regulars marched through the Massachusetts countryside.
>
> And the Americans did not mass in front of them but instead chose to slither on their bellies—these Yankee scoundrels, as the British called them—and fired from behind trees and stone walls. And not come out into the kind of open gentle-

man's fight that the British expected, and instead, took a devastating toll on the British regiment.

This concept has taken up a direct parallel in *guerrilla marketing,* where startup businesses use unconventional marketing techniques to promote their products and services on relatively small budgets. Examples of this type of marketing include PR stunts and viral videos, often taking direct aim at larger competitors, much like guerrilla warriors taking aim at a larger army. As an example, Dollar Shave Club, a subscription razor service, launched its product with a viral video. While it couldn't compete on the bigger businesses' terms (e.g., expensive TV and print ads), its edgy launch video entitled "Our Blades Are F***ing Great" immediately put the company on the map, setting it on a rapid path ultimately to a one-billion-dollar acquisition.

© marketoonist.com

One adage to keep in mind when you find yourself in a guerrilla warfare situation is that **generals always fight the last war**, meaning that armies by default use strategies, tactics, and technology that worked for them in the past, or in their *last war.* The problem is that what was most useful for the last war may not be best for the next one, as the British experienced during the American Revolution.

The most effective strategies, tactics, and especially technologies change over time. If your opponent is using outdated tactics and you are using more modern, useful ones, then you can come out the victor even with a much smaller force. Essentially, you use your tactical advantage to change the game without their realizing it; they think they are still winning a war of attrition.

On May 27 and 28, 1905, Japan's navy decisively beat Russia's navy in the Battle of Tsushima, sinking twenty-one ships, including seven battleships, with more than ten thousand Russian troops killed, injured, or captured, compared with just three torpedo boats sunk and seven hundred troops killed or injured for Japan.

Admiral Tōgō Heihachirō of Japan used advanced tactics for the time and his fleet easily overcame his Russian counterparts, who were clearly fighting the last war. Japan's ships were twice as fast as those of the Russians and equipped with much better guns, shooting 50 percent farther, using mostly high-explosive shells, causing significantly more damage on every hit. It was also the first naval battle where wireless telegraphy was used, and while both sides had some form of it, the Japanese version functioned much better and was more useful in fleet formations.

Decisive battles have been won on the back of superior technology like this many times in military history. *Don't bring a knife to a gunfight.* This concept is far-reaching, describing any situation where circumstances have changed significantly, leaving the status quo unequipped to deal with new threats.

In business, many well-known companies have lost out because they were focused on the old way of doing business, without recognizing rapidly evolving markets. IBM famously miscalculated the rise of the personal computer relative to its mainframe business, actually outsourcing its PC operating system to Microsoft. This act was pivotal for Microsoft, propelling it to capture a significant part of the profits of the entire industry for the next thirty years. Microsoft, in turn, became so focused on its Windows operating system that it didn't adapt it quickly enough to the next wave of operating system needs on the smartphone, ceding most of the profits in the smartphone market to Apple, which is now the most profitable company in history.

Once you start looking, you can find generals fighting the last war all over the place: politicians failing to adapt to new campaign strategies (like John McCain's somewhat staid online presence versus Barack Obama's modern use of social media in the 2008 U.S. presidential campaign); finance professionals missing the signs of the 2007/2008 financial crisis (because they thought the past could predict the future); or the U.S. education curriculum misreading the staying power of the digital economy (and continuing to fail to incorporate enough engineering).

Employing guerrilla warfare is an example of **punching above your weight**. In boxing, competitors are grouped by *weight*, because large differences in weight, all other things being equal, make a fight unfair. This takes us back to the physics models we discussed in Chapter 4 (see *inertia*). Heavier boxers pack more powerful *punches* and are generally harder to knock over. A boxer who punches above their weight intentionally fights in a heavier class, taking on larger competitors on purpose.

As a mental model, punching above your weight occurs any time you try to perform at a higher level than is expected of you, even outside a competitive context. Examples include joining a group made up of more accomplished members or writing an op-ed on a subject on which you are not yet a recognized expert. On the macro scale, whole countries punch above their weight when they engage in prominent roles on the world stage, such as Ireland serving as a tax haven for major corporations.

Given the inherent disadvantage of being the smaller player, you should engage in this type of fight only when you can deploy guerrilla tactics that you believe will tilt the game in your favor. If that's the case, though, you may actively seek out these types of conflicts because punching above your weight can have many benefits. These include the obvious benefit of increasing your chances to reach your goals faster, but also potential exposure to large audiences and opportunities to absorb knowledge from world-class experts. However, following the metaphor can also get you punched hard in the face, so it is inherently risky. It's like when a new TV show gets marketed to the mainstream but does not retain sufficient viewership and gets quickly canceled—*not ready for prime time.*

When deploying such tactics, you will want to reevaluate your odds as the game goes on, to make sure you are on the right track. Are your odds improving? Are you effectively changing the game to be in your favor?

ENDGAME

In chess, once most of the pieces have been removed from the board, you enter a stage called the **endgame**. This concept has been extended to refer to the final stage of any course of events. Whether you started a conflict or were drawn into one, at some point most conflicts will *end* and you need an effective plan either to lock in your gains or minimize your losses.

Your credible *strategy* to *exit* a situation is called your **exit strategy**. In a military context, the exit-strategy concept has more recently been highlighted with a negative framing in instances where there wasn't a well-thought-out exit plan, e.g., after the U.S. lost troops in a U.N. peacekeeping mission in Somalia and with U.S. involvement in Iraq and Afghanistan. In a business context, an exit strategy usually describes how a company and its investors will get a payoff through either an acquisition, a buyout, or an initial public offering (IPO). In public policy, devising an exit strategy means thinking about the practicalities and consequences of how an entity might get out of certain situations, such as European countries withdrawing from the eurozone.

As applied to your personal life, an exit strategy can be thought of in terms of how you will get out of long-term relationships you don't want to be in or obligations you no longer wish to be burdened with. What is your strategy to make an eventual graceful exit from something you're involved in? For example, if you are on the board of an organization, your exit strategy might involve finding your replacement and setting that person up for success. Your exit strategy doesn't always require a full exit, however. You can also try to find a way to hand off onerous responsibilities to another team member while holding on to the parts that you do enjoy.

In any case, coming up with a well-defined exit plan will keep you from doing things you might later regret. For instance, given the benefits of *preserving optionality* (see Chapter 2), you should probably come up with an exit strategy that avoids *burning bridges*, or ruining relationships with individuals or organizations in a way that thereafter commits you not to going back to them (to cross that *bridge* ever again). The short-term satisfaction you might receive from these acts is rarely worth the risk of the escalation, severing of ties, and resulting fallout. Similar acts to avoid are *scorched-earth* tactics, which refers to burning (*scorching*) the ground (*earth*) so it isn't of use to anyone (including yourself)—for example, destroying records.

Sometimes, though, you may just have to exit with the best strategy you can come up with at the moment, even if it means that your exit isn't that clean or graceful, recognizing that the long-term outcomes of staying the course are worse. If a solid exit strategy isn't forthcoming, one tactic is to throw a **Hail Mary pass**, a last-ditch, long-shot final effort for a successful outcome. The concept comes from a final touchdown attempt in American football where the quarterback throws a really long *pass* into the end zone in the hope of scoring the final game-winning points. The phrasing became popular after a successful attempt in a 1975 NFL playoff game between the Dallas Cowboys and the Minnesota Vikings after which Cowboys quarterback Roger Staubach recounted throwing the ball: "I closed my eyes and said a *Hail Mary*."

Spanish explorer Hernán Cortés made a counterintuitive Hail Mary pass by actually eliminating his expedition's default exit strategy. In 1519, Cortés started a war with the Aztecs that led to the destruction of their empire. However, he had only six hundred men, whereas the Aztecs controlled most of modern-day Mexico. The odds were obviously thought to be heavily against the Spanish, and many of Cortés's soldiers were reasonably wary of his plans.

To secure their motivation, Cortés sank his ships to make sure they had no option but to succeed or die. Without the *escape hatch* of going back to Spain on the boats, the soldiers' best option was to fight with Cortés. Translation errors led some to believe he burned the boats, but now we know he just had them damaged to the point of sinking. Nonetheless, **burn the boats** lives on as a mental model for crossing the *point of no return*. (Sometimes people also say *crossing the Rubicon*, referencing Julius Caesar's crossing of the Rubicon River with his troops in 49 B.C., deliberately breaking Roman law, making armed conflict inevitable and ultimately leading to him becoming dictator of Rome.)

Game theory can again help you work through your potential exit strategies, assessing likely long-term outcomes and evaluating how various tactics might affect them. While not all situations parallel game-theory models (like the prisoner's dilemma or the ultimatum game), most can still fruitfully be examined through a game-theory lens.

In any conflict, whether in the endgame stage or otherwise, we encourage you to list the choices currently available to all the "players," along with the consequences and payoffs. This method should help you decide whether a game is worth playing (or continuing), how to approach playing it, and whether there is some way to change the game so the outcome leans in your favor.

Thinking this way also helps you with diplomacy, because using a game-theory lens means you must think about how other players will move and react to your moves, which is a *forcing function* (see Chapter 4) to empathize with their goals and motivations. And through this same process you might also better clarify your own goals and motivations.

KEY TAKEAWAYS

- Analyze conflict situations through a game-theory lens. Look to see if your situation is analogous to common situations like the **prisoner's dilemma**, **ultimatum game**, or **war of attrition**.

- Consider how you can convince others to join your side by being more persuasive through the use of influence models like **reciprocity, commitment, liking, social** proof, scarcity, and **authority**. And watch out for how they are being used on you, especially through **dark patterns**.

- Think about how a situation is being framed and whether there is a way to frame it that better communicates your point of view, such as **social norms** versus **market norms**, **distributive justice** versus **procedural justice**, or an **appeal to emotion**.

- Try to avoid direct conflict because it can have uncertain consequences. Remember there are often alternatives that can lead to more productive outcomes. If diplomacy fails, consider **deterrence** and **containment** strategies.

- If a conflict situation is not in your favor, try to change the game, possibly using **guerrilla warfare** and **punching-above-your-weight** tactics.

- Be aware of how **generals always fight the last war**, and know your **best exit strategy**.

8

Unlocking People's Potential

THE 1992 OLYMPICS WAS THE first to allow active professional basketball players from the National Basketball Association (NBA) to compete. The United States fielded a team dubbed the "Dream Team," which the Naismith Memorial Basketball Hall of Fame has called "the greatest collection of basketball talent on the planet." The team included legendary players Michael Jordan, Larry Bird, and Magic Johnson. In fact, eleven of the twelve players are in the Hall of Fame today. Collectively they defeated their opponents by an average of 44 points, including a 32-point victory against Croatia in the finals. Needless to say, it was a spectacle to watch.

The 1996 Olympics had a similar result, with the U.S. team returning five members of the original Dream Team to join new stars like Shaquille O'Neal and Reggie Miller. Again in 2000 the United States won gold with relative ease. But then in 2004 something curious happened. Despite having the most talented players (including LeBron James, Dwyane Wade, and Allen Iverson), the U.S. team lost three games (the most ever for the U.S.) and left with only the bronze medal. In fact, it lost the first game of the tournament to Puerto Rico by a score of 92–73, the biggest loss ever recorded for any U.S. Olympic basketball team.

Argentina then beat the United States in the semifinals in one of the most surprising upsets in Olympic history and went on to win the gold medal that year. Though Argentina had several NBA players itself, including Manu Ginóbili, hardly anyone expected it to be victorious.

Why did the talented U.S. team fall short of the gold? The historical analysis converges on the fact that the U.S. "team" wasn't much of a team at all—more like a loose collection of individual stars. They practiced together only for a few weeks before the tournament, not enough time to get used to playing with one another. They also didn't have enough players with experience in all the different positions. By contrast, other countries selected players to complement one another, and then those players worked together for years, honing their collective playing styles and eventually gelling as teams.

We relate this story because most of us are not able to put together or be part of a dream team packed with the most talented people in their fields the world over. **Joy's law** is a mental model named after Sun Microsystems cofounder Bill Joy, who remarked at an event in 1990, *No matter who you are, most of the smartest people work for someone else.* Former U.S. Secretary of Defense Donald Rumsfeld said something similar, known as *Rumsfeld's Rule*: *You go to war with the army you have. They're not the army you might want or wish to have at a later time.*

Both Joy and Rumsfeld acknowledge that organizations hardly ever have perfect resources, nor can they always afford to wait until they have better ones before moving forward. Joy's law further stresses that great people are unlikely to be concentrated in a single organization.

Don't be discouraged, though. With the right leadership, a well-constructed team can accomplish incredible things, as Argentina and Puerto Rico did in the 2004 Olympics. As another example, startup companies that disrupt large incumbents routinely start with relatively tiny amounts of resources, often a hundred to a thousand times less. Yet they become successful because they are the right group of people led in the right way. Instagram had only thirteen employees when Facebook bought it for one billion dollars in 2012; a few years later Facebook bought WhatsApp, with fifty-five employees, for a whopping nineteen billion dollars.

In the startup world, you will sometimes hear about a **10x engineer**, an exceptional engineer who produces many times the output of an average engineer: a world-class all-star. Ten isn't an exact number here—it's just meant to signify that a person is much, much better than average, a true outlier. (Of course, this concept applies beyond engineering, as there are top performers in every field.)

Organizations are always on the lookout for 10x individuals because they can be the ingredients of a true dream team. Keeping Joy's law in mind, however, reminds you that just seeking out 10x people is a trap for two reasons. First, they are extremely rare; not every organization can hire world-class talent, because there just isn't enough to go around.

The second reason is subtler. There are many excellent people who, despite not being world-class, can achieve 10x output in certain situations, but that output may not be replicated when they switch roles, projects, or organizations. In other words, when you see outsized output by an individual, such as on a resume or via a reference, it is usually because they have many things working in their favor all at once to produce that outsized impact: role in the organization or team, personality as applied to this role, types of tasks assigned, resources provided, and the value of their unique set of skills and relationships in that particular situation. When one or more of those variables change, the person may not be able to produce at the same level.

We actually view this as a positive. It means that such outsized output can be created within an organization, not by recruiting world-class all-stars, but by crafting the right projects and roles, ones that allow excellent people to reach extraordinary performance given their unique set of characteristics. As a manager, if you can help your team members in this way, you can create a **10x team** around you.

A 10x team arises when you've helped to arrange everything so that multiple people on your *team* become *10x* contributors all at once. These are the teams that *punch above their weight* (see Chapter 7), as in defeating a U.S. Olympic Dream Team in basketball, competing successfully against much bigger organizations, and achieving other impressive and unexpected accomplishments. If the members of the team were on different projects, in different roles, or embedded in different organizations, they might not perform this well, but on this particular team, you've helped everyone achieve their full potential. That's the dream of management in any situation.

This chapter is about using mental models to form and lead such incredible teams, 10x teams. A February 4, 1996, quote from former U.S. senator Bill Bradley in *The New York Times* is apt: "Leadership is unlocking people's potential to become better." When you foster a 10x team, you draw on people's different skills and abilities, allowing each person to play their unique part and collectively achieve outsized impact.

IT TAKES A VILLAGE

To work toward a 10x team, you must recognize that people are not interchangeable. On the same team, one person's 10x role on a project might be another person's 0.1x role on the same project. In figuring out who goes where, you must appreciate the nuanced differences between people, and in particular, appreciate each individual's unique set of strengths, goals, and personality traits so you can craft roles for them that best utilize those characteristics and motivate them.

First, consider personality traits. Both of us are **introverts**. We strongly prefer small group interactions to large group ones, as we can easily be overstimulated or drained of energy by larger social activities. At the same time, we are totally fine and even thrive when working alone for long periods of time. So we enjoy roles that involve things like reading, writing, planning, and building things like programs and spreadsheets.

By contrast, **extroverts** gain energy from large group interactions. They tend to avoid solitary situations when possible, preferring synchronous interaction. A team role that involves frequent interfacing with others (like many sales roles) and appearing in large group settings (e.g., conferences) is therefore well suited for an extrovert. And conversely, a team role that involves solitary work, like many programming roles, is well suited for an introvert.

Where personality traits come from is subject to debate, and that debate is generally referred to as **nature versus nurture**. *Nature* refers to traits being explained by genetics, and *nurture* refers to traits being explained by all the environmental factors that don't come from your genes (parenting, physical environment, culture, etc.). Studies have shown that many personality dimensions (like introversion/extroversion) arise out of a combination of the two.

Regardless of the root causes of people's differences, the key insight to remember is that people really are different. What's going on in your head isn't the same as what's going on in someone else's head. You will approach and interpret the same situation differently, filtered through your personality, culture, and life experiences (see *frame of reference* in Chapter 1).

Also, even if derived largely from nurture, most personality traits aren't quick to change once established. That means an introvert isn't likely to become an extrovert (or vice versa) when put in a new situation. You should therefore look to accommodate these traits in the roles you select for yourself or for other people.

You should also know that there are other personality dimensions besides introversion versus extroversion, though we find that one to be the most actionable on a day-to day basis. There is no widespread agreement on the aspects of personality to focus on, but Lewis Goldberg presented one leading theory in "The Structure of Phenotype Personality Traits" that suggests there are five key factors:

1. Extroversion (outgoing versus reserved)
2. Openness to experience (curious versus cautious)
3. Conscientiousness (organized versus easygoing)
4. Agreeableness (compassionate versus challenging)
5. Neuroticism (nervous versus confident)

Beyond personality, you're probably familiar with **IQ** (intelligent quotient), a measure of general intelligence. A form of intelligence that you might not know about is emotional intelligence, measured by **EQ** (emotional quotient). People with high EQ are typically more empathetic, correlated with high abilities in these areas:

- Perceiving complex emotional states in others
- Managing these emotions in themselves and others
- Using emotions (including their own) to facilitate conversations

Thus, roles that involve group dynamics, coordination, or empathy (e.g., project management, leadership, sales, marketing) are best suited for people with high EQ. (Note that

"A-ha, I've proven them wrong! The computer, my one and only friend, says I have high EQ!"

IQ and EQ are independent traits, meaning the same person could have any combination of high or low IQ and EQ.)

When considering people for roles, you must also consider their individual goals and strengths, which can vary widely. A few mental models can help you make some useful distinctions. For example, some people wish to know a little about a lot (**generalists**) while others wish to go deeper in one area (**specialists**).

Specialist vs. Generalist

Think about physicians: primary care physicians are generalists and do a bit of everything, serving as the starting point for the diagnosis of any ailment. But for specific conditions, they will refer their patients to specialist physicians, trained and experienced to treat in one area, such as infectious disease or oncology. Or take retail stores: Sometimes you want to go to a general store like Walmart or Target to get a variety of things. Other times a specialty store like Home Depot (home improvement), Best Buy (electronics), or AutoZone is more appropriate.

In your organization, you will need people who lean toward one side or the other depending on the situation. In very small organizations, for example, specialists are more of a luxury. You will want generalists because so many types of problems need to be solved but you have only a few people to address them. In these cases, problems that require specialists are often not frequent enough to justify full-time positions, and so organizations usually rely on outside resources to solve them. By contrast, larger organizations employ many specialists, who can usually get better outcomes than generalists because of their long-term specialist experience.

A similar model from author Robert X. Cringley in his book *Accidental Empires* describes three types of people required in different phases of an organization's life cycle—**commandos**, **infantry**, and **police**.

> Whether invading countries or markets, the first wave of troops to see battle are the commandos. . . . A startup's biggest advantage is speed, and speed is what commandos live for. They work hard, fast, and cheap, though often with a low level of professionalism, which is okay, too, because professionalism is expensive. Their job is to do lots of damage with surprise and teamwork, establishing a beachhead before the enemy is even aware that they exist. . . .
>
> Grouping offshore as the commandos do their work is the second wave of soldiers, the infantry. These are the people who hit the beach en masse and slog out the early victory, building on the start given them by the commandos. . . . Because there are so many more of these soldiers and their duties are so varied, they require an infrastructure of rules and procedures for getting things done— all the stuff that commandos hate. . . .
>
> What happens then is that the commandos and the infantry head off in the direction of Berlin or Baghdad, advancing into new territories, performing their same jobs again and again, though each time in a slightly different way. But there is still a need for a military presence in the territory they leave behind, which they have liberated. These third-wave troops hate change. They aren't troops at all but police. They want to fuel growth not by planning more invasions and landing on more beaches but by adding people and building economies and empires of scale.

This model applies equally to well to projects. As entrepreneur Jeff Atwood put it in a June 29, 2004, post on his blog, *Coding Horror*:

> You really need all three groups through the life cycle of a project. Having the wrong group (commandos) at the wrong time (maintenance) can hurt you a lot more than it helps. Sometimes being a commando, even though it sounds really exciting, actually hurts the project.

People who like rules and structure are much better suited for police roles, whereas anti-establishment types gravitate toward and excel in commando roles. If you put a commando person in a police role (e.g., project manager, compliance officer, etc.), they will generally rebel and make a mess of everything, whereas if you put a police person in a commando role (e.g., a position involving rapid prototyping, creative deliverables, etc.), they will generally freeze up and stall out.

Another mental model that helps you consider people's strengths is **foxes versus hedgehogs**, derived from a lyric by the Greek poet Archilochus, translated as *The fox knows many things, but the hedgehog knows one big thing.* Philosopher Isaiah Berlin applied the metaphor to categorize people based on how they approach the world: *hedgehogs*, who like to frame things simply around grand visions or philosophies; and *foxes*, who thrive on complexity and nuance. Hedgehogs are big picture; foxes appreciate the details.

Like other dichotomous pairs, foxes and hedgehogs excel in different situations. For example, in his book *Good to Great*, Jim Collins noted that most of the "great" companies profiled were run by hedgehogs who built up massive companies in dogged pursuit of one simple vision:

> Those who built the good-to-great companies were, to one degree or another, hedgehogs. They used their hedgehog nature to drive toward what we came to call a Hedgehog Concept for their companies. Those who led the comparison companies tended to be foxes, never gaining the clarifying advantage of a Hedgehog Concept, being instead scattered, diffused, and inconsistent.

However, many of those "great" companies no longer exist. They were great only for a short period of time, often because times had changed while they held on to the same Hedgehog Concept. By comparison, Pulitzer Prize–winning journalist Nicholas Kristof, writing in *The New York Times* on March 26, 2009, described research detailing why foxes often make better predictors:

> Hedgehogs tend to have a focused worldview, an ideological leaning, strong convictions; foxes are more cautious, more centrist, more likely to adjust their views, more pragmatic, more prone to self-doubt, more inclined to see complexity and nuance. And it turns out that while foxes don't give great sound-bites, they are far more likely to get things right.

Again, each type of person should be placed in roles that suit them. For example, a hedgehog will be better at marketing roles, communicating a vision clearly and succinctly. A fox will be better at strategic roles, wading through the nuances of uncertainty and complexity. And you will need both types of people on your teams.

Because 10x teams perform at such a high level, leaders should be actively thinking of ways to create and maintain them. Members of 10x teams tend to have different skills and backgrounds because this gives the team variety in perspectives (see *divergent thinking* in Chapter 6) and the ability to assign team roles and responsibilities to people well suited for them. This means that at the organizational level, you benefit from diversity because you can create multiple 10x teams by arranging people the right way, drawing on their wide array of skills and other individual traits that diversity provides.

For leaders, when constructing these teams, the starting point is knowing and appreciating the unique characteristics of your team members. Then you can craft team roles and responsibilities based on what will work best for the specific people available. As needed, you can recruit additional people with complementary skills who can further strengthen the team.

You also need to keep individual characteristics in mind when you manage the people on these teams, and adjust your management accordingly. We call this **managing to the person**, as opposed to managing to the role or managing everyone the same. In other words, good people management is not one-size-fits-all.

As with many challenges, *Maslow's hammer* (see Chapter 6) can convince you that you should take the technique that worked for one person and apply it to all the other members of the team. But this is not effective; managing two different people will involve two different sets of behaviors, each individually calibrated to their unique characteristics and situations.

This model can be extended to other settings: teaching to the student, parenting to the child, etc. Our two children are very different, and parenting techniques that work well with one child seldom work as well with the other. Approaching each relationship as unique will help you better appreciate its individual attributes and use that knowledge to ultimately create more effective relationships and teams.

WHO GOES WHERE

The strongest teams have the right people in the right roles, allowing them to amplify their individual strengths and skill sets. Conversely, when people are in the wrong roles, you can get dysfunctional teams. At the very least, you don't want people in obviously wrong roles. That sounds easy to achieve, but in practice it is not.

Educator Laurence Peter introduced the concept of the **Peter principle** in his 2009 book of the same name, which has become known by the phrase *managers rise to the level of their incompetence.* What he's saying is that people get promoted to a new role based on how they performed in their previous role; however, the abilities required of their new role may be completely different, and possibly ill-suited for them. Eventually, they will be promoted into a role that will not suit them ("the level of their incompetence"), where they will struggle.

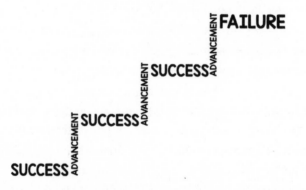

When people are excelling, it's natural to reward them with promotions for their excellent performance. However, you need to keep the Peter principle in mind when doling out those promotions, so that you don't put people in roles where they are unlikely to succeed. This can be more problematic the longer a person succeeds in your organization. Often higher roles involve different skills, such as more people management and less individual contribution, which may cut against someone's strengths or career goals. To counteract the Peter principle, organizations can develop multiple career tracks, such as a technical leadership track that doesn't require people management.

In addition, higher roles tend to involve more **strategy** than **tactics**. Generally, strategy is the big picture; tactics are the details. Strategy is the long term, defining what ultimate success looks like. Tactics are short term, defining what we're going to do next to get there. The Peter principle factors in because promoting someone who is great tactically into a strategic role can be problematic if that person is not strong strategically.

A related difficulty arises when a person wants a role that they are ill-suited for. In that case, you must determine whether they could grow into the new role over time. If you think they can, you can promote them and give them the support they need to grow. On the other hand, if you think the new role will be forever ill-fitting (perhaps because of personality or other factors that are hard to change), you should help them attain satisfaction in their current role or craft a wholly different role that both fulfills them and works for the organization.

However, just because someone doesn't fit a role initially doesn't mean that they will be forever ill-suited for it. Given time and practice, they might even excel at it. And there are several strong reasons why you might want to help people learn and grow into new roles rather than always hire outside the organization.

First, it often takes a significant amount of time for new employees to *ramp up* and become truly effective contributors within your organization. This time length is obviously dependent on the job and organization, but as roles get more complex and involve learning a wide variety of new information and internal processes, it can easily be six to eighteen months. You could instead use this amount of time to help an existing team member rise to the same set of responsibilities.

Second, if an organization doesn't provide career paths to existing team members, many will leave for other organizations where they think they can get better opportunities. When they leave, they take with them some of the organization's **institutional knowledge**, the collective *knowledge* shared by the entire *institution*.

Your best people know how to be effective within your organization. They know the organizational history, who to go to for different pieces of knowledge, and ultimately how to get things done. When these people leave, their institutional knowledge *walks out the door with them*, and the whole organization becomes less effective. For example, Lauren continued to get questions about her projects at GlaxoSmithKline long after she left her position, even after one of the drugs she worked on had been purchased by another corporation. She answered them, but there is no guarantee that your former employees will be as accommodating.

A third reason to try to grow people into new, expanded roles instead of hiring externally is that organizations often craft unrealistic job postings. Such a position can be filled only by a **unicorn candidate**, a term that was coined to signify that finding such a *candidate* might be as rare as finding a *unicorn* (essentially impossible). It's like people who have unrealistic or too specific requirements for a significant other or political candidate.

If you try to fill a role for a long time and you aren't seeing any qualified candidates, then you might be looking for a unicorn candidate (assuming there isn't some other issue, such as the compensation offered mismatches the role, or your company has a negative reputation). Unrealistic hiring expectations are a form of *grass-is-greener mentality,* covered in Chapter 6: "If only our organization could hire the perfect person for this role, things would be great." In these situations, the organization may need to split the role and hire multiple people, focus on growing people from within, or do some combination of the two.

Another critical endeavor for your organization is making the boundaries around roles and responsibilities crystal clear. Apple is known for popularizing a mental model called **directly responsible individual**, or **DRI** for short. After every meeting, it is made clear that there is one DRI who is responsible and accountable for the success of each action item. DuckDuckGo similarly assigns a DRI to every company activity—from the smallest task to the largest company objective.

DON'T MIND US -- WE'RE JUST PASSIVE BYSTANDERS

The DRI concept helps avoid *diffusion of responsibility*, also known as the **bystander effect**, where people fail to take *responsibility* for something when they are in a group, because they think someone else will take on that responsibility. In effect, they act like *bystanders*, and the responsibility *diffuses* across all the members of the group instead of being concentrated in one person who is held accountable.

You can see the bystander effect in many situations, including when people need help in an emergency. In a famous 1968 study, "Bystander Intervention in Emergencies: Diffusion of Responsibility," John Darley and Bibb Latané had a group of subjects participate in a group discussion about their lives, communicating with one another electronically from separate rooms. Unbeknownst to them, all the other "participants" were prerecorded, and the size of the group varied from two (with one prerecorded voice) to six (with five prerecorded voices). Each "participant" took turns speaking, and one of the prerecorded voices on their first turn revealed they were prone to life-threatening seizures. On the second turn, that same "participant" had a fake seizure, with their prerecorded voice saying, "I'm . . . I'm having a fit . . . I . . . I think I'm . . . help me . . . I . . . I can't . . . Oh my God . . . er . . . if someone can just help me out here . . . I . . . I . . . can't breathe p-p-properly . . . I'm feeling . . . I'm going to d-d-die if . . ."

Darley and Latané found that people were much less likely to try to help someone if they perceived that at least one other person was also hearing them struggle. In the one-on-one configuration, 85 percent of the subjects sought help before the recording ended, but only 31 percent did so when they thought there were four or more other participants.

Studies like this one have since been replicated in many other configurations and situations. An everyday example just mentioned is the set of next steps that emerges from a work meeting—everyone attending might assume someone else will do them, and so they don't get done in a timely manner. The DRI concept is a simple and powerful way to cut through this natural inclination by clearing up who is responsible for what.

In other scenarios, sometimes people step up right away, especially when they are particularly motivated by the task at hand or want to showcase their abilities. An organization can take advantage of this self-selection for roles and responsibilities by using a controlled **power vacuum**. This mental model is an analogy to the natural concept of a *vacuum*, a space devoid of all substance, including air. If you make a vacuum, say by pumping air out of an empty container, and then you open that container, air will quickly rush into it, *filling the vacuum*, normalizing the air pressure.

In a power vacuum, the "vacuum" is created when someone who had *power* suddenly departs, leaving the opportunity for someone else to quickly fill the void. Throughout history, power vacuums have been common when despotic leaders are deposed, and others then rush in to seize their power (see *hydra effect* in Chapter 2).

In a controlled setting, an organization can deliberately create a power vacuum, and actively try to get people to fill it. For example, leadership can carve out a set of responsibilities and offer people an opportunity to take them over. In other cases, leaders may wait to see if anyone steps up naturally. Setting up a controlled power vacuum like this can help determine who is intrinsically attracted to a role. By watching what people do as they step into the power vacuum, you can see how well suited they are for the role before officially giving it to them.

However you decide to do it, discovering the right roles and responsibilities for the members of your team is a step worth taking. The ideal situation for any group setting is one where you have clearly delineated roles and responsibilities, and people who are well suited for each and intrinsically motivated to excel at them. Those are the ingredients for a 10x team.

PRACTICE MAKES PERFECT

Crafting the right role for an individual—whether for yourself or for a colleague—doesn't guarantee that they will reach their full potential. People, especially those in new roles, need guidance and mentorship to achieve at the highest level. If you've ever been on either side of a successful coaching or mentorship relationship, you probably know what we mean. In any case, you should be aware of several mental models to help you think about how to receive or provide such guidance and mentorship.

Psychologist K. Anders Ericsson has made a career studying the fastest way to get good at something, a model he calls **deliberate practice**. It works by *deliberately* putting people in situations at the limit of their abilities, where they are constantly *practicing* increasingly difficult skills and receiving consistent real-time feedback. As Ericsson noted in "The Role of Deliberate Practice in the Acquisition of Expert Performance": "The differences between expert performers and normal adults reflect a life-long period of deliberate effort to improve performance in a specific domain."

Deliberate practice is more intensive than what you think of as regular practice. A kids' soccer practice where the children spend the beginning of the session passing the ball back and forth is passing practice. However, it is not deliberate passing practice because the kids are not practicing at the edge of their abilities and also are not receiving real-time feedback on how to improve.

Deliberate Practice

Deliberate passing practice could take multiple forms. One example would be repeatedly trying to hit a target and getting coached on mistakes after each few tries. The goal could be to hit the target an increasing number of times in a row: first once, then three times, then five times, and so on. Once the last goal has been reached, then the target could be moved further away and the process repeated. This more focused type of passing practice is a more efficient way to improve passing skills.

You may have heard of the so-called "10,000-Hour Rule," which Malcolm Gladwell popularized in his book *Outliers*. Gladwell draws on Ericsson's work and notes that world-class experts usually required ten thousand hours of deliberate practice to achieve world-class status. Please be aware that Ericsson and others have noted that this is not a hard-and-fast "rule," in that actual hourly amounts vary depending on the subject you are practicing, how deliberate the practice, how good your coaches are, and the degree of mastery you are seeking.

Regardless, it is clear that in any field, deliberate practice is the fastest way to move from being a novice to being an expert. It is difficult to do alone, however, because it relies on continuous specific feedback about what you could be doing better. Unless there is a simulated environment where such feedback can be usefully received (e.g., some online chess programs), at least one other person needs to be involved.

Ideally, this person is a true expert who can provide direct feedback and identify the best goals, practice environments, and coaching methods. Think of someone like a personal trainer, sports coach, or music teacher. In a professional setting, this person could be a manager or mentor who is helping you take on more and more responsibility, coaching you consistently along the way.

Deliberate practice puts you outside your comfort zone. That is both mentally and physically taxing. Trying to impose deliberate practice on someone is therefore a losing battle. It is better to get buy-in from both the mentor and mentee before committing to this model.

A related model is the **spacing effect**, which explains that learning *effects* are greater when that learning is *spaced* out over time, rather than when you study the same amount in a compressed amount of time. That is, "cramming" is usually a suboptimal strategy, as we noted in Chapter 3. To really learn something, you must reinforce it over and over again.

The spacing effect further holds that spacing between reinforcements can be increased over time. Think about when you learn a new word. The first day you learn it, you really need to study it. Then you might want to remind yourself of its meaning the next day or a couple of days later to make sure you've got it, but you don't need to do that every day for the rest of your life. If you never use the word again, though, you'll likely eventually forget it, and so occasionally you need to be reminded of it. This is exactly how many modern online learning platforms, such as Duolingo for learning languages and Quizlet for learning facts.

The spacing effect should inform your deliberate practice. You don't completely master a skill and move on. Rather, you must rotate among skills, reinforcing what you've learned over time. It's like going to the gym and rotating among all the muscles in your body, gradually taking on more intense workouts that involve more weight and complicated movements.

The spacing effect has more wide-reaching implications, such as that spacing out advertisements is more effective than showing them back-to-back. Also, spacing out topics within a textbook is more effective than the standard mechanism of covering each topic in its own, single chapter. For example, in an elementary math textbook, if you teach fractions in different chapters, kids learn how fractions can be applied across different contexts and the concept is better reinforced than it would be if taught in a single chapter.

To make deliberate practice work in an organizational context, you need to find a way to provide people the continual feedback and reinforcement learning they need. One way to do this is through a **weekly one-on-one** standing meeting with a manager, mentor, or coach. This meeting can serve as a *forcing function* to deliver such feedback on a regular basis (as we noted in Chapter 4). These can be relatively unstructured meetings where you discuss current projects, as well as discussions about skill development and career growth.

In her book *Radical Candor*, Kim Scott describes a model of the same name for how to approach giving feedback in one-on-ones, weekly or otherwise, using the trusty 2 × 2 *matrix* (see Chapter 4).

Radical Candor

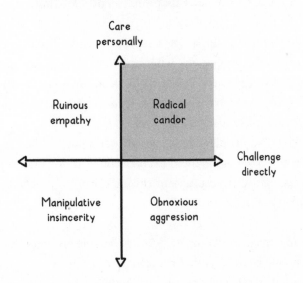

The two axes for this matrix are "challenge directly" and "care personally." When you give feedback to someone, you can give it in a vague, abstract way ("I think you could do a better job at communication"), or in a specific, actionable way where you challenge directly ("This sentence you said was confusing, here's why, and here's what I think you should have said"). Being vague and abstract is much easier to do because it avoids the hard work of identifying specific examples and the psychological stress of debating the nuances around those specifics. Many people thus take the easy way out. But for your feedback to be effective, you are going to need specifics.

Caring personally involves nurturing the relationship you've built prior to giving feedback. If you've consistently shown that you have this person's best interests at heart, then you've laid the groundwork for that person to be receptive to your constructive criticism. On the other hand, if you don't have much of a relationship at all, or worse, have a negative one, your feedback is not likely to be accepted. It is too easy at that point for the receiver to disregard it.

Radical candor is giving feedback in a way that both challenges directly and cares personally (upper right quadrant of the matrix). Your feedback is completely *candid* and gets to the root of an issue, its *radical* form. It goes hand in hand with deliberate practice because this type of feedback is exactly the type that should be given in a deliberate practice session: a specific account of what the person could be doing better at a particular skill they are trying to improve.

The other quadrants create suboptimal feedback patterns:

- *Ruinous empathy* (upper left quadrant)—when you care personally but don't challenge directly. This occurs when you aren't specific enough in your feedback.
- *Obnoxious aggression* (lower right quadrant)—when you challenge directly but don't care personally. This type of feedback is often brushed off because the lack of caring can make it seem insincere.
- *Manipulative insincerity* (lower left quadrant)—when you neither challenge directly nor care personally. This takes the form of vague criticism that isn't actionable enough to be useful and can be off-putting because of the lack of a strong foundational relationship.

When you engage in deliberate practice outside an organization, you and your coach can design practice sessions that are specially tuned to your goals and skill level. Think about the soccer practice where you can arrange the cones just so. Inside an organization, by contrast, constructing these ideal practice sessions is more challenging because you do not control the environment. For example, you might want to work on your presentation skills, but you may have only so many possibilities to do so given your position. Additionally, these real-world situations come with constraints and consequences. However, you can still try your best to find learning opportunities.

An excellent start would be declaring your intention to engage in deliberate practice for a particular skill set and recruiting a mentor who is willing to coach you regularly. Then you and your mentor can look out for situations where you can work on improving your skills without much consequence to the organization. For example, you can take a role where you practice your skills on a project that won't have a big impact on the company. Of course, you can also find additional practice opportunities in your time outside the organization.

How can the organization help you determine which projects are suitable for practicing your skills, or, as a mentor yourself, how can you help determine the same for your team members? Venture capitalist Keith Rabois developed a related mental model, called the **consequence-conviction matrix**, to do just that. As he explained in his lecture "How to Operate":

> You basically sort your own level of conviction about a decision on a grate, extremely high or extremely low. There are times when you know something is a mistake and there's times when you wouldn't really do it that way, but you have no idea whether it's the right or wrong answer. And then there is a consequence dimension. There are things that if you make the wrong decision are very catastrophic to your company and you will fail. There are things that are pretty low impact. At the end of the day they aren't really going to make a big difference, at least initially.
>
> Where there is low consequence and you have very low confidence in your own opinion, you should absolutely delegate. And delegate completely, let people make mistakes and learn. On the other side, obviously where the consequences are dramatic and you have extremely high conviction that you are right, you actually can't let your junior colleague make a mistake.

Conviction-Consequence Matrix

	High conviction	Low conviction
High consequence	Don't delegate	Delegate sometimes
Low consequence	Delegate sometimes	Delegate completely

The consequence-conviction matrix can help you free up your time as a leader, and also categorize situations into learning opportunities for your team members. You can even apply this matrix to family situations. For example, we try to have our kids attempt things that won't cause much harm if they fail, such as buying something at a store themselves or making their own lunch.

Tying it all together, activities in the high-conviction, low-consequence quadrant are perfect to help someone (or yourself) with deliberate practice. These are times when what should be done is known, so that coaching can happen effectively, and at the same time it won't be so consequential to the organization if the associated tasks initially fail. These situations are perfect deliberate practice exercises where the particular tasks that are on (or just outside) the edge of someone's ability are delegated, and then that person is given radically candid feedback about how to improve. That's a compelling method to help people grow quickly, including in new roles.

UNLOCKING POTENTIAL

Certain psychological mental models repeatedly arise when you are helping people unlock their potential. First, even if someone agrees to the idea of pursuing deliberate practice and receiving radically candid feedback, the process simply doesn't work very well if the person doesn't have the right mindset. Psychologist Carol Dweck developed the **fixed mindset versus growth mindset** model, which explains this wrong-versus-right frame of mind, popularized in her book *Mindset: The New Psychology of Success*.

A **fixed mindset** means you believe that your personal attributes and abilities are *fixed*, with no ability to grow or change. For example, you may believe that you are "just bad at math," and this lack of ability is "just part of who you are." Of course, if you believe that your abilities (or lack thereof) are fixed, then you are naturally going to resist feedback to improve them.

The opposite of the fixed mindset is the **growth mindset**, where you believe that you can grow and change over time. When you have a growth mindset, you are more open to critical feedback, since you believe that you can grow your abilities and recognize that receiving and acting on constructive criticism is a necessary part of the process.

You have to be careful about your mindset, especially with things you're already pretty good at. The reason is that when you're good at something (e.g., math), being good at that thing can become part of your identity ("I am a person who is good at math"). Yet effectively growing that skill, such as through deliberate practice, requires consistently getting out of your comfort zone and periodically failing. If you have a fixed mindset, this process is perceived as an attack on your identity ("How can I be a person who is good at math and keep failing at these math problems?").

As you start looking at whether people have a fixed or growth mindset, you will find that these concepts can apply selectively to certain characteristics (e.g., public speaking, athletics, etc.), though for certain people a fixed or growth mindset can be pervasive across most of their endeavors. What do you personally have a fixed or growth mindset about?

Originally, Dweck theorized that delivering educational instructions in school might encourage one mindset over another. For example, telling children they are smart encourages a fixed mindset because then students may take fewer educational risks in an effort to protect their "smartness." On the other hand, praising students for working hard encourages a growth mindset because then they want to put in more effort, including taking on new challenges.

Since Dweck's original studies in the 1970s, many others have been conducted. A recent meta-analysis in March 2018 in *Psychological Science* found that these types of "growth-mindset interventions" have a positive effect, though a modest one. However, there is an opportunity to replace these subtle interventions, like praising hard work instead of intelligence, with a much more direct approach, which is simply talking through this model explicitly with the person being coached. You will reap significant benefits if you can get someone to commit to having a growth mindset for a particular skill.

It is similarly important for you to believe in the growth potential of your team members, as your expectations may influence their performance. The **Pygmalion effect** is a model that states that higher expectations lead to increased performance, as people try to meet the expectations set for them. (It's named after the Greek myth of Pygmalion, a sculptor who crafted his ideal spouse, whom Aphrodite then gave life to as Galatea.) Conversely the **golem effect** is the phenomenon where lower expectations lead to lower performance. (That one's named after a clay creature in Jewish mythology that came to life, grew increasingly corrupt and violent, and eventually had to be destroyed.) Both are types of *self-fulfilling prophecies*.

As with fixed and growth mindsets, there is an ongoing debate on the strength of these effects across different circumstances. The original studies in classroom settings have also been criticized, but stronger effects have been shown in other settings, such as organizational leadership. For example, a meta-analysis in the October 2009 issue of *Leadership Quarterly* found the Pygmalion leadership style to be the most effective of the methods studied. This meta-analysis of two hundred different studies on leadership methods was sponsored by the U.S. Department of Defense and compared Pygmalion leadership interventions with traditional methods (popular ideas from the 1970s and earlier) as well as newer techniques described variously as charismatic, inspirational, transformational, or visionary methods. Setting high expectations came out on top.

If you set high expectations for your kids or colleagues, that alone will likely not be enough to propel them to reach their full potential. But setting low expectations or lacking expectations altogether will likely create a significant barrier for them and prevent them from reaching their full potential. Again, being explicit can help: if people understand what they are shooting for, they can *rise to the occasion*.

However, setting high expectations for people and repeatedly putting them into challenging situations can be exhausting or unsettling for them. You may have experienced these feelings yourself. Effective leaders need to be sensitive to this reality and put support systems in place to help people overcome the psychological barriers that can arise.

There are several psychological models to look out for in these settings. First is **impostor syndrome**, in which someone is plagued with the feeling that they are an *impostor*, fearing being exposed as a fraud, even though in reality they are not. Surveys indicate that 70 percent of people become inflicted with impostor syndrome at some point in their careers. Have you?

When people fall victim to impostor syndrome, they dismiss their successes as luck or deception and focus on their failures or fear of failure. This constant focus on failure can

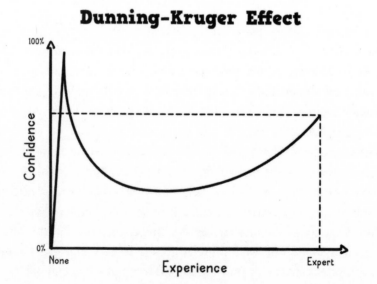

Dunning-Kruger Effect

lead to high stress and anxiety, and negative behaviors like overexertion, perfectionism, aggression, or defeatism.

You can take the following steps to help people overcome impostor syndrome:

- Highlight its prevalence ("Everyone's felt this way before; *I've* felt this way before").
- Explain that small failures are expected when you are operating out of your comfort zone. This explanation can help people recharacterize mistakes as learning opportunities.
- Connect them with other peers or mentors who have faced impostor syndrome.

A second model to consider is the **Dunning-Kruger effect**, named after social psychologists David Dunning and Justin Kruger. This model describes the confidence people experience over time as they move from being a novice to being an expert.

You usually make a lot of progress when you start out learning something, because there is so much new to learn. For example, you can learn to juggle three tennis balls relatively quickly. This quick progress up the *learning curve* propels you to have high confidence in your abilities. However, you may trick yourself into thinking that this must be a really easy skill, when in reality you are not yet fully grasping everything you don't know about the skill and how you could be better.

Your confidence plummets and, as you learn more, you start to realize everything you don't know, and see how much effort it will take to truly become an expert at the skill. For juggling, trying to juggle more than three balls or switching to different objects quickly drives this point home. Then your confidence gradually builds back up as you put in that effort and gain meaningful experience.

As a coach, you should keep in mind the Dunning-Kruger effect and be aware of where your team members are along the curve. When you are working with people who have less expertise, help them properly recognize their level of abilities so they don't become overconfident, but at the same time praise their learning progression so they don't become discouraged. It's a balancing act. As they get closer to the middle of the curve, they will need more and more encouragement as their confidence plummets. And don't forget to also keep the model in mind when you are learning a skill yourself.

While the Dunning-Kruger effect explains what happens psychologically across the whole learning curve, it is often used to refer to just the first spike, i.e., the phenomenon where low-ability people think they are high-ability, unable to recognize their own skill level (or lack thereof) in a particular area. This is really the opposite of impostor syndrome: instead of thinking they are much worse than they are, they think they are much better than they are.

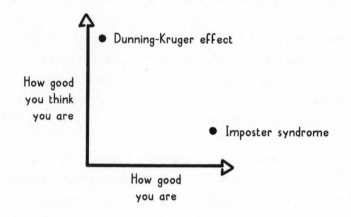

A third mental model about psychological barriers was proposed by psychologist Abraham Maslow (of Maslow's hammer fame) in his 1943 paper "A Theory of Human Motivation," and is now known as **Maslow's hierarchy of needs**. Maslow says that to reach your full potential (a state he calls "self-actualization"), you first need to satisfy basic psychological and material needs: physical (food, water, etc.), safety (shelter, freedom from fear, etc.), love (relationships, support, etc.), and self-esteem. He represents these categories of needs as a hierarchy, with self-actualization at the top.

Maslow's Hierarchy of Needs

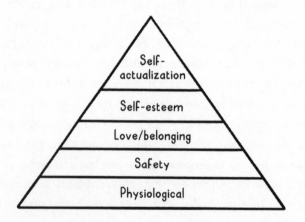

Maslow suggests that you can focus on self-actualization (the top layer) only once all of the more basic needs are met (bottom layers). Through the lens of this model, impostor syndrome reflects an unmet need in the esteem part of the hierarchy, since you feel somehow undeserving of success. Thus, it is preventing your growth into ultimate success at the top layer.

A couple of other examples: If you're in the middle of a tumultuous personal relationship (like breaking up), then the middle-layer needs (love/belonging) may be unmet. Or children who live with food insecurity or in a violent environment may have trouble learning due to their safety-layer needs being unmet.

Critics have raised questions about whether Maslow's hierarchy differs across cultures or circumstances, or even if there is an actual hierarchy at all. Nevertheless, thinking about this model can help you identify why you or others are not reaching full potential.

Finally, let's suppose you're coaching someone and together you have been able to work through all their psychological barriers. You are helping them engage in deliberate practice. You are actively providing actionable feedback on a regular basis. When you are helping them analyze past situations to give such feedback, you still need to consider another psychological phenomenon: that sometimes your memories of the past, even the very recent past, can be biased or distorted.

We covered some of these biases way back in Chapter 1 with *availability bias* and the like. One other mental model to consider is **hindsight bias**, where, after an event occurs, in *hindsight*, there is a *bias* to see it as having been predictable even though there was no real objective basis on which it could have been predicted. *Monday morning quarterbacking* and *hindsight is twenty-twenty* are formulations of the same concept.

Turn on the TV after any major event to see hindsight bias in action. Talking heads will explain why something occurred, and yet, if you had watched coverage before the event, you would not have found many predicting it ahead of time. Think of the 2007/2008 financial crisis or the U.S. 2016 election cycles.

Hindsight bias arises in many other situations: judges weighing evidence in court cases, historians analyzing past events, and physicians assessing earlier clinical decisions. For example, in negligence cases, for guilt to be found, it must be shown that the person who committed the negligent act would have known that their actions would endanger others. When experimental subjects are presented with various negligence scenarios, they typically rate an outcome as more foreseeable the worse the outcome is, even when the negligent act is the same. In other words, the worse the outcome, the worse the hindsight bias.

In the context of leadership and learning new roles, hindsight bias can keep you from learning from past events. If you believe an event was predictable when it was not, you may take away that you made the wrong choices leading up to the event, when in reality you may have made the right choice given the information available at the time.

For example, if you make an investment in a new technology or even personally in a stock or startup company, and it doesn't work out, it doesn't mean it wasn't a good bet at the time. The odds may have been in your favor, but the luck of the draw simply didn't go your way. The questions to ask are how accurate your risk assessment was at the time, and whether it could have been any more accurate given the time and resources available. Answering these questions moves you away from black-and-white thinking (the event was totally predictable or not) and into more nuanced thinking (considering how predictable it really was).

Counterfactual thinking (see Chapter 6) can reduce hindsight bias because it forces you to consider other ways events could have unfolded. Ask yourself how things would have changed if you had done X, Y, or Z instead. Another related model is *survivorship bias* (see Chapter 5), which, as applied here, tells you that when looking to see what past failures had in common, you should consider that past successes might have also had these things in common. For instance, when analyzing past investment decisions, you need to look at how your decision-making criteria applied to the winners and the losers as a whole, and not just to one of those subgroups, or else you may take away the wrong message.

Another way to counteract hindsight bias is to take notes as events occur in real time. That way you have a more objective record of what happened and are not relying solely on potentially compromised recollections. Of course, literal recordings are the most objective record and are increasing in popularity. Some organizations record some meetings or produce structured notes, journalists record interviews with sources, and police are increasingly using body cams to document encounters.

It is important to realize, though, that hindsight bias can affect you only in instances where the outcome could not be foreseen. Hindsight bias is not a factor when you are reviewing the many instances of predictable errors out there. The key is distinguishing between the two situations. *Self-serving bias* (see Chapter 1) suggests that you will be more inclined to say that your own or your group's mistakes could not have been predicted ("Who could have known?") and you are more likely to apply hindsight bias to be critical of others.

The mental models from this section can help correct psychological mischaracterizations (e.g., impostor syndrome), artificial roadblocks (e.g., fixed mindset), and misinformation (e.g., hindsight bias), all in the service of helping people, including yourself, think objectively about current performance and ways to improve.

TOGETHER WE THRIVE

So far in this chapter, we've covered the mental models that help people reach their full potential and thrive as members of 10x teams. There is another set of mental models, however, that can dramatically increase (or decrease) the likelihood of creating these special teams—those related to the makeup of organizational **culture**.

Every group of people has a culture. Often described on an ethnic, national, or regional level, culture as a concept also applies to smaller groups: organizations, immediate family units, extended families, groups of friends, and offline and online communities built around common interests. Culture describes the common beliefs, behavioral patterns, and social norms of group members. For example, different families have different norms for resolving disputes: some talk openly about emotions, some hardly ever; some have heated discussions, some much less so. What is the norm in your family?

Similarly, two highly functioning organizations can have widely different norms and processes for information control (open versus need-to-know), communication delivery (spoken versus written), how new ideas get proposed (ad hoc versus formal), punctuality (always on time versus flexible), and many other dimensions.

In any group setting, it is important to understand the culture, including whether it is one that prefers **high-context** or **low-context** communication. A low-context culture is

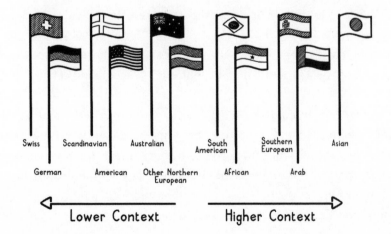

High-Context/Low-Context Continuum

Swiss   Scandinavian   Australian   South American   Southern European   Asian

German   American   Other Northern European   African   Arab

← Lower Context   Higher Context →

explicit and direct with information, preferring that you *be real* and *tell it like it is*. You need a *low* amount of *context* to understand low-context communication, because most everything you need to know is clearly expressed.

At the other extreme, in a high-context culture, information is conveyed much more indirectly, less confrontationally. For example, how things are going in a project or role is communicated less explicitly. You need a *high* amount of additional *context* to fully understand such high-context communication, appreciating the nuances of nonverbal cues, voice intonation, and adherence (or lack thereof) to usual processes as clues. In other words, what isn't said is just as important as what is said, if not more so. This high-context/low-context continuum applies to all cultures, from small-group ones all the way up to the cultures of whole countries.

As with personality traits, there are many dimensions that sociologists use to describe culture. Some other commonly cited dimensions besides low context versus high context include the following:

- Tight (many norms and little tolerance for deviation from those norms) versus loose: In a loose organizational culture, you might see people doing the same thing (like organizing a project) in many different ways, whereas tight cultures develop stricter rules and procedures.
- Hierarchical (lines of power are clear) versus egalitarian (more shared power): You will see more consensus and group decision making in an organization with a more egalitarian culture.
- Collectivist (group success is more important than individual success) versus individualist: Performance-ranking systems like stacked ranking (where managers are forced to rank their direct reports) occur in individualist organizational cultures.
- Objective (favoring empirical evidence) versus subjective: Organizational cultures that are more data-driven fall on the objective side of this spectrum.

In any case, when you recruit new members to your organization, it may take significant time for them to adapt to its culture. For example, someone who is used to extremely low-context environments will expect you to be very direct, whereas someone used to extremely high-context environments may be offended by your directness, and such low-context communication could potentially hurt their morale.

While new hires can grow accustomed to a new culture, they may be resistant initially.

So the more up-front you are about the culture of the organization, the better. In fact, being explicit about your cultural norms is one of the most *high-leverage activities* you can do as an organizational leader (see Chapter 3). It can help prospective team members figure out whether your organization is a good fit for them. Strengthening cultural norms also helps existing team members work together more efficiently.

It's sometimes said, "Culture is what happens when managers aren't in the room." It's what people do when they're *left to their own devices*. And that's exactly why it is so high-leverage to develop and reinforce culture: You can't look over people's shoulders all the time. It takes time and energy that is usually best spent elsewhere. If your team makes progress in the way you want only when you're scrutinizing them, then they won't get very far in the direction you desire.

Additionally, if you don't shape your organization's culture, it will shape itself, and may develop in ways you don't want. Some organizations, such as Uber, were at one time infamous for having a *toxic culture*. Characteristics of a toxic culture include preoccupation with status, territorialism, aggression, poor communication, fear of speaking up, unethical behavior, harassment, and general unhappiness.

Fortunately, there are many straightforward ways to positively shape culture:

- Establishing a strong vision—"Our *north star,* our vision for the future, is X" (see Chapter 3).
- Defining a clear set of values—where your organization sits along the various cultural dimensions, e.g., "Our organization values taking calculated risks, even if they fail."
- Reinforcing that vision and those values through frequent communications—including at all-hands meetings and through team-wide broadcasts.
- Creating processes that align with that vision and those values—such as how you decide on hiring new team members.
- Leading by example—making sure leaders adhere to the norms and values you want everyone else to adhere to.
- Establishing traditions—gatherings that celebrate stated values, such as holiday celebrations, group volunteer events, or recurring award ceremonies.
- Fostering accountability—e.g., reviewing previous experiences for lessons learned in *post-mortems* (see Chapter 1) or giving honest feedback on performance reviews.
- Rewarding people for exhibiting exemplary cultural behaviors—giving them promotions, awards, etc.

Taken together, these techniques clearly express cultural norms to everyone in the organization and show that they are taken seriously. They also convey that a person who aligns with the organization's vision, values, and related cultural norms and processes is more likely to excel within the organization.

Winning hearts and minds is a related mental model. It was first introduced in 1895 in a military context by French general Hubert Lyautey as part of a strategy to counter the Black Flags rebellion along the Indochina–Chinese border. It is a recognition that making direct appeals to people's *hearts* and *minds* through communication can effectively *win* them over.

In relatively recent history, the U.S. has led *hearts-and-minds campaigns* that directly explain its perspective to the populations of foreign countries like Vietnam and Iraq. In a business context, the concept has been successful when upstarts like Airbnb have made direct appeals to citizens to contact their representatives and lobby against regulations that would negatively impact consumer (and business) interests.

Establishing and communicating a shared vision, values, and cultural norms helps organizations win the hearts and minds of its members, and thus intrinsically motivates them to reach their full potential. Otherwise, motivation tends toward the extrinsic, such as compensation and title.

Venture capitalist Fred Wilson uses the idea of **loyalists versus mercenaries** to explain the way members view an organization. According to a June 23, 2015, blog post, he believes *loyalists* are devoted to an organization even in the face of adversity. *Mercenaries*, by contrast, are in it primarily for the money, and are much more likely to leave for greater rewards elsewhere. Wilson explains some factors that draw more loyalists:

1. Leadership. At the end of the day, people are loyal to a leader they believe in. . . .
2. Mission. People are loyal to a mission. I've seen super talented people walk away from compensation packages 2–3x what they currently make because they believe in what they are working on and think it will make a difference in their lives and the lives of others.
3. Values and Culture. . . . People want to work in a place that feels right to them. They need to feel comfortable at work. In the way that a welcoming home with comfortable furniture is pleasant to be in, a company with good values and culture is pleasant to work in.
4. Location. . . . In the Bay Area and NYC, your employees are constantly getting hammered to leave for more cash, more equity, more upside, more responsi-

bility, and eventually it leads to them becoming mercenaries. . . . If you are building your company in Ljubljana, Waterloo, Des Moines, Pittsburgh, Detroit, or Indianapolis, you have a way better chance of building a company full of loyalists than if you are building it in the Bay Area or NYC.

As Wilson notes, culture is one of the key ways to attract and retain loyalists, which should be the goal if you're seeking 10x teams for the long term. When working to craft a positive organizational culture, there are a few tactical models to keep in mind as well.

First, you can show employees that you value their contributions by understanding that people in different positions need different kinds of support to make progress on challenging efforts. Consider what startup investor Paul Graham, in a July 2009 blog post, called the **manager's schedule versus maker's schedule**:

> The manager's schedule is for bosses. It's embodied in the traditional appointment book, with each day cut into one-hour intervals. You can block off several hours for a single task if you need to, but by default you change what you're doing every hour. . . .
>
> But there's another way of using time that's common among people who make things, such as programmers and writers. They generally prefer to use time in units of half a day at least. You can't write or program well in units of an hour. That's barely enough time to get started.
>
> When you're operating on the maker's schedule, meetings are a disaster. A single meeting can blow a whole afternoon, by breaking it into two pieces each too small to do anything hard in. Plus you have to remember to go to the meeting. That's no problem for someone on the manager's schedule. There's always

something coming on the next hour; the only question is what. But when someone on the maker's schedule has a meeting, they have to think about it.

When you work with people who could benefit from a maker's schedule, you must work to create a culture that allows them these long uninterrupted blocks of time. To do so, you need to ensure that people on the manager's schedule are not consistently interrupting the flow of people on the maker's schedule. Gabriel's company (DuckDuckGo) has a policy of no standing meetings on Wednesdays and Thursdays, which facilitates schedules that incorporate *deep-work* blocks (see Chapter 3). Another approach is to allow people to work in environments more conducive to deep work, such as away from the central office, where they will get fewer interruptions from colleagues.

Next, you must be wary of culture eroding as your organization grows. Consider **Dunbar's number**—150—which is the maximum group size at which a stable, cohesive social group can be maintained. (It's named after anthropologist Robin Dunbar.) The idea behind Dunbar's number is that at about 150 group members and below, you can relatively easily know everyone in the group and their roles within it. Above this number, however, you cannot easily remember everyone and what they do.

Organizational processes that worked before Dunbar's number is reached all of a sudden seem to break down when it is exceeded, and new ones need to be constructed for the organization to be similarly effective again. A group of more than 150 people needs more explicit structures.

This concept of the stability of group dynamics being dependent on the size of the group extends to smaller groups as well. Two other well-known breakpoints are when the size of a small organization or team reaches about ten to fifteen people and when it further expands to between thirty and fifty.

When your group consists of only a few people, such as an immediate family unit or a tiny company, everyone can be involved in most major decisions and understand everything relevant to the group. At ten to fifteen people, though, this simple system breaks down, and you need some more organizational structure (subgroups, discrete projects, etc.), or chaos ensues. At thirty to fifty people, the same thing happens again—you need to create even more structure (teams, formal management, etc.) to avoid another round of disruption. And when you get to 150, Dunbar's number, you start to need more traditional corporate structure (strict policies and procedures, processes to interact with other departments, etc.).

If you are a leader in a growing organization or team, you need to plan for periods of adjustment when you cross these thresholds. You should also be wary of growing your organization too fast. If you have too many new people—who by definition aren't ingrained in your culture—come in at once, then that culture you've worked so hard to craft can quickly become diluted and much less effective. Anecdotally, this type of hyper-growth scenario risks significant trouble if an organization grows its team more than 50 percent in one year.

Another model to keep in mind that can quickly erode culture and morale is **the mythical man-month**. It comes from computer scientist Fred Brooks, who originally presented it in a book with the same name. *Man-month*, or person-month, is a unit of measurement for how long projects take (e.g., this project will take ten person-months). Brooks declares that this entire way of measurement is flawed, based on a *myth* that you can simply add more people (person-months) to a project and get it done faster.

A silly though memorable example is gestating a baby, which takes about nine months no matter how many people you try to add! The same is true for more mundane projects, especially the later it is in the project life cycle.

If you bring someone in to a project late, you need to *get them up to speed*, and usually this onboarding actually slows down the project timeline. Often it is just faster for the existing people to complete the project. However, you run the risk of burning out the team, especially if you have a strict deadline. But if you extend the deadline and do bring people in, you risk demoralizing the team that way as well, since you had to *bring in reinforcements*. Better planning can prevent you from ending up in this no-win situation.

A final tactical model to keep in mind when building positive culture is another military one: **boots on the ground**. It refers to actual troops on the *ground* in a military conflict, who are wearing *boots* as part of their uniforms. It is often referenced in the context of making the point that you need boots on the ground to be successful in a military campaign, and that conducting a war just from afar—for example, using only air power—will not achieve the ultimate goals.

A military case is also often made that to really win hearts and minds, you need boots on the ground to interact with the population and humanize the outside intervention. That is, you cannot just broadcast and enforce your message from afar. This concept has taken hold within the U.S. through community policing, where police spend time in the community building ties and therefore trust with the population they are policing.

The same is true in an organizational setting when you want people to buy in to your organization's vision and culture. You can't just define the culture from afar and hope that it will take hold. Instead, leaders must lead by example and put their own boots on the ground. This is way more effective than leaders who are always set apart, seen as sitting *in their ivory tower*. There are several common phrases that showcase the desired behavior: *rolling up your sleeves*, getting *in the trenches*, showing that you are *one of us*.

As a leader, your job of winning hearts and minds and setting your teams up for success is never done. You must continually reinforce vision and values, doing your best to evolve culture in a more optimal direction, setting up the conditions for those around you to grow. If you can do that well, then the culture you create will help set up your organization to be one that supports and cultivates 10x teams.

KEY TAKEAWAYS

- People are not interchangeable. They come from a variety of backgrounds and with a varied set of personalities, strengths, and goals. To be the best manager, you must **manage to the person**, accounting for each individual's unique set of characteristics and current challenges.

- Craft unique roles that amplify each individual's strengths and motivations. Avoid the **Peter principle** by promoting people only to roles in which they can succeed.

- Properly delineate roles and responsibilities using the model of **DRI (directly responsible individual)**.

- People need coaching to reach their full potential, especially at new roles. **Deliberate practice** is the most effective way to help people scale new learning curves. Use the **consequence-conviction matrix** to look for learning opportunities, and use **radical candor** within **one-on-ones** to deliver constructive feedback.

- When trying new things, watch out for common psychological failure modes like **impostor syndrome** and the **Dunning-Kruger effect**.

- Actively define group **culture** and consistently engage in **winning hearts and minds** toward your desired culture and associated vision.

- If you can set people up for success in the right roles and well-defined culture, then you can create the environment for **10x teams** to emerge.

Flex Your Market Power

IN 2016, HATCHIMALS WERE the hottest toy of the Christmas season. They are cute little electronic bird toys that you can take care of, kind of like a modern Furby. Supply was short, and people went to great lengths to get their hands on them. As RetailMeNot reported on December 6, 2016:

> Last Sunday, Toys "R" Us stocked its shelves with Hatchimals, and shoppers lined up overnight to get their hands on the toys. Toys "R" Us handed out tickets to those in line, and reports revealed that some people turned right around to sell those tickets for over $100 to others in line. Long story short, you should likely expect to have to camp out for these toys, especially if Target decides to implement a ticket system. You don't want to (literally) be left out in the cold.

While Hatchimals retailed for about $60 at the time, they were selling for as much as $1,200 on eBay. As you can see, people will pay very inflated prices when the supply available for a product is low relative to its demand.

With that type of profit opportunity, enterprising individuals perennially buy Christmas-season toys from retail stores so that they can resell them at higher prices on secondary markets (like ticket scalpers do for desirable concert tickets). When you take advantage of price differences for the same product in two different settings, it's called **arbitrage**.

Completely out of diapers and facing a
seven-hour layover, Marsha happens upon
a diaper scalper.

Back in the nineties, when eBay launched, it created numerous arbitrage opportunities by connecting newly minted salespersons to customers anywhere in the world. In college, Lauren found eBay to be a great source for making spare cash by pairing small-town anime lovers, who didn't have anime shops in their own towns, with products she bought at a local anime shop near MIT.

Sometimes she would even find arbitrage opportunities within eBay itself. She found she could make a profit by relisting items in a better category or by using better keywords so that more people would find the listing. For example, she once found a designer wedding gown on sale for fifty dollars in the dress-up and costume section but thought she could resell it for hundreds of dollars if she listed it in the pre-owned wedding dress section. She was right—it went for more than two hundred dollars!

Price differences like these tend to not last very long, because others notice and pursue the same discrepancies until they no longer exist. It can certainly be profitable to take advantage of these short-term opportunities, but you need to keep finding new ones to continue turning a profit.

In this chapter we explore the opposite of arbitrage: **sustainable competitive advantage**. This mental model describes a set of factors that give you an *advantage* over the *competition* that you can *sustain* over the long term. A working *flywheel* (see Chapter 4) can drive such advantage—think of what Amazon has on its competition with regard to shipping because of its size and investments in warehousing and delivery.

The signature of sustainable competitive advantage is what economists call **market power**, the *power* to profitably raise prices in a *market*. For instance, when Amazon has raised its Prime price, it hasn't lost many customers. An extreme showing of market power is a *monopoly*. Monopolies have vast market power because they have little competition.

As an example, consider the EpiPen, a medical device needed by people with severe allergies to treat potentially fatal allergic reactions. In 2016, Mylan, the company behind this well-known brand, controlled more than 90 percent of the market for these types of devices. From 2007, when it bought the brand from Merck, through 2016, its market share hadn't decreased despite having raised the price for the device by more than 500 percent. This price increase is an incredible showing of market power, aided by the recall of a competitor's device and the U.S. Food and Drug Administration's rejection of another one during this time frame.

If a monopoly raises its prices, you can either pay the higher price or forgo its product, which in many cases (such as for needed life-saving devices) is not an attractive option. The other extreme is *perfect competition*, markets where many competitors provide the exact same product, perfect substitutes (also known as *commodities*). A thirty-two-ounce bottle of isopropyl alcohol is thirty-two ounces of isopropyl alcohol no matter whom you buy it from. If a commodity supplier raises prices, you just buy from another supplier at the lower price. Consequently, these commodity providers have no market power.

Market power also applies to you personally in the labor market. If you are just starting out in an industry and have only basic, undifferentiated skills, *you* can be a commodity. That means you have no advantage over other potential employees for the same job. From the employer's perspective, you are interchangeable with other applicants for the position. In this situation, you have no ability to negotiate compensation and must accept the market rate for your services.

However, this situation doesn't necessarily mean you get paid minimum wage. As with the Hatchimals, market price, in this case compensation, is a function of *supply and demand*. Plenty of people right out of school can make good money because the demand is high for their services. For example, there are many newly minted nurses each year, but nurses are in high demand right now (at least in the U.S.), so new graduates can find work at attractive starting salaries. On the other hand, even though the number of new graduates with PhDs in history is relatively small, there are even fewer tenure-track teaching positions available for them, and consequently it is very difficult even to secure one of these jobs.

When you are undifferentiated—with no sustainable competitive advantage and therefore no market power—you are completely subject to the supply-and-demand forces in the market, and the price they deliver to you. That speaks to picking an industry in high demand for the long term, such as nursing. It also speaks to the need to differentiate yourself from your peers by developing a unique set of skills that the market values. Then you have the opportunity to demand higher compensation by demonstrating the distinctive value you bring to your employers or clients. For example, in nursing, such differentiation could be achieved by a combination of experience and continuing education in a nursing specialty like critical care, anesthesiology, or pain management.

Of course, if there is no demand for your special set of skills, then there is no oppor-

tunity for you to flex market power. For example, many Olympic athletes need day jobs because there just isn't enough market demand for their sport. They cannot support themselves on their extraordinary skills alone.

Having market power—individually or organizationally—is an attractive position because you can use your advantages to sustain profit for a long time. That's why it is called *sustainable* competitive advantage.

Nothing lasts forever, though. New technologies arise that disrupt the old. Monopolies fall. Patents expire. Regulations evolve. New job skills crop up, supplanting the way things were done before. In Chapter 4, we examined how to watch out for, anticipate, and even engender such change. In this chapter, we examine super models to help you find and hang on to market power.

SECRET SAUCE

Major life, career, and organizational choices can be thought of as bets on the future. You can be either right or wrong in those bets. If wrong, you won't achieve the success you wanted; if right, you will. However, to achieve a really high degree of success, you need something extra: to be contrarian in your bet. In "Demystifying Venture Capital Economics, Part 1," venture capitalist Andy Rachleff summarized this concept, originally formulated by investor Howard Marks, with the **consensus-contrarian matrix**:

> The investment business can be explained with a two-by-two matrix. On one dimension you can be either right or wrong. On the other you can be consensus or [contrarian]. Obviously you don't make money if you're wrong. . . . The only way to generate outstanding returns is to be right and [contrarian].

Consensus-Contrarian Matrix

	Wrong	Right
Consensus	No return	Regular-sized returns
Contrarian	No return	Outsized returns

Rachleff elaborates:

> Being willing to intelligently take this leap of faith is one of the main differ-
> ences between the venture firms who consistently generate high returns—and
> everyone else. Unfortunately, human nature is not comfortable taking risk;
> so, most venture capital firms want high returns without risk, which doesn't
> exist. As a result they often sit on the sideline while other people make the big
> money from things that most people initially think are crazy. The vast majority
> of my colleagues in the venture capital business thought we were crazy at Bench-
> mark to have backed eBay. "Beanie babies . . . really? How can that be a
> business?"

Consider the analogy of horse racing. If everyone bets on the same winning horse, no one gets a big payout. If you make the same choice as everyone else, a consensus bet, then there isn't much ability for you to individually stand out, and so you can at most get a modest success. Venture capitalist Bill Gurley put it this way: "Being 'right' doesn't lead to superior performance if the consensus forecast is also right."

But if you like a horse at fifty-to-one and she wins, then you have achieved a remark-able success. It is the difference between coming up with the next hot idea and being the fifth self-serve frozen yogurt franchise in your town. As Charlie Munger said in *Poor Char-lie's Almanack*, "Mimicking the herd invites regression to the mean" (see Chapter 5). His investing partner Warren Buffett puts it this way in *Warren Buffet Speaks*: "Most people get interested in stocks when everyone else is. The time to get interested is when no one else is. You can't buy what is popular and do well."

In horse betting, the *crowdsourced* odds (see Chapter 6) reflect how many people agree with your bet. As a result, you get the highest returns when you bet on a horse that hardly anyone else is betting on. However, there is likely a good reason that no one is betting on that horse. As Jeff Bezos said at *Vanity Fair*'s New Establishment Summit on October 20, 2016, "You just have to remember that contrarians are usually wrong."

A contrarian bet is therefore most likely to be successful when you know something that almost everyone else doesn't. In other words, you know that the chance of being right is much greater than the crowd realizes, such as when you know a particular bet has a 10 percent chance of success, but the crowd thinks it's 1 percent.

"This really is an innovative approach, but I'm afraid
we can't consider it. It's never been done before."

Jeff Bezos again, in a 1997 letter to shareholders:

> Given a ten percent chance of a 100 times payoff, you should take that bet every time. But you're still going to be wrong nine times out of ten. We all know that if you swing for the fences, you're going to strike out a lot, but you're also going to hit some home runs.

Knowing something that is important yet mostly unknown or not yet widely believed is what investor Peter Thiel calls a **secret**. This has the same meaning as its colloquial use, just applied to innovation. As Thiel wrote in his 2014 book, *Zero to One*:

> Great companies can be built on open but unsuspected secrets about how the world works. Consider the Silicon Valley startups that have harnessed the spare capacity that is all around us but often ignored. Before Airbnb, travelers had little choice but to pay high prices for a hotel room, and property owners couldn't easily and reliably rent out their unoccupied space. Airbnb saw untapped supply and unaddressed demand where others saw nothing at all. The same is true of private car services Lyft and Uber. Few people imagined that it was possible to build a billion-dollar business by simply connecting people who want to go places with people willing to drive them there. We already had state-licensed taxicabs and private limousines; only by believing in and looking for secrets could you see beyond the convention to an opportunity hidden in plain sight.

A secret can be an idea that no one else has thought of, but it can also be an idea about how to achieve something that everyone else currently thinks is too risky. It is possible that an idea is not as risky as it seems, and by taking a *first-principles* approach you can come to a more correct risk assessment (see Chapter 1).

Many investors actually passed on Airbnb because both sides of an Airbnb transaction seemed so risky that they thought there wouldn't be a market for it. After all, an Airbnb transaction on one side calls for letting a stranger sleep in your home, and on the other side involves sleeping in a stranger's home. Of course, the investors who passed were wrong; plenty of people were happy to bear those risks once Airbnb set up a marketplace to do so.

The opposite can be true as well, in that people can substantially underestimate risks, such as in the 2007/2008 U.S. housing crisis, which led to a global financial crisis. The few people who correctly assessed this risk and bet on their secret knowledge made a lot of money, as depicted in the 2015 film *The Big Short*, based on a 2010 book of the same name by author Michael Lewis.

A secret can also be how to turn someone else's good idea into a great idea. Thomas Edison didn't invent the lightbulb, but his concerted efforts made it long-lasting and commercially viable. You could similarly have a chance for great success if you see a viable path for an idea that everyone else is missing.

Most currently central ideas in academic fields started out as secrets. You can find examples throughout this book, from the *paradigm shifts* of continental drift and germ theory in Chapter 1, to the statistics in Chapter 5 that we now take for granted, to all the influence models from Chapter 7, such as *reciprocity*.

Mental models themselves are somewhat secret. The central theme of this book is that certain models from different fields can be applied to help you solve problems in other areas. Common knowledge in one field can be a secret in another. In another book by Michael Lewis, *Moneyball*, he explains how the Oakland Athletics baseball team was one of the first to use statistics to identify undervalued players by focusing on previously underappreciated statistics like on-base and slugging percentage. As a result, they assembled a world-class team with much less money than their competition. Now most professional sports teams employ a squad of statisticians to look for such anomalies.

As Thiel says, many secrets are similarly hidden in plain sight. You just need to know where to look. Science fiction writer William Gibson put it like this: "The future is already here—it's just not very evenly distributed." By studying future-facing pockets of people and knowledge across different fields, you can get closer to secrets. Technologies that people use every day started their growth among small groups of innovators many years before they became commonplace.

For example, long before computers were everywhere, enthusiasts gathered into groups such as the Homebrew Computer Club in Silicon Valley, which included Steve Wozniak (cofounder of Apple) and Jerry Lawson (inventor of the video game cartridge) among its members. Academic advances and groundbreaking ideas in every area follow a similar pattern, starting with innovators and early adopters before moving into the mainstream (see the *technology adoption life cycle* in Chapter 4). Find the Homebrew Computer Club equivalent for whatever area you're interested in and you'll find active discussions of secrets.

Seeking out groups like these puts you in the know. You are then in the position to jump on an innovation bandwagon early and be among the groundbreakers in a new field or industry. However, if you aren't set on changing the world, secrets can also be used on a smaller scale. Knowing about new technologies can help you improve your day-to-day life, through such current innovations as virtual assistants, new delivery services, or telemedicine. For instance, knowing about new medical advances can help you make better medical decisions, and knowing about the latest car technologies can help you make a safer vehicle choice.

Just discovering a secret is not enough; your timing must also be right. Pushing on an idea too soon can result in a lot of wasted time and money, possibly leading you to miss out on the opportunity altogether. Unfortunately, new ideas and ways of doing things can face a lot of challenges that make this timing difficult to get right. A contrarian idea will almost inevitably face a fight against the *inertia* from the consensus idea (see Chapter 4). This inertia can be a barrier against both the spreading of the idea and the ability to raise capital to fund it. New ideas also often face technological barriers to mass adoption.

Uber's widespread adoption was possible only once everyone had a smartphone. YouTube became a mainstream possibility only once broadband access was prevalent. In both cases there were earlier attempts to accomplish similar things that failed because the timing wasn't right. The rest of the world wasn't yet sufficiently equipped with the necessary technology.

Apple famously introduced the Apple Newton tablet device in 1993 and discontinued it in 1998 after lackluster sales. More than a decade later, Apple introduced a new tablet device—the iPad—which had the fastest initial adoption rate of any mainstream electronic device up to that point, even ahead of the iPhone and the DVD player. What changed? For one thing, the internet: you could do so much more with the iPad relative to the Newton, given the previous twenty years of internet advances.

Similarly, in 1995, *Newsweek* published a now-infamous opinion piece by Cliff Stroll entitled "The Internet? Bah!" which basically said that the internet's potential impact was wildly overstated. Cliff Stroll was neither a Luddite nor a noob in the tech world. As stated in his piece, he was an early adopter, having been on the internet already for two decades, even famously catching a hacker. He just couldn't see that 1995 was the right time for mainstream internet adoption. While it wasn't yet the right time for a mainstream tablet like the Newton, enough people were coming online to enable sites like Amazon (founded in 1994) and eBay (founded in 1995) to become viable.

It is certainly fair and reasonable to question hype, especially because so many over-hyped ideas fizzle out before they take off. Additionally, some of the ideas best primed for takeoff aren't hyped much at all. Psychologist Robert Sternberg explained to *Psychology Today*: "Creative ideas usually get a weak reception, at least initially . . . but contrarians give their lives meaning by attempting to change the way things are to the way they think they should be."

William Brody, former president of Johns Hopkins University, told a story in a 2004 faculty newsletter about giving a presentation about digital radiography as a young faculty member in the late 1970s to a standing-room-only crowd at an international meeting. The promise of this new technology was the totally "filmless" radiology department, and he had some interesting results to share.

Next door, a new imaging technology was presented to only a handful of people, most of whom were collaborators or family of the presenter. While decades later the medical community was still waiting for filmless radiology departments, the other presenter, Sir Peter Mansfield, went on to win a Nobel Prize in 2003 for his contributions to the invention of magnetic resonance imaging (MRI) technology.

To address this timing question more systematically, ask yourself **why now?** This simple yet powerful mental model comes from venture capital firm Sequoia Capital, early investors in Apple, Oracle, PayPal, YouTube, Instagram, Yahoo!, WhatsApp, and many more business ideas that went on to become household names. For every rocket-ship startup, there is a good answer to this question underpinning it, usually based on some rapidly unfolding secret due to a confluence of recent advances and adoption of underlying technology.

The same concept applies for almost any change you want to make, from trying out a new organizational process to pursuing a new career. *Why now?* Would it make a difference if you waited longer? What would you be waiting for in particular? Given the array of things you can work on, is there another change you should be making right now?

You can also consider this question using *inverse thinking* (see Chapter 1). Instead of asking *why now?*, ask *now what?* When you see something change in the world around you, ask yourself what new opportunities might open up as a result. From the political sphere to the personal and organizational, many sweeping changes happen in the wake of a real or impending crisis.

Politician Rahm Emanuel offers this perspective: "You never want to let a serious crisis go to waste. And what I mean by that [is] it's an opportunity to do things you think you could not do before."

The *why now* model also explains why there are often concurrent academic discoveries across the world and similar startups independently emerging simultaneously. Wikipedia has a huge list of instances like these, and there is a name for the concept: **simultaneous invention**, or *multiple discovery*.

Modern calculus was independently formulated around the same time in the seventeenth century by Isaac Newton and Gottfried Leibniz. And as we mentioned in Chapter 4, Charles Darwin and Alfred Wallace jointly published the theory of *natural selection* after independent discovery. The underlying conditions were ripe for these ideas, and often more than one person will act on the same secret once they have determined the time is right to pursue the opportunity.

VISION WITHOUT EXECUTION IS JUST HALLUCINATION

Unfortunately, even knowing a secret at the right time still isn't enough to guarantee success. People with great, timely insights often fail to achieve great returns due to poor execution. In this section we will explore mental models that can improve your chances of successful execution. The title of this section is a modern take on an old Japanese proverb, "Vision without action is a daydream. Action without vision is a nightmare."

Successful, world-changing ideas almost always involve changing the behavior of a large group of people: how they live, work, entertain themselves, or even how they think. For example, as noted earlier, Airbnb has changed the way many people travel. Whether your idea is business-focused or not, you can think of the people whose behavior it seeks to change as your "customers."

In this context, your secret is the insight you have on how the behavior of your customers should be changed, e.g., people should be able to rent out rooms directly from one another. Your "product" is therefore how you specifically are using your secret to cause a behavioral change in your customers, e.g., creating a marketplace of rentable rooms over the internet.

Even if you are the first to market with the idea, you will still lose out to the competition if your product cannot create the necessary behavioral change. The first person or organization to try to capitalize on a secret can indeed have a **first-mover advantage**, crafting a competitive *advantage* derived from being the *first* to *move* into a market with a product. However, they can also experience a **first-mover disadvantage** if they make a lot of mistakes. Fast-followers can copy the first mover, learn from their mistakes, and then quickly surpass them, leaving the first mover ultimately *disadvantaged* even though they were first.

For a first mover, the difference between success and failure hinges on whether they can also be first to achieve **product/market fit**. That's when a *product* is a such a great *fit* for its *market* that customers are actively demanding more. This model was also developed by Andy Rachleff, who explained in "Demystifying Venture Capital Economics,

Part 3," "First to market seldom matters. Rather, first to product/market fit is almost always the long-term winner. . . . Once a company has achieved product/market fit, it is extremely difficult to dislodge it, even with a better or less expensive product."

A company without product/market fit finds it extremely hard to obtain customers; in contrast, a company with product/market fit finds it relatively easy to obtain customers. This concept can be widened to "fits" in a variety of situations: person/organization fit, member/group fit, culture/strategy fit, message/audience fit, etc.

As we explored in Chapter 8, a person in just the right role can produce amazing results, and an organizational strategy attuned perfectly to its culture can be a quick and resounding success. Similarly, a message can strike just the right tone for a specific audience such that it will deeply resonate. You see this phenomenon repeatedly in politics when certain candidates hit a nerve with a segment of the population, as Bernie Sanders and Donald Trump did in the U.S. 2016 presidential election cycle.

A model that captures these phenomena is **resonant frequency**. This model comes from physics and explains why glass can break if you play just the right note: Each object has a different *frequency* at which it naturally oscillates. When you play that frequency, such as the right tone for a wineglass, the energy of the wave causes the glass to vibrate more and more until it breaks.

When you achieve product/market fit, the effect is similar. When this happens, results are not just a little better, they're dramatically better. Product is flying off the shelves. That's what you're looking for with product/market fit or any other fit—signs of real *reso-*

Resonance

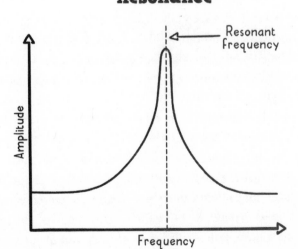

nance. In Chapter 8, we also discussed *10x teams.* True resonance is like that: not one or two times better, but many, many times better.

One way to increase your chances of getting to product/market fit is through **customer development**, a product *development* model established by entrepreneur Steve Blank that focuses you on taking a *customer*-centric view. Customer development's goal is to help you find a sustainable business model by applying the *scientific method* (see Chapter 4) through rapid experimentation with your customers. You set up a quick feedback loop with them to learn as much as you can about their needs, resulting in a repeatable process to acquire and retain them.

Way back in Chapter 1 we explained how you want to *de-risk* an idea by testing your assumptions as cheaply as possible. Customer development is one way to do that, by talking directly to customers or potential customers. As Blank says, "There are no facts inside the building so get the hell outside!" If you can ask the right questions, you can find out whether you have something people really want, signaling product/market fit.

Of course, you probably won't make something people really want on the first shot. That's why you build an *MVP* (again, see Chapter 1) and run experiments with customers to see how it is actually used (if at all), continually refining your product as you incorporate real-world feedback via this rapid experimentation process.

Customer development works in a wide variety of situations: Talk to residents before you move somewhere. Interview current employees before you take a job. Poll a community before enacting a new policy. For any idea you have, think about who the "customer" is and then go talk to them directly about your "product." Think focus groups, surveys, interviews, etc.

When you are trying to act on a secret by delivering a product or service, you are in a race against your competition for product/market fit. To give yourself the best chance of winning this race, you must engage in customer development the fastest. A model from the military can help: the **OODA loop**, which is a decision *loop* of four steps—**observe, orient, decide, act (OODA)**.

U.S. Air Force colonel John Boyd developed the OODA loop to assist fighter pilots in dogfights, where there isn't time for analysis between actions. Each pilot is trying to quickly outmaneuver the other, reacting to the other's moves and surrounding circumstances. Boyd showed repeatedly that the pilot who can adjust more quickly—who moves faster through the OODA loop—will usually win. They take an *observing* glance at the changing conditions, immediately re-*orient* their assessment of the situation, *decide* the next best course of action, *act* on it without hesitation, and then repeat this loop.

OODA Loop

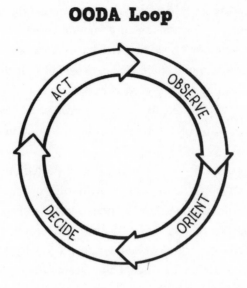

The faster you can make your OODA loop, the faster you can incorporate external information, and the faster you'll reach your destination, be that product/market fit or something else. The OODA loop applies best in situations where rapid learning will give you an advantage; not every situation is so uncertain and ever changing, though many are.

One area that is always changing and evolving is technology, making it a great example of an area where OODA loops are particularly effective. Increasingly, all major businesses, not just traditional "tech" companies, are trying to utilize technology to gain an edge on their competition. As a result, creating fast OODA loops is becoming more important over time. The organization with the fastest OODA loop learns faster than its competitors, consistently makes better decisions, and adapts faster to the unfolding technology landscape.

OODA loops may call *natural selection* to mind (see Chapter 4). Species that have faster life cycles evolve faster, so you might say they have a faster OODA loop. For example, some bacteria can create a new generation in fifteen minutes. This is a primary reason why it doesn't take long for bacteria to become resistant to the drugs designed to fight them. Similarly, having a faster OODA loop helps you adapt faster to changing circumstances, including reaching product/market fit before your competitors.

If, after extensive customer development, you still cannot find this promised land of product/market fit, then you must **pivot** to something different. A pivot is a change in course of strategic direction, and there are many famous examples. You may be surprised to know that Twitter started as a podcasting network or that Nintendo actually dates back to 1889, when it was founded as a playing-card manufacturer.

Over the course of Nintendo's history, it tried its hand at a variety of businesses with limited success (taxi service, motel chain, TV network, instant rice sales). After its stock price bottomed out in 1964 as playing-card sales dropped, it was saved by a pivot to the toy industry after a maintenance engineer, Gunpei Yokoi, invented the Ultra Hand toy. Yokoi thereafter took a leading role in transitioning Nintendo into a video game powerhouse.

Some pivots are less extreme. For example, PayPal started out as a way to beam payments physically between handheld devices before finding product/market fit with online payments. Similarly, Starbucks started out selling roasted whole coffee beans and equipment. In fact, Starbucks didn't sell its first latte until thirteen years after the company was founded. After a trip to Italy, employee and future CEO Howard Schultz persuaded the founders to test the coffeehouse concept after seeing the popularity of espresso bars in Milan. Schultz eventually bought the company from them and expanded Starbucks to what it is today.

Pivoting is usually difficult because it cuts against organizational inertia, involves openly admitting failure, and requires finding a better direction, all at the same time. But it can also be necessary. Pivoting is appropriate when your current strategy is not going to bring you the results you are seeking. Consulting advisers, who can more easily see your situation objectively, can help you determine whether a pivot is a good move. More broadly, pivoting can apply across all areas of life: your career path, a difficult relationship, how you're approaching meeting your child's educational needs, and so forth.

When considering a pivot, you can use a few mental models to help you decide what to do. Harvard Business School professor Clayton Christensen named and championed the model of **jobs to be done**, which asks you to figure out the real *job* that your product *does*, which can be different than what you might initially think. An oft-cited example by Christensen is a power drill: "Customers want to 'hire' a product to do a job, or, as legendary Harvard Business School marketing professor Theodore Levitt put it, 'People don't want to buy a quarter-inch drill. They want a quarter-inch hole!'"

Knowing the real job your product does helps you align both product development and marketing around that job. Apple does this exceptionally well. For instance, it introduced the iPod in 2001 amid a slew of MP3-player competitors but chose not to copy any of their marketing lingo, which was focused on technical jargon like gigabytes and codecs. Instead, Steve Jobs famously framed the iPod as "1,000 songs in your pocket," recognizing that the real job the product was solving was letting you carry your music collection with you.

In a December 8, 2016, podcast with *Harvard Business Review*, Christensen describes another illustrative example, this one about milkshakes served at a particular fast-food restaurant. You might assume that a milkshake's job is to be a special treat to cap off a meal. While it is true that many parents order shakes as an after-dinner family treat, this restaurant learned that almost half of their shake customers were using them for a different job—to make their long morning commutes more interesting. People felt their trips were more enjoyable as they sipped milkshakes while moving through traffic.

Doing two jobs at once sounds great, but that usually means at least one job isn't being done particularly well. In this case, parents didn't like how long it took their kids to drink the shakes. Yet that was one of the key features for the commuters.

The restaurant chain realized they needed two different products to do the two different jobs well. They decided to further improve the shake for the commuters by making it even thicker, adding more chunks, and moving the shake machine to the front of the stores for the fast on-the-go service that commuters wanted. They then needed to market a wholly different dessert product to kids and their parents.

When you truly understand what job people are really trying to get done by using your product, then you can focus your efforts on meeting that need. Asking customers what job they really want done can tell you the root of their problem and eliminate faulty assumptions on either side, ultimately resulting in a solution with a higher chance of success. In your analysis, you want to figure out what job your product is really currently doing and where it might be miscast, as in the milkshake example (see *5 Whys* in Chapter 1 for a tactical technique).

When you talk to customers, beware of their focus on a specific solution instead of on the problem they're trying to solve. For example, as a statistician, Lauren has often been asked to perform statistical analyses using a specific computational technique. However, the particular techniques suggested are often the wrong ones. That's because non-statisticians are usually unable to determine the best statistical plan on their own, and so instead they suggest a technique they know, regardless of whether it is appropriate (see *Maslow's hammer* in Chapter 6).

Telling a client or colleague that they are proposing to solve a problem in completely the wrong way can at times be difficult. Lauren recognizes, though, that using a particular technique is not really the job the client wants done. The client really wants a correct analysis, and will gladly accept that analysis from Lauren regardless of how she gets there.

To approach these situations, Lauren tries to get the client to *take a step back* and define their ultimate objective, using layman's terms.

Outside of business, you can ask yourself the same questions in the context of any personal connection ("What does this person really want out of this relationship?") or anywhere you are contributing ("What did they really hire me to do?"). From this perspective, you can determine whether you are really getting the job done with your current strategy. Is there a different approach that might do the job better? Understanding the answer to these questions will help you determine whether you need to make a pivot.

Another clarifying model is **what type of customer are you hunting?** This model was created by venture capitalist Christoph Janz, in a November 4, 2016, post on his *Angel VC* blog, to illustrate that you can build large businesses by *hunting* different size *customers*, from the really small (flies) to the really big (elephants).

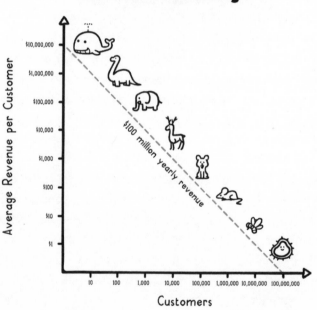

What Type of Customer Are You Hunting?

Janz notes that to get to $100 million in revenue, a business would need 10 million "flies" paying $10 per year, or 1,000 "elephants" paying $100,000 per year. Believe it or not, there are successful $100 million revenue businesses across the entire spectrum, from those seeking "amoebas" (at $1 per year) to those seeking "whales" (at $10 million per year).

More commonly, with any project, and certainly with a business, you want to define what success looks like and whether it is achievable under reasonable assumptions and time frames.

Janz's framing steers you toward a particular quantitative evaluation: How many "customers" will it take to achieve success? And what exactly do you need them to "pay" (or do)? Once you answer these questions, you can then ask whether there are enough of these types of customers out there. If not, you might consider pivoting toward bigger or smaller types of customers.

A key reason why this model matters is because how you interact with your customers depends on the type of customer you are hunting. If you need to reach ten million people, you can't do that by talking individually to each one. Additionally, it is challenging to get ten million people to pay a high "price" for a product. In contrast, you can deal individually with one thousand customers and get each of them to "pay" you more.

In the business context, hunting different customers means deciding to put out a free or minimally priced service to millions of people (like Spotify or Snap) versus selling a high-priced product to large enterprises (like Oracle or Salesforce). Or, within an industry, it's deciding between customer segments that choose to pay much different amounts, such as Rolls-Royce and Lamborghini versus Kia and Hyundai in the automobile sector.

In a political context, a candidate in a local election can try to meet all their constituents, but this type of outreach becomes impossible in larger elections. And in those larger elections, fundraising becomes increasingly important because of the need to turn to TV and the internet to reach everyone, which is relatively expensive. This political reality has the consequence that statewide and national politicians need to focus considerable attention on courting (hunting) deep-pocketed individuals (whales/dinosaurs/elephants) to foot the bill for this advertising.

A quantitative evaluation like this one is an example of a **back-of-the-envelope calculation**, a quick numerical assessment that you can *calculate* literally on the *back of an envelope*. A simple spreadsheet is the modern-day equivalent. This type of exercise forces you to quantify your assumptions and can quickly result in clarifying insights.

With *jobs to be done*, you are asking what stakeholders are "hiring" you for. With *what type of customer are you hunting?* you are asking how many "customers" you need to be hired by and what you want them to give you in exchange for your doing the job. Like customer development, both of these models ask you to think from the customer perspective. Thinking this way can also help you develop **personas**, fictional characters that *personify* your ideal customers, which will help you better reason through a realistic assessment of your idea.

What kind of people are your customers exactly—what are their demographics, likes versus dislikes, and hobbies? If you did customer development right, your personas should be modeled on characteristics of real people you've already met. Once constructed (say Bob and Sally are your personas), you can ask yourself: Would Bob and/or Sally do X?

Thinking in terms of actual people, fictional or otherwise, can really ground you in the customer perspective and help you apply these assessment models more effectively. However, be careful not to allow *availability bias* (see Chapter 1) to limit the factors you consider for creating these personas. The most easily collected or available data might not lead to the most useful personas.

Looking at the totality of these models, you should now know what success looks like (how many customers you need and what you need them to do) and whether you see a realistic path toward that goal. So, should you pivot?

If the answer is still unclear, one litmus test is this: Do you have any **bright spots**, positive signs in a sea of negative ones? In a business context, this would be a small subset of customers who really like what you're doing and are highly engaged with your product. Outside of business, you might look to the bright spots in your current job when considering the prospect of pivoting your career: What are the things you really like about your job? Are there enough of them to make you stay? What aspects would you like to retain if you do choose to pivot?

If you have no bright spots after some time, it is likely you do need to pivot. It's like the old phrase "You don't have to go home, but you can't stay here." If you do have some bright spots, you can try to figure out why things are working there and focus on growing out from that base. This is actually a useful strategy for advancing any idea, struggling or otherwise, drawing on the military concept of the **beachhead**. That's where a military offense takes and defends a *beach* so that more of their force can move through the beachhead onto the greater landmass.

In other words, a beachhead is getting a foothold and using it as a launching point. Amazon's beachhead was books. Tesla's was its Roadster. These were positions they could stake out in the market, and then use to expand into adjacent markets. For your career, your beachhead might be your current skills and position, which you could use to launch toward a better position or more fulfilling career.

A beachhead strategy is only one way to navigate the process of taking your secret and turning it into a product that achieves product/market fit. More broadly, this process can be compared to navigating a maze, what investor Balaji Srinivasan calls the **idea maze**. Imagine a physical maze, as in a corn maze at a fall festival or a hedge maze in a formal garden. The entrance is you starting out on your idea, and the exit is your idea's ultimate success. Within the maze are lots of dead ends, and it is your job to navigate the maze and successfully get to the other side. As he said in a lecture:

> A good founder is capable of anticipating which turns lead to treasure and which lead to certain death. A bad founder is just running to the entrance of (say) the "movies/music/filesharing/P2P" maze or the "photosharing" maze without any sense for the history of the industry, the players in the maze, the casualties of the past, and the technologies that are likely to move walls and change assumptions.

Josh Kopelman, another investor, equates founders who can successfully navigate the perils of finding product/market fit with **heat-seeking missiles**. As he wrote on his *Redeye VC* blog on August 2, 2010:

> It doesn't matter where the missile is aimed pre-launch. Successful entrepreneurs are constantly collecting data—and constantly looking for bigger and better targets, adjusting course if necessary. And when they find their target, they're able to lock onto it—regardless of how crowded the space becomes.

These metaphors can apply to navigating any path in life. Successfully navigating the idea maze means understanding how best to interact with the people in your life through understanding what you want and need from them and what they want and need from you. It's recognizing when you are on the wrong path in the maze, deciding when and how to pivot, and having the resilience to find a way to navigate obstacles put in your path.

ACTIVATE YOUR FORCE FIELD

Once you achieve product/market fit or whatever type of fit you are trying to achieve, it is time to protect your position. Warren Buffett popularized the term **moat**, making an analogy to the deep ditch of water surrounding a castle to describe how to shield yourself from the competition, thereby creating a sustainable competitive advantage.

Moats are situationally dependent. The following are some cases in which they are used (not mutually exclusive):

- Protected intellectual property (copyright, patents, trade secrets, etc.)
- Specialized skills or business processes that take a long time to develop (for example, Apple's vertically integrated products and supply chain, which meld design, hardware, and software)
- Exclusive access to relationships, data, or cheap materials
- A strong, trusted brand built over many years, which customers turn to reflexively
- Substantial control of a distribution channel
- A team of people uniquely qualified to solve a particular problem
- *Network effects* or other types of *flywheels* (as described in Chapter 4)
- A higher pace of innovation (e.g., a faster OODA loop)

Elon Musk notably sparred with Warren Buffett on the concept of moats. In Musk's words from a May 2, 2018, Tesla earnings call: "Moats are lame," and "If your only defense against invading armies is a moat, you will not last long." He was pointing out that, in his opinion, the most important sustainable competitive advantage is creating a culture that supports a higher pace of innovation, because that higher pace of innovation can overcome traditional moats.

In our opinion, though, a higher pace of innovation is really just another type of moat, and the metaphor of the moat shouldn't be taken too literally. Instead of a static moat, consider the sci-fi equivalent of a force field or a deflector shield, which allows you to move at warp speeds while still offering protection. You can both continue innovating (at warp speed) and also employ other types of moats (for increased defenses).

The Eastman Kodak Company is a great case study on how to build a moat. Founded in 1888, Kodak dominated the camera market for a hundred years. It arguably had significant moat protection in all the categories mentioned above, successfully fending off competitors and reaping outsized profits for a century:

- *Protected intellectual property:* It held many photography patents and trade secrets.
- *Specialized skills or business processes that take a long time to develop:* They had a vertically integrated supply chain serving all sides of the market, from cameras to film to printing.
- *Exclusive access to relationships, data, or cheap materials:* It had many exclusive business deals, and being the biggest in the industry, it could negotiate to secure supplies more cheaply than competitors.
- *A strong, trusted brand built over many years:* Everyone knew the name of Kodak and what it specialized in.
- *Substantial control of a distribution channel:* It had the prime shelf space at retail locked in.
- *A team of people uniquely qualified to solve a particular problem:* In Kodak Research Laboratories, it had the widest expertise in its technology areas and developed many advances in the field.
- *Network effects or other types of flywheels / A higher pace of innovation:* While Kodak had no real network effects, it had a major flywheel going with its research and development department. Since it made outsized profits, it could invest more than anyone else in research and development, which kept its outsized profits going via faster innovation.

When assessing your possible sustainable competitive advantages, be explicit. A list like the one above can be a big help. What are you doing that competitors can't copy? What will keep the competition at bay and allow you to exercise your market power for the long term?

Any single advantage could serve as the basis for your moat, but, as you can see from the Kodak example, several advantages can also work together, amplify one another, and produce an even bigger moat (force field). As we will see in a bit, though, even the biggest moats don't last forever.

These same moat types can apply to your personal place in an organization or field as well. For example: You can have the biggest personal network (exclusive access to relationships). You can build a personal following (strong, trusted brand). You can become the expert in an in-demand area (unique qualifications). You can create a popular blog (substantial control of a distribution channel). Each of these and more can create a moat that protects your place in a competitive landscape.

Organizations and individuals that control working moats create **lock-in** when customers are *locked in* to their services because perceived **switching costs** are so high. There are many ways to create switching costs, such as cancellation fees, trusted relationships, new equipment costs, learning curves, *network effects* (see Chapter 4), brand affinity, etc.

Many people feel locked into Facebook because this is how many of their friends and family choose to share photos and updates of what is going on in their lives. Employers can feel locked into certain key employees, which gives these employees leverage to ask for raises or other benefits. Some employees are so critical to a business's operations that there is a whole class of insurance products called key person insurance, which pays out if these key people become incapacitated.

These concepts also apply well beyond business situations. Many people feel locked into personal relationships, since the perceived costs (including emotional and psychological costs) of these changes are so high. Or you may feel locked into your housing situation, given the costs of physically moving and the *opportunity cost* (see Chapter 3) of spending your time on picking a new place, packing your things, making new friends, etc. Even countries get locked into diplomatic arrangements with high switching costs, as in the case of Brexit.

A related pair of concepts resulting from moats are **barriers to entry** and **barriers to exit**, which prevent people or companies from either *entering* or *exiting* a situation or market. A new mobile operating system wanting to compete with Apple's iOS or Google's Android would need to re-create an app store populated with thousands of useful apps, a large barrier to entry. Some careers have high barriers to entry, such as expensive years of schooling required. Similarly, some personal contracts, such as noncompetes, partnership agreements, or even marriage, create significant barriers to exit.

As with switching costs, barriers to entry and exit can come in many forms, such as trade secrets, like the Coca-Cola formula; high capital investment, like the cost of a huge factory; and government regulations that protect incumbents. A specific model centered on barriers to entry due to regulation is called **regulatory capture**, in which *regulatory* agencies or lawmakers get *captured* by the special interest groups they are supposed to be regulating, ultimately protecting these entities from competition.

In 2012, Jeff Donn reported on a year-long Associated Press investigation of the U.S. Nuclear Regulatory Commission [NRC], resulting in a lengthy four-part series that noted:

Federal regulators have been working closely with the nuclear power industry to keep the nation's aging reactors operating within safety standards by repeatedly weakening those standards, or simply failing to enforce them. . . .

Examples abound. When valves leaked, more leakage was allowed—up to 20 times the original limit. When rampant cracking caused radioactive leaks from steam generator tubing, an easier test of the tubes was devised, so plants could meet standards.

Failed cables. Busted seals. Broken nozzles, clogged screens, cracked concrete, dented containers, corroded metals and rusty underground pipes—all of these and thousands of other problems linked to aging were uncovered in the AP's yearlong investigation. And all of them could escalate dangers in the event of an accident.

Yet despite the many problems linked to aging, not a single official body in government or industry has studied the overall frequency and potential impact on safety of such breakdowns in recent years, even as the NRC has extended the licenses of dozens of reactors.

Industry and government officials defend their actions, and insist that no chances are being taken. But the AP investigation found that with billions of dollars and 19 percent of America's electricity supply at stake, a cozy relationship prevails between the industry and its regulator, the NRC.

The disheartening part about this example is that nuclear power done right can be a safe and essentially unlimited source of low-carbon energy. Not regulating it effectively foments fears of nuclear energy and sets back the entire industry.

Nobel Prize–winning economist Joseph Stiglitz pioneered the model of regulatory capture. One reason for its common occurrence is that special interest groups often collectively lobby regulators via lobbyists, whereas the individuals affected do not tend to put together strong lobbying efforts due to their lack of organization. Another reason is that the regulators themselves often operate in a *revolving-door* pattern in which, after their time as regulators, they take highly compensated jobs in the industry they were just regulating.

Regulatory capture can happen outside the government as well, such as in occupational licensing, where certain occupations restrict the supply of professionals through control of their licensing boards and processes. For example, according to a Brookings report, in the U.S. about one-quarter of current jobs require a license, up from just 5 percent in the 1950s. These licenses cover occupations that you might think they should, such as medicine, and also those you might not think of, such as cosmetology. Critics contend that while some licensing can make sense, the trend is to require too much money and time to acquire these licenses, which protects people who already have them at the expense of competition. For example, they found the "number of days to obtain a cosmetology license varies from 232 in New York to 490 in Iowa."

"AT FILMORE HOLDINGS, WE DON'T BREAK THE LAW. WE DONATE to POLITICIANS to CHANGE THE LAW."

Another common example is nonprofit or community boards that get overrun by the personal interests and motivations of friends or family. In its worst form, regulatory capture is just plain corruption, though it often also occurs naturally with good-faith intentions through regulators not seeking broad enough input from their constituents or not conducting comprehensive impact assessments (see *availability bias* and *confirmation bias* in Chapter 1).

There are ways to diminish regulatory capture. As U.S. Supreme Court justice Louis Brandeis famously wrote in *Other People's Money*, "Sunlight is said to be the best of disinfectants," meaning that allowing people to see and understand regulation and its effects—increasing transparency—can lead to less regulatory capture by special interests. When people are held accountable and made to explain their actions, change can more easily occur.

Strong moats, including those built upon regulatory capture and especially those built on network effects, can also lead to **winner-take-most markets**. This is where one company, once it reaches *critical mass* (see Chapter 4) through its network or dominant position based on another sustainable competitive advantage, effectively *wins* the *market* by *taking most* of the customers within it. For example, with more than two billion people on Facebook, a competitor won't find it easy to re-create that network and compete with Facebook's core offerings.

Just because you won the market, however, doesn't mean you will win in perpetuity. Andy Grove, former CEO of Intel, famously wrote in his 1999 book of the same name, "**Only the paranoid survive**." Intel's early dominance was in memory chips; however, by the mid-1980s, Japanese manufacturers had effectively erased much of its competitive advantages in this market. But at the height of its dominance, Intel foresaw this existential competitive threat.

As a result, it pivoted the focus of the company into microprocessors and reestablished a long-lasting moat ("Intel Inside"). Grove's words serve as a reminder that even if you establish a working moat, you must be constantly evaluating the strength of it, and even when you have a strong product/market fit, your moat may give way and you may need to eventually pivot. And Intel's new moat did in fact eventually give out with the rise of the chips that power the smartphone and other smaller devices.

Remember Kodak? Its moat was also disrupted, though it didn't pivot in time as Intel did from memory chips. In the 1990s, Kodak was rapidly disrupted by digital photography, and it ultimately declared bankruptcy in 2012 after a century of market dominance. You might think that it got caught off guard, but that isn't true, just as it usually isn't true in similar cases.

As mentioned, Kodak's investment in research and development was part of its moat. Kodak actually developed the very first digital camera, way back in 1975! But the timing wasn't right for digital photography to prosper then, due to lack of a supporting ecosystem—graphics cards were not fully developed, physical hard drive size was too big, etc. Meanwhile, Kodak had been making most of its money from selling film. Digital photography of course has no film, and once it prospered, it fundamentally disrupted Kodak's profitable analog model.

When disruptive technologies like this first emerge, they are usually inferior to the current technologies in the ways that most buyers care about. For decades, digital photography was comparatively expensive and produced lower-quality photographs than film; however, its convenience (in not having to develop pictures) appealed to some buyers and allowed the market to progress. Slowly but surely, the price and performance gap between digital and film closed. Once it crossed the *tipping point* (see Chapter 4) of being attractive to most consumers, the digital camera market exploded.

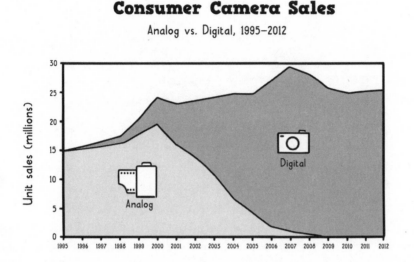

Consumer Camera Sales
Analog vs. Digital, 1995–2012

Kodak wasn't blind to these developments either. Initially it was even the market leader in digital cameras too, with a 27 percent share in 1999. However, it didn't invest heavily enough in the technology relative to its competitors, the way Intel did when pivoting to microprocessors. Kodak simply wasn't paranoid enough.

The overall market for photography quickly and fundamentally shifted from the high-margin film business to a highly commoditized digital camera business, and Kodak simply wasn't fast enough to adapt. It didn't use its flywheel from the film business to fuel its path to domination in digital, and its share of the exploding digital photography market fell as a result. In 2007 Kodak was number four in digital photography and by 2010 they fell to seventh, at 7 percent market share, behind Canon, Sony, Nikon, and others.

Just as this happened, these same digital camera manufacturers were similarly disrupted by Apple, Samsung, and others producing smartphone cameras. Same story: First, these new "cameras" were relatively expensive and produced lower-quality photographs, but they were more convenient. Over time, however, the quality kept increasing and there were more and more reasons to have a smartphone, leaving not enough reasons to have a separate digital camera.

It is an interesting question in *counterfactual thinking* (see Chapter 6) to ask what

Consumer Camera Sales
Digital vs. Smartphone, 2002–2016

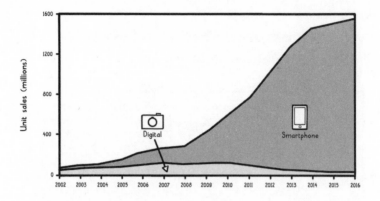

would have happened if Kodak had tried to develop the digital photography market earlier. Would it have been able to dominate that market? Would we all have had digital cameras years earlier? Could it have eventually pivoted into a role powering the cameras in most smartphones or pivoted even more drastically and created a product like Instagram? We'll never know.

In Clayton Christensen's seminal work *The Innovator's Dilemma*, he lays out the framework for how such **disruptive innovations** ripple through industries, ushering new industry entrants into power while leaving dead incumbents in their wake.

The incumbent's dilemma is whether to embrace the disruptive technology, usually at the great cost of the existing business. That's what Intel did but Kodak didn't do. If Kodak had more readily embraced digital camera technology, it would have directly cannibalized its outsized profits in analog film technology. Similarly, many companies are right now facing difficult decisions about whether to embrace new disruptive innovations like artificial intelligence, solar power, streaming video, driverless vehicles, and electric cars.

Individual workers face comparable issues. Over the past decades, globalization has dramatically changed the job responsibilities and prospects for many across a wide swath of industries. Employees who were essential at one time saw their moats destroyed. Similarly, automation and artificial intelligence are poised to disrupt many more jobs over the coming decades.

If you see disruption on the horizon in your field, you ought to prepare to respond sooner rather than later. Maybe that means investing in a new set of skills; maybe it means switching responsibilities; maybe it means pivoting to another field altogether. Unfortunately, truly embracing a disruptive innovation usually means major upheaval to the company or person itself: major losses of revenue in the short term, retraining from the ground up—a major pivot.

There have been many instances where pivots have been advisable at the height of market dominance or earning potential. Unfortunately, market dominance can correspond with complacency. That's why only the paranoid survive—you have to be paranoid to perceive the threat of something so small or far off in the future when you are in such good shape. When you embrace this model, you must therefore pay attention to a lot of small threats, most of which will turn out to be harmless. How do you distinguish *the signal from the noise*?

One approach is to closely monitor the progression of new threats as they progress from being used just by early adopters to being taken up by the mainstream, along the curve of the *technology adoption life cycle* as described in Chapter 4. Many technologies or ideas often capture some interest by innovators or early adopters, but very few actually make the jump to the early majority of the mainstream.

Business strategist Geoffrey Moore named this jump **crossing the chasm** in a book by the same name. The *chasm* here refers to the fact that many ideas, companies, and technologies fail to make it from one side to the other. That's because there is a huge gulf in expectations between early adopters and the early majority, which most things fail to meet. Early adopters like to tinker with things or are a small subset of people who really need something, but to cross the chasm into the early majority, a product has to solve a real ongoing need for a lot more people. And most products just aren't compelling enough to *cross* this gulf and truly spread into the mainstream.

Crossing the Chasm

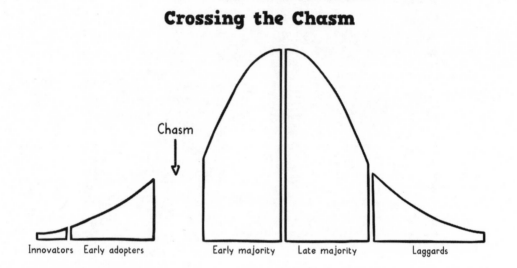

But if you think a competitive threat does have a decent chance of crossing the chasm, you should pay close attention. That's because if they do cross the chasm, it will mark a tipping point of significant and much more rapid adoption. You need to be prepared when that happens, not caught off guard like Kodak.

This process of maintaining your market power is never ending. You are constantly assessing new threats, bolstering the strength of your moats, and pivoting as needed over time. If you let your guard down, you will surely be disrupted. On the other hand, if you focus on maintaining your market power, which may involve some major pivots, you may be able to reap its benefits indefinitely.

- Find a **secret** and build your career or organization around it, searching via **customer development** for **product/market fit** (or another "fit" relevant to the situation).

- Strive to be like a **heat-seeking missile** in your search for product/market fit, deftly navigating the **idea maze**. Look for signs of hitting a **resonant frequency** for validation.

- If you can't find any **bright spots** in what you're doing after some time, critically evaluate your position and consider a **pivot**.

- Build a **moat** around yourself and your organization to create **sustainable competitive advantage**.

- Don't get complacent; remember **only the paranoid survive**, and keep on the lookout for **disruptive innovations**, particularly those with a high probability of **crossing the chasm**.

Conclusion

AS WE SAID IN THE INTRODUCTION, this is the book we wish someone had given us when we were starting out in our careers. That's because mental models unlock the ability to think at higher levels. We hope that you've enjoyed reading about them, and that our book has helped you in your super thinking journey.

Since many of these concepts may be new to you, you will need to practice using them to get the most out of them. As Richard Feynman famously wrote in his 2005 book, *What Do You Care What Other People Think?*, "I learned very early the difference between knowing the name of something and knowing something."

A related mental model is the **cargo cult**, as explained by Feynman in his 1974 Caltech commencement speech:

> In the South Seas there is a cargo cult of people. During the war they saw airplanes land with lots of good materials, and they want the same thing to happen now. So they've arranged to imitate things like runways, to put fires along the sides of the runways, to make a wooden hut for a man to sit in, with two wooden pieces on his head like headphones and bars of bamboo sticking out like antennas—he's the controller—and they wait for the airplanes to land. They're doing everything

right. The form is perfect. It looks exactly the way it looked before. But it doesn't work. No airplanes land. So I call these things cargo cult science, because they follow all the apparent precepts and forms of scientific investigation, but they're missing something essential, because the planes don't land.

Feynman is describing a real group of people in Melanesia and how they acted after coming into contact with more advanced technology. They believed, in a *cultish* fashion, that imitating what they saw from the technologically advanced people would bring them great wealth, or *cargo*. However, they didn't really understand how to behave in a way to get the results they wanted. They thought that if they built the runway just right, that would mean the planes would automatically start arriving with free goods. Of course, that didn't happen, because they didn't really understand what was attracting the planes in the first place, let alone the actual technologies needed to allow them to land safely.

When people don't really understand what they're doing, they are cargo cultists, unlikely to get the results that they seek. For example, cargo-cult entrepreneurs might constantly go to startup networking events, but never actually build a viable company. Cargo-cult science appears to be a scientific endeavor, but it does not rigorously follow the *scientific method* (see Chapter 4). Cargo-cult investors might try to copy what they see others investing in, but they do not understand the reasons behind the investments, and so their investments don't perform as well in the long run.

You don't want to be a cargo-cult super thinker, using mental models without really understanding them, and therefore not getting their benefits. For example, you don't want to use the wrong ones for a given situation or take away the wrong messages. To avoid these traps, you need to think deeply about whether and how a given mental model applies to a situation. We have a couple of steps for you to take in order to do so and ensure that you become a real super thinker.

First, get a partner in super thinking. Thinking about complicated topics in isolation does not yield the best results. It's much better to share your ideas with someone and get their feedback. It doesn't have to be the same person for all topics. You could talk to one person for political topics, someone else for economic topics, etc. But talking to people who are interested in the core truth of a particular subject is essential.

Second, try writing. Even if you never publish anything, the act of writing clarifies your thinking and makes you aware of holes in your arguments. You can combine writing and finding a partner by participating in an online forum or blog where the complex topics that interest you are discussed and analyzed.

Over time, your efforts will expand what Warren Buffett calls your **circle of competence**. The inside of the *circle* covers areas where you have knowledge or experience—where you are *competent*—and in those areas, you can think effectively. In areas outside the circle, you cannot. The most dangerous zone is just outside your circle of competence, where you might think you are competent but you really are not. Buffett wrote in a 1999 shareholder letter:

> If we have a strength, it is in recognizing when we are operating well within our circle of competence and when we are approaching the perimeter. . . .

Anywhere in life, your success rate will drop if you operate out of your circle of competence. You can suffer from the *Dunning-Kruger effect* (see Chapter 8), where you make mistakes because you don't know what you don't know. For example, you can fail to recognize or misapply *design patterns* (see Chapter 3). You also may apply the few techniques you know well to try to solve all your problems, inevitably in suboptimal ways (see *Maslow's hammer* in Chapter 6).

The good news is that the mental models in this book will expand your circle of competence. Interacting with people who already know how to successfully apply them can help you correct your mistakes and expand your circle even faster. With that in mind, we feel it is apt to conclude with a couple more quotes from Charlie Munger. Our super

Circle of Competence

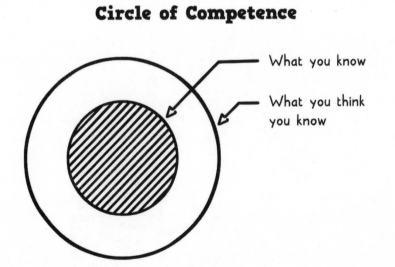

What you know

What you think you know

thinking journey began after we heard his speech, and we hope he can offer the same inspiration to you. The first is from *Poor Charlie's Almanack*, the second from a May 2007 commencement speech at the University of Southern California Gould School of Law:

> In my whole life, I have known no wise people (over a broad subject area) who didn't read all the time—none, zero. You'd be amazed at how much Warren [Buffett] reads—and how much I read. My children laugh at me. They think I'm a book with a couple of legs sticking out.
>
> Since the really big ideas carry 95% of the freight, it wasn't at all hard for me to pick up all the big ideas in all the disciplines and make them a standard part of my mental routines. Once you have the ideas, of course, they're no good if you don't practice. If you don't practice, you lose it. So I went through life constantly practicing this multidisciplinary approach.
>
> Well, I can't tell you what that's done for me. It's made life more fun. It's made me more constructive. It's made me more helpful to others. It's made me enormously rich. You name it. That attitude really helps.

Acknowledgments

THANK YOU TO OUR KIDS, Eli and Ryan, for bearing with us while we were writing this book. Thank you to Michael Zakhar and Stephen Hanselman, as well as everyone else at Portfolio and Penguin for editing support, especially Vivian Roberson, Leah Trouwborst, and Kaushik Viswanath. Thank you to Madé Dimas Wirawan for his illustrations.

Image Credits

Page xi: Adapted from *The Avengers*, dir. Joss Whedon (Marvel Studios, 2012).

Page 4: Adapted from *Apollo 13*, dir. Ron Howard (Imagine Entertainment, 1995).

Page 8: Based on a meme from "What is the next step with our MVP?" Gerry Claps, Quora, September 10, 2015, www.quora.com/what-is-the-next-step-with-our-mvp.

Page 11: Adapted from Creative Commons image: Ghiles, "Somewhat noisy linear data fit to both a linear function and to a polynomial of 10 degrees," Wikimedia Commons, March 11, 2016, https://commons.wikimedia.org/wiki/File:Overfitted_Data.png.

Page 12: Cartoon by Wiley Miller.

Page 13: Headlines from August 31, 2015, on foxnews.com and cnn.com. Both early headlines have since been altered, though the final stories from the following day are still available: "Atlanta-Area Police Officer Shot after Responding to Wrong Home," Fox News, September 1, 2015, www.foxnews.com/us/atlanta-area-police-officer-shot-after-responding-to-wrong-home; Eliott C. McLaughlin and Holly Yan, "Police: Friendly Fire Likely Wounded Officer in Wrong-House Encounter," CNN, September 1, 2015, www.cnn.com/2015/09/01/us/georgia-wrong-house-shooting/index.html.

Page 14: Adaped from Texas Roadhouse menu, http://restaurantfood.menu/menu/image/allbrandlogo/Texas%20Roadhouse.jpg.

Page 16 (top): U.S. Customs and Border Protection, as cited by Christopher Ingraham, "There's

No Immigration Crisis, and These Charts Prove It," *Washington Post*, June 21, 2018, www
.washingtonpost.com/news/wonk/wp/2018/06/21/theres-no-immigration-crisis-and-these
-charts-prove-it.

Page 16 (bottom): Justin McCarthy, "Most Americans Still See Crime Up Over Last Year," Gallup,
November 21, 2014.

Page 17: Sarah Lichtenstein et al., "Judged Frequency of Lethal Events," *Journal of Experimental
Psychology* 4, no. 6 (November 1978).

Page 18: DuckDuckGo, "There are no 'regular results' on Google anymore," October 10, 2012,
Vimeo video, 1:21, https://vimeo.com/51181384.

Page 23: Adapted from "Addition using number bonds," OnlineMathLearning.com, www.online
mathlearning.com/addition-number-bonds.html.

Page 24: Adapted from a map by the U.S. Geological Survey, May 5, 1999, https://pubs.usgs.gov
/gip/dynamic/continents.html.

Page 25: Claude Allègre, *The Behavior of the Earth: Continental and Seafloor Mobility*, trans. Debo-
rah Kurmes Van Dam (Cambridge, Mass.: Harvard University Press, 1988), 7.

Page 27: Cartoon by Clive Goddard.

Page 29: Meme adapted from https://78.media.tumblr.com/7f4ed380aadc01351b024959008f6e02
/tumblr_mg3mhsUlOz1rhf11x01_500.png.

Pages 37 and 233: Cartoons by Betsy Streeter.

Page 40: Sandra W. Roush et al., "Historical Comparisons of Morbidity and Mortality for Vaccine-
Preventable Diseases in the United States," *Journal of the American Medical Association* 298,
no. 18 (November 14, 2007).

Page 43: Environmental Defense Fund, "How Cap and Trade Works," January 7, 2009, YouTube
video, 1:13, www.youtube.com/watch?v=EKT_ac4LPkU.

Pages 45, 65, 204, and 307: Cartoons by Harley Schwadron.

Page 51: © 2002 Kenneth and Gabrielle Adelman, California Coastal Records Project, www
.californiacoastline.org.

Page 52: Jonathon W. Penney, "Chilling Effects: Online Surveillance and Wikipedia Use," *Berkeley
Technology Law Journal* 31, no. 1 (September 8, 2016): 148.

Page 56: Cartoon by Greg Perry.

Page 57: Based on a meme tweeted by Kristian Hellang, "Just tried to explain technical debt to a
customer, had to pull this out again . . . ," Twitter, July 30, 2015, 4:29 A.M., https://twitter.com
/khellang/status/626716128379830273.

Pages 61, 240, and 311: Cartoons by Tom Fishburne.

Page 64: Cartoon by Mark Godfrey.

Page 67: Adapted from Craig Brown, "The Little Dipper and the Earth's Tilt and Rotation," *Craig's*

Sense of Wonder: Into a Curious Mind, November 17, 2012, https://craigssenseofwonder.word press.com/tag/insolation.

Page 68: Adapted from Creative Commons image: Ashley Dace, "Star Trail above Beccles, near to Gillingham, Norfolk, Great Britain," Wikimedia Commons, May 13, 2010, https://commons .wikimedia.org/wiki/File:Star_Trail_above_Beccles_-_geograph.org.uk_-_1855505.jpg.

Page 74: Cartoon by Roy Delgado.

Page 75: Adapted from U.S. Congressional Budget Office, "The Federal Budget in 2015," info-graphic, January 6, 2016, www.cbo.gov/sites/default/files/cbofiles/images/pubs-images/50xxx /51110-Land_Overall.png.

Page 80: Adapted from National Institute for Health Care Management Foundation, "Concentra-tion of Health Spending Among Highest Spenders," infographic, 2013.

Page 84: Angela Liao, "A Field Guide to Procrastinators," *Twenty Pixels*, September 6, 2013, www .20px.com/blog/2013/09/06/a-field-guide-to-procrastinators.

Page 88: Eric Johnson and Daniel Goldstein, "Do Defaults Save Lives?" *Science* 302, no. 5649 (No-vember 21, 2003).

Page 96: Cartoon by Mike Shapiro.

Page 98: *The Argyle Sweater* © 2010 Scott Hilburn. Dist. by Andrews McMeel Syndication. Reprinted with permission. All rights reserved.

Page 100: Adapted from Creative Commons image: Martinowsky and Chiswick Chap, "Natural selec-tion in action: light and dark morphs of the peppered moth, *Biston betularia*," Wikimedia Commons, February 18, 2007, https://commons.wikimedia.org/wiki/File:Lichte_en_zwarte_versie _berkenspanner_crop.jpg.

Page 101: Cartoon by Larry Lambert.

Page 102: "Inertia - Demotivational Poster," Fake Posters, July 22, 2009, www.fakeposters.com/posters /inertia.

Page 106: Communic@tions Management Inc., "Sixty Years of Daily Newspaper Circulation: Can-ada, United States, United Kingdom," (May 6, 2011), http://media-cmi.com/downloads/Sixty _Years_Daily_Newspaper_Circulation_Trends_050611.pdf.

Page 108: Adapted from a Creative Commons image. Birmingham Museums Trust, "Richard Trevithick's 1802 steam locomotive," Wikimedia Commons, August 11, 2005, https://en.wiki pedia.org/wiki/Flywheel#/media/File:Thinktank_Birmingham_-_Trevithick_Locomotive(1) .jpg.

Page 111: Adapted from public domain image. Damian Yerrick, "Illustration of a roly-poly toy viewed from the side. The red and white bullseye represents the figurine's center of mass (COM)." Wikimedia Commons, August 15, 2009, https://commons.wikimedia.org/wiki/File :Poli_Gus_N_rocked.svg.

Page 114: "How does a Nuclear Bomb work?" Figure 1: The Nuclear Fission Chain Reaction, guernseyDonkey.com, February 24, 2012.

Page 115: Peter Leyden, "Historical Adoption Rates of Communication Technologies," infographic.

Page 118 (top): Justin McCarthy, "Record-High 60% of Americans Support Same-Sex Marriage," Gallup (May 19, 2015).

Page 118 (bottom): Adapted from a Creative Commons image. Woody993, "Diagram showing the network effect in a few simple phone networks," Wikimedia Commons, May 31, 2011, https://en.wikipedia.org/wiki/Metcalfe's_law#/media/File:Metcalfe-Network-Effect.svg.

Page 121: J. L. Westover, "The Butterfly Effect," *Mr. Lovenstein,* https://www.mrlovenstein.com/comic/50.

Pages 123 and 211: Cartoons by Theresa McCracken.

Page 126: Randall Munroe, "Fuck Grapefruit," *XKCD,* https://xkcd.com/388.

Page 127: Cartoon by Bradford Veley.

Page 131: Adapted from *Raiders of the Lost Ark,* dir. Steven Spielberg (Lucasfilm Ltd., 1981).

Page 134 (top): Adapted from *Willy Wonka & the Chocolate Factory,* dir. Mel Stuart (Wolper Pictures Ltd., 1971).

Page 134 (bottom): Randall Munroe, "Correlation," *XKCD,* https://xkcd.com/552.

Page 135: Creative Commons license. Tyler Vigen, "Spurious Correlations," www.tylervigen.com/spurious-correlations.

Page 138: Cartoon by Fran.

Page 140: *Dilbert* © 2001 Scott Adams. Used by permission of Andrews McMeel Syndication. All rights reserved.

Page 141: Adapted from a Creative Commons image. McGeddon, "Illustration of hypothetical damage pattern on a WW2 bomber," Wikimedia Commons, November 12, 2016, https://commons.wikimedia.org/wiki/File:Survivorship-bias.png.

Page 142: Cartoon by Nate Fakes.

Page 145: Stephen Pinker, *The Better Angels of Our Nature* (New York: Viking Books, 2011).

Page 147: Philip A. Mackowiak, Steven S. Wasserman, and Myron M. Levine, "A Critical Appraisal of 98.6°F, the Upper Limit of the Normal Body Temperature, and Other Legacies of Carl Reinhold August Wunderlich," *Journal of the American Medical Association* 268, no. 12 (September 1992), 1578–80.

Page 148: U.S. Census Bureau, "HINC-06. Income Distribution to $250,000 or More for Households," www.census.gov/data/tables/time-series/demo/income-poverty/cps-hinc/hinc-06.2016.html.

Page 150: Center for Disease Control, "Anthropometric Reference Data for Children and Adults: United States, 2011–2014," *Vital and Health Statistics* series 3, no. 39 (August 2016).

Page 151 (bottom): Common Probability Distributions, Cloudera Engineering Blog, Sean Owen, December 3, 2015.

Page 153: Mark L. Berenson, David M. Levine, and Timothy C. Krehbiel, *Basic Business Statistics: Concepts and Applications* (Upper Saddle River, N.J.: Prentice Hall, 2006).

Page 161: Randall Munroe, "Significant," *XKCD*, https://xkcd.com/882.

Pages 176 and 287: Cartoons by Aaron Bacall.

Pages 183 and 199: Cartoons by Shaun McCallig.

Page 184: Cartoon by Mike Baldwin.

Page 196: Adapted from Shivshanker Singh Patel, "local optimal success{ordinals of life 2.0}," *Destiny exiles me*, May 16, 2013, http://destinyexilesme.blogspot.com/2013/05/local-optimal-sucessordinals-of-life-20.html.

Page 200: Adapted from a Creative Commons image: Dhatfield, "Diagram of Schrödinger's cat thought experiment," Wikimedia Commons, June 26, 2008, https://commons.wikimedia.org/wiki/File:Schrodingers_cat.svg.

Page 202: Cartoon by Joseph Farris.

Page 210: Georgetown University Center on Education and the Workforce, as cited in Debra Humphreys and Anthony Carnevale, "The Economic Value of Liberal Education," slideshow, 2013, www.slideshare.net/aacu_/the-economic-value-of-liberal-education.

Page 212: Adapted from James M. Kilts, "Fuck Everything, We're Doing Five Blades," *The Onion*, February 18, 2004, www.theonion.com/fuck-everything-were-doing-five-blades-1819584036.

Page 216: Adapted from Joshua L. Kalla and David E. Broockman, "Campaign Contributions Facilitate Access to Congressional Officials: A Randomized Field Experiment," *American Journal of Political Science* 60, no. 3 (July 2016).

Page 218 (top): Sacred Heart University, "SHU Just the Facts," Facebook page, www.facebook.com/shujustthefacts.

Page 235: Adapted from a Creative Commons image. Nyenyec, "Illustration of domino theory (20th century foreign policy theory, promoted by the government of the United States)," Wikimedia Commons, November 10, 2010, https://commons.wikimedia.org/wiki/File:Domino_theory.svg.

Page 249: Adapted from Jeff Wysaki, *Pleated Jeans*, http://sanctuarycounseling.com/wp-content/uploads/2014/06/977fcc90fb0909b04e1a594d8142045f.jpg.

Page 251: Cartoon by Andrew Toos.

Page 258: Cartoon by Will Dawbarn.

Page 261: Based on the theory of deliberate practice, as presented by Anders Ericsson and Robert Pool, *Peak* (New York: Eamon Dolan Books, 2017).

Page 263: Kim Scott, "What is Radical Candor?" www.radicalcandor.com/about-radical-candor.

Page 270 (top): Jessica Hagy, "Two annoying problems," *Indexed* (blog), May 9, 2012, thisisindexed .com/2012/05/two-annoying-problems.

Page 273: Adapted from Katie Stouffs Grimes, "High and Low Context Cultures - Developing Cultural Fluency," National Association of Realtors, January 26, 2015, http://theglobalview.blogs .realtor.org/2015/01/26/high-and-low-context-cultures-developing-cultural-fluency.

Page 277: *Dilbert* © 2012 Scott Adams. Used by permission of Andrews McMeel Syndication. All rights reserved.

Page 282: Cartoon by John McPherson.

Page 284: Adapted from *Taken*, dir. Pierre Morel (EuropaCorp, 2008).

Page 293: Adapted from a Creative Commons image. Sjlegg, "Graph of the amplitude of an oscillator against its frequency, showing the significance of the resonant frequency," Wikimedia Commons, April 15, 2009, https://en.wikibooks.org/wiki/A-level_Physics_(Advancing_Physics) /Resonance#/media/File:Resonant_frequency_amplitude.svg.

Page 298: Adapted from an illustration by Christoph Janz, "Three more ways to build a $100 million business," *The Angel VC* (blog), November 4, 2014, https://christophjanz.blogspot.com /2014/11/three-more-ways-to-build-100-million.html.

Page 304: Cartoon by Dave Whamond.

Page 309: Based on data from the Camera & Imaging Products Association, as cited by Stephan Dolezalek and Josh Freed, "An American Kodak Moment," Third Way, April 17, 2014, www .thirdway.org/report/an-american-kodak-moment.

Page 310: Based on data from the Camera & Imaging Products Association and Gartner, as cited by Michael Zhang, "This Latest Camera Sales Chart Shows the Compact Camera Near Death," *PetaPixel*, March 3, 2017, https://petapixel.com/2017/03/03/latest-camera-sales-chart-reveals -death-compact-camera.

Page 312: Geoffrey A. Moore, *Crossing the Chasm*, 3rd ed. (New York: HarperBusiness, 2014).

Index

babies, 198, 279
    sleep and, 131–32
babysitters, 222
backfire effect, 26
back-of-the-envelope calculation,
    299
bacteria, 47–49, 295
bait and switch, 228, 229
bandwagon effect, 202
barriers to entry and barriers to
    exit, 305
baseball, 83, 145–46, 289
base rate, 157, 159, 160
base rate fallacy, 157, 158, 170
BATNA (best alternative to a
    negotiated agreement), 77
Battle of Heraclea, 239
Battle of Tsushima, 241
Bayes' theorem and Bayesian
    statistics, 157–60
beachhead, 300–301
Beatles, 105
Beautiful Mind, A, 213
beliefs, 103, 107
bell curve (normal distribution),
    150–52, 153, 163–66, 191
Bell Labs, 89
benefit of the doubt, 20
benefits:
    cost-benefit analysis, 177–86,
        189, 194
    eliminating, 224
    net, 181–82, 184
Berlin, Isaiah, 254
Bernoulli distribution, 152
best practices, 92
beta, 162, 182
Better Angels of Our Nature, The
    (Pinker), 144
Bezos, Jeff, 61–62, 286–87
bias, 3, 139
    availability, 15–18, 30, 33, 300
    confirmation, 26–28, 33, 103, 159
    disconfirmation, 27
    groupthink, 201–3
    hidden, 139–43
    hindsight, 271–72
    nonresponse, 140, 142, 143
    observer-expectancy, 136, 139
    optimistic probability, 33
    present, 85, 87, 93, 113
    publication, 170, 173
    response, 142, 143
    selection, 139–40, 143, 170

    self-serving, 21, 272
    survivorship, 140–43, 170, 272
Big Short, The (Lewis), 289
bike-shedding, 75, 93
Bird, Larry, 246
birth lottery, 21–22, 69
black-and-white thinking, 126–28,
    168, 272
black boxes, 94–95
Black Flags rebellion, 276
blackouts, electric, 120
black swan events, 190–91, 193
Blank, Steve, 294
bleeding them dry, 239
blinded experiments, 136
Blockbuster, 106
blowback, 54
Boaty McBoatface, RSS, 35
body mass index (BMI), 137
body temperature, 146–50
boiling frog, 55, 56, 58, 60
bonds, 180, 184
Bonne, Rose, 58
Boot, Max, 239
boots on the ground, 279
Boston Common, 36–38, 42
Boyd, John, 294
Bradley, Bill, 248
brainstorming, 201–3
Brandeis, Louis, 307
breast cancer, 156–57, 160–61
Breathalyzer tests, 157–58, 160
Brexit, 206, 305
bright spots, 300
bring in reinforcements, 279
British Medical Journal (*BMJ*), 136–37
broken windows theory, 235–36
Broderick, Matthew, 230
Brody, William, 290–91
Brookings Institution, 306
brute force solution, 93, 97
Bryson, Bill, 50
budget, 38, 74–75, 81, 95, 113
    national, 75–76
Buffett, Warren, viii, 69, 286, 302,
    317, 318
burning bridges, 243
burnout, 82, 83
Burns, Robert, 49
burn the boats, 244
Bush, George H. W., 104
business case, 207
butterfly effect, 121, 122, 125, 201
Butterfly Effect, The, 121

Butterworth, Brian, x
buyout, leveraged, 79
bystander effect, 259

cable television, 69, 100, 106
Caesar, Julius, 244
calculus, 291
call your bluff, 238
cameras, 302–3, 308–10
campaign finance reform, 110
Campbell, Donald T., 49–50
Campbell's law, 49–50
cancer:
    breast, 156–57, 160–61
    clusters of, 145
    lung, 133–34, 137
cap-and-trade systems, 42–43
capital, cost of, 76, 77, 179, 182
careers, 300–301
    decisions about, 5–6, 57, 175–77,
        201, 207, 296
    design patterns and, 93
    entry barriers and, 305
    licensing and, 306–7
Carfax, 46
Cargill, Tom, 89
cargo cults, 315–16
caring personally, 263–64
car market, 46–47
Carrey, Jim, 229
carrot-and-stick model, 232
cascading failures, 120, 192
casinos, 220, 226
cast a wide net, 122
catalyst, 112–13, 115, 119
Catherine II, Empress, 228
causal loop diagrams, 192–93
causation, correlation and, 134, 135
cellphones, 116–17
center of gravity, 112
central limit theorem, 152–53, 163
central tendency, 147
chain reaction, viii, 114, 120
Challenger, 31–33
challenging directly, 263–64
change, 100–101, 112–13, 129
    resistance to, 110–11
chaos, 124
    balance between order and, 128
chaos theory, 121
chaotic systems, 120–21, 124, 125
Chatelier's principle, 193–94
cheating, 50
Chekhov, Anton, 124

delayed gratification, 87
deleveraging, 78–79
deliberate practice, 260–62, 264, 266
Democratic National Committee, 97
de-risking, 6–7, 10, 294
design debt, 56–57
design patterns, 92–93, 97, 226, 317
Detecting Lies and Deceit (Vrij), 13–14
deterrence, 231–32, 237, 238
Detroit, Mich., 41
Devil's advocate position, 28–30, 202
diagrams, 192–93
dice, 170
Dick, Philip K., 201
diet, 1, 87, 102, 103, 130
Difficult Conversations (Stone, Patton, and Heen), 19
Diffusion of Innovation (Rogers), 116
diffusion of responsibility, 259
digital photography, 308–10
Dilbert, 140
diminishing returns, 81–83
diminishing utility, 81–82
dinosaurs, 103
diplomacy, 231
directly responsible individual (DRI), 258–59
disclosure law, 45
disconfirmation bias, 27
discounted cash flow, 85
discounting, hyperbolic, 87
discounting the future, 85–87
discount rate, 85–87, 180–82, 184, 185
discoveries, multiple, 291–92
Disney World, 96–97
dispersion, 147
disruptive innovations, 308, 310–11
distribution, *see* probability distributions
distributive justice versus procedural justice, 224–25
divergent thinking, 203
diversity debt, 57
diversity of opinion, 205, 206, 255
divide and conquer, 96
divorce, 231, 305
Dollar Shave Club, 240
domino effect, 234–35, 237
done, calling something, 89–90
Donne, John, 209
don't bring a knife to a gunfight, 241
drinking, 217, 218
drunk drivers, 157–58
drugs, 236

DuckDuckGo, 18, 32, 68, 258, 278
Dubner, Stephen, 44–45
Dunbar, Robin, 278
Dunbar's number, 278
Dunning, David, 269
Dunning-Kruger effect, 268–70, 317
Dweck, Carol, 266, 267

early adopters, 116–17, 289, 290, 311–12
early majority, 116–17, 312
Eastman Kodak Company, 302–3, 308–10, 312
eBay, 119, 281, 282, 290
echo chambers, 18, 120
Ecker, Ullrich, 13
economies of scale, 95
Economist, 14–15
economy, 122, 125
    inflation in, 179–80, 182–83
    financial crisis of 2007/2008, 79, 120, 192, 271, 288
    recessions in, 121–22
Edison, Thomas, 289, 292
education and schools, 224–25, 241, 296
    expectations and, 267–68
    mindsets and, 267
    school ranking, 137
    school start times, 110, 111, 130
    selection bias and, 140
    textbooks in, 262
    see also college
effective altruism, 80
egalitarian versus hierarchical, in organizational culture, 274
80/20 arrangements, 80–81, 83
Einstein, Albert, 8, 11
Eisenhower, Dwight, 72
Eisenhower Decision Matrix, 72–74, 89, 124, 125
elections, 206, 218, 233, 241, 271, 293, 299
Ellsberg, Michael, 220
email spam, 161, 192–93, 234
Emanuel, Rahm, 291
emotion, appeal to, 225, 226
emotional quotient (EQ), 250–52
empathy, 19, 21, 23
    ruinous, 264
employee engagement survey, 140, 142
endgame, 242, 244
endorsements, 112, 220, 229

endpoints, 137
ends justify the means, 229
energy:
    activation, 112–13
    potential, 111–12
engineering, 247
Enron, 228
entrepreneurs, 301
    cargo cult, 316
entropy, 122–24
entry, barriers to, 305
environmental issues, 38
    climate change, 42, 55, 56, 104, 105, 183, 192
EpiPen, 283
EQ (emotional quotient), 250–52
equilibrium, 193
Ericsson, K. Anders, 260, 261
error bars, 155, 156
escalation of commitment, 91
escape hatch, 244
Ethernet, 118
Etsy, 119
European Union, 59
evolution, 99–100, 133
execution, 292
exercise, 85, 87, 88, 102, 111, 113, 130
exit:
    barriers to, 305
    strategy for, 242–43
expectations, 267–68
experimenter bias (observer-expectancy bias), 136, 139
experiments, 135–36, 161–63, 173
    A/B testing, 136
    alpha in, 161, 182
    beta in, 162, 182
    blinded, 136
    endpoints in, 137
    power of, 162
    randomized controlled, 136
    replication of, 168–72
    sample size in, 143, 160, 162, 163, 165–68, 172, 182
    thought, 199–201
    see also polls and surveys; research
expected value, 186–89
expertise, 109, 115, 269
    deliberate practice and, 260–62, 264, 266
    externalities, 41–42, 47
    negative, 41–43, 47
extroverts, 249–50

hammer, Maslow's, xi, 177, 255, 297, 317
Hanlon's razor, 20
harassment, 53
Harvard Business Review, 297
Hatchimals, 281, 284
hazard, 43–45, 47
head in the sand, 55
Health and Human Services, U.S. Department of, 48
healthcare, 41, 54–55
  HealthCare.gov, 107
  insurance, 42, 46, 47, 190
  spending on, 80, 81
health information, 53
heart rhythms, 139
heat death of the universe, 124
heat-seeking missiles, 301
hedgehogs versus foxes, 254–55
Heen, Sheila, 19
Heifer International, 109
height, 150–51, 156, 191–92
Heilbroner, Robert, 49
helplessness, learned, 22–23
Heraclea, Battle of, 239
herd immunity, 39–40, 46
heroin, 36
heuristic, 94
Hick, William, 62
Hick's law, 62, 63
hierarchical versus egalitarian, in organizational culture, 274
hierarchy of needs, 270–71
high-context communication, 273–74
high-leverage activities, 79–81, 83, 107, 113
hindsight bias, 271–72
hiring, 258
histogram, 147–48, 150
Hitler, Adolf, 237
HIV, 233
Hoffman, Reid, 7
Hofstadter, Douglas, 89
Hofstadter's law, 89
hold the line, 236
hollow victory, 239
home:
  being locked into housing situation, 305
  insurance on, 156
  new-construction, 228
  purchase of, 79, 178
  repairs on, 56, 185–89
  security services for, 229

Homebrew Computer Club, 289
Homeland Security, U.S. Department of, 97
homelessness, 22
homeostasis, 110–12, 194
honeypot, 234
hornet's nest, 51–52
horse racing, 91, 286
hospital rankings, 50
hotels, 217, 228
house, *see* home
Housing First, 22
Houston, Tex., 192
Hyman, Ray, 62
hydra effect, 51, 52
hyperbolic discounting, 87
hypothesis, 136, 161
  alternative, 163, 164, 166, 167
  null, 163, 164
    see also experiments
hysteresis, 194

IBM, 241
iCloud, 97
idea maze, 301
ignorance, veil of, 21
"I Know an Old Lady" (Bonne and Mills), 58
immigration, 15–16
immune system, 194
imposter syndrome, 268–72
incentives, 55
  perverse, 50–51, 54
income, U.S. household, 148–49, 191
independence, 205
India, 50–51, 235
individualist versus collectivist, in organizational culture, 274
inertia, 102–3, 105–8, 110, 112, 113, 119, 120, 129, 290, 296
infantry, in organizations and projects, 253
inflation, 179–80, 182–83
inflection point, 115
Influence: The Psychology of Persuasion (Cialdini), 215
influence models, 215, 220, 221, 226, 229, 230, 289
  authority, 219–20, 226
  commitment, 216, 220
  liking, 216–17, 220
  reciprocity, 215–16, 220, 222, 229, 289

scarcity, 219, 220
  social proof, 217–20, 229
information asymmetry, 45–47
information overload, 60, 146
Ingham, Harrington, 196
in-group favoritism, 127, 217
Inkster, James A., 91
innovations, 302
  disruptive, 308, 310–11
innovators, in technology adoption life cycle, 116–17, 289, 311
Innovator's Dilemma, The (Christensen), 310
insincerity, manipulative, 264
Instagram, 220, 247, 291, 310
instant gratification, 87
institutional knowledge, 257
insurance, 43, 46, 191
  health, 42, 46, 47, 190
  key person, 305
Intel, 308, 310
intelligence quotient (IQ), 138, 250–52
interest, compound, 69, 85
interest rates, 85, 182–83
internalizing, 41–42
internet, 290
  messaging services, 119
introverts, 249–50
intuition, 30–31, 33, 132
invention, simultaneous, 291–92
inverse fallacy, 156–57
inverse thinking, 1–2, 291
investments, investors, 180–84, 192, 272, 288
  cargo cult, 316
Invisible Armies (Boot), 239
iPad, 290
iPod, 296–97
IQ (intelligence quotient), 138, 250–52
Iraq, 196, 234, 243, 276
irreversible decisions, 61–62, 223–24
Iverson, Allen, 246

Jacobi, Carl, 1
James, LeBron, 246
Janz, Christoph, 298–99
Japan, 241
jelly beans, 169–71
Jobs, Steve, 64, 296–97
jobs to be done, 296, 299–300
John, Tommy, 83
Johnson, Magic, 246

jokes, 35–36
Jordan, Michael, 246
Journal of Experimental Psychology, 13, 17
Joy, Bill, 247
Joy's law, 247, 248
judicial rulings, 63, 144
Jurassic Park, 121
justice, distributive versus procedural, 224–25
Justice, U.S. Department of, 97
just world hypothesis, 22

Kahneman, Daniel, 9, 30, 90
karoshi, 82
Kauffman Foundation, 122
keeping up with the Joneses, 210–11
key person insurance, 305
King, Martin Luther, Jr., 129, 225
KISS (Keep It Simple, Stupid), 10
knowledge, institutional, 257
knowns:
    known, 197
    unknown, 198, 203
known unknowns, 197–98
Knox, Robert E., 91
Kodak, 302–3, 308–10, 312
Koenigswald, Gustav Heinrich Ralph von, 50
Kohl's, 15
Kopelman, Josh, 301
Korea, 229, 231, 235, 238
Kristof, Nicholas, 254
Krokodil, 49
Kruger, Justin, 269
Kuhn, Thomas, 24
Kutcher, Ashton, 121

labor market, 283–84
laggards, 116–17
landlords, 178, 179, 182, 188
Laplace, Pierre-Simon, 132
large numbers, law of, 143–44
Latané, Bibb, 259
late majority, 116–17
lateral thinking, 201
law of diminishing returns, 81–83
law of diminishing utility, 81–82
law of inertia, 102–3, 105–8, 110, 112, 113, 119, 120, 129, 290, 296
law of large numbers, 143–44
law of small numbers, 143, 144
Lawson, Jerry, 289

lawsuits, 231
leadership, 248, 255, 260, 265, 271, 275, 276, 278–80
learned helplessness, 22–23
learning, 262, 269, 295
    from past events, 271–72
learning curve, 269
Le Chatelier, Henri-Louis, 193
Le Chatelier's principle, 193–94
left to their own devices, 275
Leibniz, Gottfried, 291
lemons into lemonade, 121
Lernaean Hydra, 51
Levav, Jonathan, 63
lever, 78
leverage, 78–80, 83, 115
    high-leverage activities, 79–81, 83, 107, 113
leveraged buyout, 79
leveraging up, 78–79
Levitt, Steven, 44–45
Levitt, Theodore, 296
Lewis, Michael, 289
Lichtenstein, Sarah, 17
lightning, 145
liking, 216–17, 220
Lincoln, Abraham, 97
Lindy effect, 105, 106, 112
line in the sand, 238
LinkedIn, 7
littering, 41, 42
Lloyd, William, 37
loans, 180, 182–83
lobbyists, 216, 306
local optimum, 195–96
lock-in, 305
lock in your gains, 90
long-term negative scenarios, 60
loose versus tight, in organizational culture, 274
Lorenz, Edward, 121
loss, 91
loss aversion, 90–91
loss leader strategy, 236–37
lost at sea, 68
lottery, 85–86, 126, 145
low-context communication, 273–74
low-hanging fruit, 81
loyalists versus mercenaries, 276–77
luck, 128
    making your own, 122
luck surface area, 122, 124, 128
Luft, Joseph, 196
LuLaRoe, 217

lung cancer, 133–34, 173
Lyautey, Hubert, 276
Lyft, ix, 288

Madoff, Bernie, 232
magnetic resonance imaging (MRI), 291
magnets, 194
maker's schedule versus manager's schedule, 277–78
Making of Economic Society, The (Heilbroner), 49
mammograms, 160–61
management debt, 56
manager's schedule versus maker's schedule, 277–78
managing to the person, 255
Manhattan Project, 195
Man in the High Castle, The (Dick), 201
manipulative insincerity, 264
man-month, 279
Mansfield, Peter, 291
manufacturer's suggested retail price (MSRP), 15
margin of error, 154
markets, 42–43, 46–47, 106
    failure in, 47–49
    labor, 283–84
    market norms versus social norms, 222–24
    market power, 283–85, 312
    product/market fit, 292–96, 302
    secondary, 281–82
    winner-take-most, 308
marriage:
    divorce, 231, 305
    same-sex, 117, 118
Maslow, Abraham, 177, 270–71
Maslow's hammer, xi, 177, 255, 297, 317
Maslow's hierarchy of needs, 270–71
mathematics, ix–x, 3, 4, 132, 178
    Singapore math, 23–24
matrices, 2 × 2, 125–26
    consensus-contrarian, 285–86, 290
    consequence-conviction, 265–66
    Eisenhower Decision Matrix, 72–74, 89, 124, 125
    of knowns and unknowns, 197–98
    payoff, 212–15, 238
    radical candor, 263–64
    scatter plot on top of, 126

quarantine, 234
questions:
    now what, 291
    what if, 122, 201
    why, 32, 33
    why now, 291
quick and dirty, 234
quid pro quo, 215

Rabois, Keith, 72, 265
Rachleff, Andy, 285–86, 292–93
radical candor, 263–64
Radical Candor (Scott), 263
radiology, 291
randomized controlled experiment,
    136
randomness, 201
rats, 51
Rawls, John, 21
Regan, Ronald, 183
real estate agents, 44–45
recessions, 121–22
reciprocity, 215–16, 220, 222, 229,
    289
recommendations, 217
red line, 238
referrals, 217
reframe the problem, 96–97
refugee asylum cases, 144
regression to the mean, 146,
    286
regret, 87
regulations, 183–84, 231–32
regulatory capture, 305–7
reinventing the wheel, 92
relationships, 53, 55, 63, 91, 111,
    124, 159, 271, 296, 298
    being locked into, 305
    dating, 8–10, 95
replication crisis, 168–72
Republican Party, 104
reputation, 215
research:
    meta-analysis of, 172–73
    publication bias and, 170, 173
    systematic reviews of, 172, 173
    see also experiments
resonance, 293–94
response bias, 142, 143
responsibility, diffusion of, 259
restaurants, 297
    menus at, 14, 62
RetailMeNot, 281
retaliation, 238

returns:
    diminishing, 81–83
    negative, 82–83, 93
reversible decisions, 61–62
revolving door, 306
rewards, 275
Riccio, Jim, 306
rise to the occasion, 268
risk, 43, 46, 90, 288
    cost-benefit analysis and, 180
    de-risking, 6–7, 10, 294
    moral hazard and, 43–45, 47
Road Ahead, The (Gates), 69
Roberts, Jason, 122
Roberts, John, 27
Rogers, Everett, 116
Rogers, William, 31
Rogers Commission Report, 31–33
roles, 256–58, 260, 271, 293
roly-poly toy, 111–12
root cause, 31–33, 234
roulette, 144
Rubicon River, 244
ruinous empathy, 264
Rumsfeld, Donald, 196–97, 247
Rumsfeld's Rule, 247
Russia, 218, 241
    Germany and, 70, 238–39
    see also Soviet Union

Sacred Heart University (SHU),
    217, 218
sacrifice play, 239
Sagan, Carl, 220
sales, 81, 216–17
Salesforce, 299
same-sex marriage, 117, 118
Sample, Steven, 28
sample distribution, 152–53
sample size, 143, 160, 162, 163,
    165–68, 172
Sánchez, Ricardo, 234
sanctions and fines, 232
Sanders, Bernie, 70, 182, 293
Sayre, Wallace, 74
Sayre's law, 74
scarcity, 219, 220
scatter plot, 126
scenario analysis (scenario
    planning), 198–99, 201–3,
    207
schools, *see* education and schools
Schrödinger, Erwin, 200
Schrödinger's cat, 200

Schultz, Howard, 296
Schwartz, Barry, 62–63
science, 133, 220
    cargo cult, 315–16
Scientific Autobiography and other
    Papers (Planck), 24
scientific evidence, 139
scientific experiments, *see*
    experiments
scientific method, 101–2, 294
scorched-earth tactics, 243
Scott, Kim, 263
S curves, 117, 120
secondary markets, 281–82
second law of thermodynamics, 124
secrets, 288–90, 292
Securities and Exchange
    Commission, U.S., 228
security, false sense of, 44
security services, 229
selection, adverse, 46–47
selection bias, 139–40, 143, 170
self-control, 87
self-fulfilling prophecies, 267
self-serving bias, 21, 272
Seligman, Martin, 22
Semmelweis, Ignaz, 25–26
Semmelweis reflex, 26
Seneca, Marcus, 60
sensitivity analysis, 181–82, 185, 188
    dynamic, 195
Sequoia Capital, 291
Sessions, Roger, 8
sexual predators, 113
Shakespeare, William, 105
Sheets Energy Strips, 36
Shermer, Michael, 133
Shirky, Clay, 104
Shirky principle, 104, 112
Short History of Nearly Everything, A
    (Bryson), 50
short-termism, 55–56, 58, 60, 68, 85
side effects, 137
signal and noise, 311
significance, 167
    statistical, 164–67, 170
Silicon Valley, 288, 289
simulations, 193–95
simultaneous invention, 291–92
Singapore math, 23–24
Sir David Attenborough, RSS, 35
Skeptics Society, 133
sleep meditation app, 162–68
slippery slope argument, 235

slow (high-concentration) thinking, 30, 33, 70–71
small numbers, law of, 143, 144
smartphones, 117, 290, 309, 310
smoking, 41, 42, 133–34, 139, 173
Snap, 299
Snowden, Edward, 52, 53
social engineering, 97
social equality, 117
social media, 81, 94, 113, 217–19, 241
    Facebook, 18, 36, 94, 119, 219, 233, 247, 305, 308
    Instagram, 220, 247, 291, 310
    YouTube, 220, 291
social networks, 117
    Dunbar's number and, 278
social norms versus market norms, 222–24
social proof, 217–20, 229
societal change, 100–101
software, 56, 57
    simulations, 192–94
solitaire, 195
solution space, 97
Somalia, 243
sophomore slump, 145–46
South Korea, 229, 231, 238
Soviet Union:
    Germany and, 70, 238–39
    Gosplan in, 49
    in Cold War, 209, 235
space exploration, 209
spacing effect, 262
Spain, 243–44
spam, 37, 161, 192–93, 234
specialists, 252–53
species, 120
spending, 38, 74–75
    federal, 75–76
spillover effects, 41, 43
sports, 82–83
    baseball, 83, 145–46, 289
    football, 226, 243
    Olympics, 209, 246–48, 285
Spotify, 299
spreadsheets, 179, 180, 182, 299
Srinivasan, Balaji, 301
standard deviation, 149, 150–51, 154
standard error, 154
standards, 93
Stanford Law School, x
Starbucks, 296
startup business idea, 6–7

statistics, 130–32, 146, 173, 289, 297
    base rate in, 157, 159, 160
    base rate fallacy in, 157, 158, 170
    Bayesian, 157–60
    confidence intervals in, 154–56, 159
    confidence level in, 154, 155, 161
    frequentist, 158–60
    p-hacking in, 169, 172
    p-values in, 164, 165, 167–69, 172
    standard deviation in, 149, 150–51, 154
    standard error in, 154
    statistical significance, 164–67, 170
    summary, 146, 147
    see also data; experiments; probability distributions
Staubach, Roger, 243
Sternberg, Robert, 290
stock and flow diagrams, 192
Stone, Douglas, 19
stop the bleeding, 234
strategy, 107–8
    exit, 242–43
    loss leader, 236–37
    pivoting and, 295–96, 298–301, 308, 311, 312
    tactics versus, 256–57
strategy tax, 103–4, 112
Stiglitz, Joseph, 306
straw man, 225–26
Streisand, Barbra, 51
Streisand effect, 51, 52
Stroll, Cliff, 290
Structure of Scientific Revolutions, The (Kuhn), 24
subjective versus objective, in organizational culture, 274
suicide, 218
summary statistics, 146, 147
sunk-cost fallacy, 91
superforecasters, 206–7
Superforecasting (Tetlock), 206–7
super models, viii–xii
super thinking, viii–ix, 3, 316, 318
surface area, 122
    luck, 122, 124, 128
surgery, 136–37
Surowiecki, James, 203–5
surrogate endpoint, 137
surveys, *see* polls and surveys
survivorship bias, 140–43, 170, 272
sustainable competitive advantage, 283, 285

switching costs, 305
systematic review, 172, 173
systems thinking, 192, 195, 198

tactics, 256–57
Tajfel, Henri, 127
take a step back, 298
Taleb, Nassim Nicholas, 2, 105
talk past each other, 225
Target, 236, 252
target, measurable, 49–50
taxes, 39, 40, 56, 104, 193–94
T cells, 194
teams, 246–48, 275
    roles in, 256–58, 260
    size of, 278
    10x, 248, 249, 255, 260, 273, 280, 294
Tech, 83
technical debt, 56, 57
technologies, 289–90, 295
    adoption curves of, 115
    adoption life cycles of, 116–17, 129, 289, 290, 311–12
    disruptive, 308, 310–11
telephone, 118–19
temperature:
    body, 146–50
    thermostats and, 194
tennis, 2
10,000-Hour Rule, 261
10x individuals, 247–48
10x teams, 248, 249, 255, 260, 273, 280, 294
terrorism, 52, 234
Tesla, Inc., 300–301
testing culture, 50
Tetlock, Philip E., 206–7
Texas sharpshooter fallacy, 136
textbooks, 262
Thaler, Richard, 87
Theranos, 228
thermodynamics, 124
thermostats, 194
Thiel, Peter, 72, 288, 289
thinking:
    black-and-white, 126–28, 168, 272
    convergent, 203
    counterfactual, 201, 272, 309–10
    critical, 201
    divergent, 203
    fast (low-concentration), 30, 70–71
    gray, 28

About the Authors

© Dave Justo

© Betsy Barron

GABRIEL WEINBERG is the CEO and founder of DuckDuckGo, the internet privacy company and private search engine. He holds a BS with honors from MIT in physics and an MS from the MIT Technology and Policy Program. Weinberg is also the coauthor of *Traction*.

LAUREN McCANN is a statistician and researcher. She spent nearly a decade at GlaxoSmithKline, where she designed and analyzed clinical trials and authored articles in medical journals, including the *New England Journal of Medicine*. She holds a PhD in operations research and a BS with honors in mathematics from MIT.

CENTRAL LIMIT THEOREM · CONFIDENCE INTERVAL · ERROR BAR
· FREQUENTISTS VS. BAYESIANS · FALSE POSITIVE · FALSE NEGA
· REPLICATION CRISIS · DATA DREDGING · PUBLICATION BIAS
GREENER MENTALITY · MASLOW'S HAMMER · COST-BENEFIT A
OUT · DECISION TREE · EXPECTED VALUE · UTILITY VALUES ·
SYSTEMS THINKING · CHATELIER'S PRINCIPLE · HYSTERESIS ·
UNKNOWN UNKNOWNS · SCENARIO ANALYSIS · THOUGHT EXPER
· BANDWAGON EFFECT · DIVERGENT THINKING VS. CONVERGENT T
· BUSINESS CASE · ARMS RACE · GAME THEORY · PRISONER'S D
SOCIAL PROOF · SCARCITY · AUTHORITY · SOCIAL NORMS V
PROCEDURAL JUSTICE · APPEAL TO EMOTION · FEAR, UNCERTA
· TROJAN HORSE · BAIT AND SWITCH · POTEMKIN VILLAGE · M
STICK · CONTAINMENT · STOP THE BLEEDING · QUARANTINE ·
BROKEN WINDOWS THEORY · GATEWAY DRUG THEORY · LOSS LE
TOLERANCE POLICY · CALL YOUR BLUFF · WAR OF ATTRITION
LAST WAR · PUNCHING ABOVE YOUR WEIGHT · ENDGAME · EX
ENGINEER · 10X TEAM · INTROVERTS VS. EXTROVERTS · NATURE V
INFANTRY, AND POLICE · FOXES VS. HEDGEHOGS · MANAGING TO
KNOWLEDGE · UNICORN CANDIDATE · DIRECTLY RESPONSIBLE I
PRACTICE · SPACING EFFECT · WEEKLY ONE-ON-ONE · RADICAL
GROWTH MINDSET · PYGMALION EFFECT · GOLEM EFFECT · IMPO
OF NEEDS · HINDSIGHT BIAS · CULTURE · HIGH-CONTEXT VS. LOW-
· MANAGER'S SCHEDULE VS. MAKER'S SCHEDULE · DUNBAR'S NU
· SUSTAINABLE COMPETITIVE ADVANTAGE · MARKET POWER · CON
INVENTION · FIRST-MOVER ADVANTAGE VS. FIRST-MOVER DISAD
DEVELOPMENT · OODA LOOP (OBSERVE, ORIENT, DECIDE, ACT) · P
· BACK-OF-THE-ENVELOPE CALCULATION · PERSONAS · BRIGHT
· LOCK-IN · SWITCHING COSTS · BARRIERS TO ENTRY AND
MARKETS · ONLY THE PARANOID SURVIVE · DISRUPTIVE INNOVAT